To The Reader:

I hope for two things to happen for us as this year of days unfolds.

The first, of course, is that each day's meditation gives you something worth taking away with you—to strengthen you, amuse you, touch you. Maybe I'll get lucky, and a few of them will do all three.

I hope also that the ancient texts upon which these reflections are based will come alive for you in a new way. The people who wrote the psalms were not magical or unnaturally good. They were not special—at least, no more special than you are. They were just people trying to make sense of their world and their own souls, as we try to make sense of ours. So we hear them complaining, rejoicing, wondering at the beauty of the world and at the annoying habits of their neighbors, green with envy and pale with fear, trusting sometimes and doubting others. Don't make them better than they were. You'll miss a lot.

I don't know the shape of your beliefs; I only know the shape of mine, and feel no particular need to do commercials for them in these pages. We each must develop our own—spiritual matters are much too important to leave to someone else! But as to pondering them, thinking along with me as I ponder, and agreeing or not, as your own wisdom decides—there are worse ways to start the day.

The things of faith and the things of life are the same things. The soul lives in the body while we are here, and nothing that concerns us is too mundane to have a spiritual significance. Family, job, friends, disappointment, triumph, memory: I have brought mine here. I honor yours.

Barbara Cawthorne Crafton
New York City, 1995

Meditations
on the
Book of Psalms

BY BARBARA CAWTHORNE CRAFTON

Finding Time for Serenity:
Every Woman's Book of Days

The Sewing Room:
Uncommon Reflections on Life, Love, and Work

*T*his book is dedicated with respect and admiration to Richard Corney, Professor of Old Testament at the General Theological Seminary, under whose instruction I and many others have studied the psalms. He ought not to be held responsible, however, for the considerable liberties I take with them, nor should this book be understood to be somehow his fault.

When many cares fill my mind, your consolations cheer my soul.
PSALM 94:19

✦

*P*age after page of advice in the magazines about sorting out your life: clutter in your closet, chaos in your checkbook, your diet, your schedule. That seems to be what January's for—a new beginning in the parts of life that need one. I have a modest proposal of my own.

Before you tackle your closets or sign up at the gym, give some serious thought to your spiritual life. Do you have a place to take the joys and sorrows that each day presents? A way to mark them, to celebrate or to mourn them? I say "before" you turn your attention to these other things because a spiritual discipline is not just another something on your to-do list. It's not another task, like remembering your vitamins and flossing. It's the thing *in which* the tasks of life happen. It's the frame of life. I have found my own life happiest when my spiritual discipline is explicit, when there are certain things I do regularly. I have found living that way much happier than the times when I have been more general about it, vaguely waiting for inspiration to find me.

A group of nuns I see regularly spends at least four hours in prayer every day. Not everybody is called to do that—there's a reason monastic life is a minority vocation! But to live by a rule, a set of practices to which one commits oneself: that is within anybody's grasp. You alone decide what will be in it. You will walk a mile and meditate while you're walking. You will read a portion of a book every day. You will pray in the morning, or at lunch. You will get away for an entire quiet day a couple of times in the coming year. You will find a spiritual friend with whom to talk things over. You will do one, three, or all of these things—or you will do something else. But a commitment to be intentional about doing something will surprise you with unexpected joy.

Some people think it's wrong to plan spiritual things. *You should be honest and spontaneous,* they think. *What if I don't feel like praying? Won't it be hypocritical to meditate if I don't feel like it? I don't want to be rigid.*

My experience and that of many, many others suggests otherwise. Discipline doesn't crush the spirit: it sets it free. It gives it a room of its own. It honors its peculiar gifts. Your discipline should not be rigid or harsh; it is intended for your joy, not to increase your guilt. It is a gift, not a job.

JANUARY 2

Out of the mouths of infants and children your majesty is praised above the heavens.

PSALM 8:2

➤✦

I am midway through my sermon when a baby in the back row begins to cry. A few yelps go by; the parents are hoping it will pass. No such luck: he was just warming up. Now he is in excellent voice and shows no signs of stopping. A few childless people and empty nesters look annoyed; most of us, though, have been there—and remember. I don't mind one way or the other; I can preach louder than most babies can yell. Admitting defeat, though, his mother slides out of the pew and carries her noisy little bundle out the door.

Yes, they are noisy. Yes, it's embarrassing if it's yours—nothing seems as loud as your own baby's cry in a quiet public place. But I visit profoundly disabled children in a city chronic-care hospital. They lie motionless in their metal beds, unable to move until an overworked nurse comes to move them. Their bodies are tiny; the arms and legs have never grown sturdy and strong from running and jumping in the sun. Many of the children are curled up into a little ball, as if still in the wombs they probably should never have left. For the most part, these children are quiet—they are past weeping, or they have never learned how. Theirs is a silent world.

One of my babies was born too soon. He did not live to be one of these silent children. I suppose that's just as well. I was home alone when he was born, suddenly, and with little warning. Instinctively, I carried him to the bathroom—to do what? Administer first aid? It was too late, of course—he was already dead. I never heard a single cry. Not a sound.

The noise of children praises God. Their messiness praises God. Their incessant demands, their banging of screen doors, their tears of frustration, their squeals of laughter—the earthly hope of the human race is made of nothing more complicated than these things. Discipline your children as best you can. Try to help them behave themselves in public places. Be considerate of other people's need for quiet. But never let anyone make you feel guilty about the noise they make.

JANUARY 3

Submit to the Lord with fear, and with trembling bow down before him.
PSALM 2:11

❧

Language like this turns a lot of people off. Women, especially, correctly point out that the Judeo-Christian tradition was recorded by some pretty warlike folks, and think it's high time we found some images of God less violent than this one, of a despotic king who likes it when his frightened subjects grovel before him.

Well, fair enough. Actually, there already *is* plenty of gentler imagery throughout our sacred texts: God is depicted at times as a shepherd, as a husband, as a mother, as a lover, as a farmer, and even as an artist, lovingly forming people out of clay. People have chosen to emphasize the aggressive images because people are aggressive, I guess, so if we decide to be otherwise we are free to emphasize something else. Nobody can make me understand God in a certain way. I must find my own way of understanding God.

The great religious traditions are custodians of our culture. It stands to reason, then, that they would contain elements of our history we no longer endorse; they conserve everything that people who have lived within them have believed, the good and the bad alike. And they will contain the contributions we add now, the good and the bad alike. Many things we do will seem quaint to those who come after us. Some of the things we do will seem offensive.

But faith is not just the custodian of culture. It can be its critic as well. Faith can call me to go beyond my upbringing, and it can give me the courage to do that when it's a lonely way to go. I don't have to leave the church because many Christians in the past were violent, any more than I have to leave it because some are today.

To live within the historical culture is like living critically in any other culture: we have the freedom and the power—and the duty, if we love the tradition and intend to stay within it—to take what is edifying and leave the rest.

Many are saying, "Oh, that we might see better times!"

PSALM 4:6

➤✦

One friend has been out of work for three years. She gets temporary jobs in her profession: a month here, three weeks there, the kind where they don't have to pay you benefits. Another was out for almost two years. She had to rely on the generosity of a wealthy friend.

The designers tell us that bright, bright colors are in style this year: neon orange blazers, hot pink mohair skirts, bright green sequined tank tops. Or pastels, they say in the fashion magazines. Lots of the women I see in New York every day, though, seem not to have picked up on this: they are still all in black, every day, just as they were last year, and the year before that, and the year before that. I go out at lunchtime and look around: occasionally something in taupe, once in a while some grey. There was a run on oatmeal last summer, but you can't count summer, really. Mostly it's black. My daughter says it has nothing to do with depression. *People just look good in black,* she says.

I am not so sure. I look at the serious young faces, the somber clothes, the work boots: it all looks pretty grim to me. I remember the glitzy fabrics and bright colors of a few years ago. I go to my closet and try some of them on. They no longer look right.

Maybe we're in mourning. The economists tell us that our standard of living is diminishing for the first time, that young people today will not surpass or even equal their parents' success, as we have always expected they would. There will be a lot more people in "temporary" jobs, like my friend—more people to whom no employer has a sense of obligation. So maybe we are mourning the death of something we thought would always be here: the dream of more and more, of better and better.

But in the last century the wearing of mourning dress was ordinarily a temporary measure. It usually lasted a year or two, as a sign that one had sustained a loss and shouldn't be expected to participate fully in the world's affairs while grieving. Then people resumed a more active life, concerning themselves again with the living. So, if our version of the American Dream has died, we shouldn't mourn forever. Yes, it does look as though the American Dream is undergoing a serious change. But eventually it's time to turn our focus from what was and get on with what is.

JANUARY 5

Lord, how many adversaries I have! How many are there who rise up against me!
PSALM 3:1

✣

It's a rare life that does not incur some enmity. Some people have lots of enemies, even seem to thrive on being at war with at least one person most of the time. Others of us are terrified at the very thought that somebody may not like us, and scurry away from the gentlest of controversies in abject fear of offending somebody we may not even like.

I am one of the latter. Now and then in the course of my professional life, it has become clear that a confrontation with another person was inevitable. A couple of times I have had to fire someone. Many times I have had to make it clear to someone that his or her behavior toward another person, or toward me, is not acceptable. I am long-suffering in the extreme, tolerating things other people wouldn't put up with for a minute. I never, never confront without very good reason. But the night before I must lower the boom, I am apt to be unable to sleep. The person will hate me. He will think I am unfair or mean. I think these things, even though I know that they are not true. There have even been times when I was frightened of my own children in this way, and there were times that I allowed them to do things I now wish I hadn't. I was so afraid of being accused of using power illegitimately that I was unable to use my legitimate power.

Most of the people I deal with would probably be better off if I weren't so afraid of incurring their ill will. Sometimes I have made a bad situation actively worse by circling it for too long, wringing my hands, instead of jumping in and kicking some derriere. But I can't help it. I'm just not a derriere-kicker.

I think I'm getting better, though. It's getting easier to make legitimate demands. I now share my fears with people who can help me stand up to them. Maybe I should be able to do this on my own, but I often find that I cannot. So what? If it's right to be tough and I can't summon enough toughness on my own, then it's right to find someone who can help me.

JANUARY 6

Give ear to my words, O Lord; consider my meditation.
PSALM 5:1

➤←

I couldn't count the number of people who have told me that they stopped trying to pray because God never heard their prayers. I assume that by that they meant that things didn't work out the way they wanted in whatever situation they were praying about. But think about it for just five seconds and it is obvious: lots of people pray and don't get everything they want. Bad things just happen to people sometimes, and prayer will not stop them from happening to you. Or to me. Prayer really isn't about things always turning out in your favor.

So what is it about, then? How will I know that God is "considering my meditation"? At first glance, the truth about prayer is disappointing to many people. It's not a talisman against misfortune. It is a guarantee of the presence of God. *Big deal,* says the widow who prayed and prayed that her husband would live. *To tell you the truth, I don't really care much about the presence of God. The absence of my life's companion is all I can feel.*

And I know she's being dead-on honest with me. We don't get much choice in many of the things that happen in our lives. But we do get a choice in the matter of whether or not we will find meaning through them. Prayer imparts meaning to life, to everything in life, even the terrible things. It doesn't make bad things good. It doesn't erase our sorrows. It won't make the widow happy that her husband has died; it won't even make it understandable. But it will connect her with a reality beyond her sorrow that is bigger than she is, a reality in which she may rest and which can comfort her if she wants to be comforted. Grief and loss are painful realities, but a new life can come out of them. It's not easy to see it, and the nature of the new life can never be predicted beforehand. You will not be the same as you were before. But you will still *be.* And prayer, listening for the God who is listening for you, helps you discover how—and who—you will be.

*I grow weary because of my groaning; every night I drench my bed
and flood my couch with tears.*

PSALM 6:6

➤←

 $\mathcal{M}$e, too, sometimes.

Bed is a great place in which to cry. Nobody will pester you to find out what's wrong and nobody will try to make you stop. You have a full eight hours in which to lose the puffy eyelids you are incurring (a cool slice of cucumber on each eye for five minutes in the morning will do the rest; try it and see). If I am sad and have some time, I go into my drawer and get one of my dad's soft old handkerchiefs, the sight of which is enough, all by itself, to bring tears. And I crawl into bed. And the tears come. I bury my face in the soft, old cloth—its owner is not here to comfort me anymore, not in the body. But I will awaken refreshed, even if whatever I'm crying about hasn't gone away; a satisfying limpness sets in after a good cry, relaxing muscles, deepening sleep, and calming nerves.

I remember crying in bed once, when I was about fourteen. I remember that my dad got up for some reason and heard me. Probably I sniffled extra loud to be sure he would. I remember that he came into my room and just sat on the bed next to me. *What's the matter?* he asked, and I told him I didn't know. Then I just rested my head in his lap for a while as he stroked my hair. Neither of us spoke. Then he went on back to bed. I have never been more profoundly comforted than I was by his wordless presence.

To admit to feeling sorrowful is hard for some people. They want to be optimistic, to see the glass as half full instead of half empty. And that is a good attitude with which to live one's life. But human beings just have sorrow sometimes, and there's no shame in showing it. You won't open the floodgates to a deluge of self-pity that never ends and drives everyone else nuts. You won't make your sorrow any greater by showing it; neither will you make it any less. And you will have the energy you are spending defending yourself against the true expression of it available for something a little more useful.

JANUARY 8

God sits in judgment every day.
PSALM 7:12
→←

A friend remembers going to church every Sunday under the eye of God, literally: there was a huge eye painted on the ceiling. She found it terrifying when she was little, that all-seeing God taking note of every sin and marking it down to be used against her later. And that's the setup you see in cartoons and endless religion jokes: *So, this guy comes up to St. Peter at the pearly gates, right? And Peter looks in his book. . . .* The whole idea of heaven and hell, in fact, is based on the idea that God judges us harshly. This is not encouraging news: when you stop and think about it, there is no one who has done everything perfectly. We all fall short somewhere along the line. So if God is ready to cast us into hell for our sins, we're probably all headed there.

My guess, though, is that this concept was considerably enlarged by people as our religious tradition developed. It proved useful in getting people to behave themselves. Or did it? Were people really more righteous when more of them thought they would fry if they weren't? I'm not sure. They may have been better than we are in some ways, but every age has its failures. The 1930s may have had the Waltons, but they also had Jim Crow—and unlike the Waltons, Jim Crow is a matter of historical fact. The Victorians may have had rigid standards about propriety, but they also had child labor. So much of what we have taken for absolute morality turns out in retrospect to have been merely local custom.

It drives some people crazy to hear talk like that. But it's true: human values change from age to age. The meaning of righteousness changes, and it has always changed. You could own slaves in the antebellum South and consider yourself a moral person, and you would have had no trouble finding people who agreed with you. Only a few short years ago, you could light up a cigarette in an enclosed room and think it nobody's business but your own. Just try doing it today. Some of today's virtues will be tomorrow's sins.

JANUARY 9

For the needy shall not always be forgotten, and the hope of the poor shall not perish for ever.
PSALM 9:18

✦

*W*e may need hope in order to live. *What do you want for your future?* a baffled police officer asked the thirteen-year-old boy he had just arrested for the fourth or fifth time. The boy shrugged expressionlessly and said nothing. I don't think he thought he had a future. And, it turned out, he didn't: his bullet-ridden body was found in a doorway just a few weeks later. His short life, which had consisted mainly of running away from whatever makeshift living arrangement he happened to be in, was over.

Experience had taught that sad and angry child not to hope for anything. If you have no hope for the future, there really is no reason to try for something better. There is nothing more important to teach a child than the relationship between her own effort and her achievement. Unless I think I can make a difference in my life by what I do, I have no incentive to do anything at all.

Oddly, this neglected, hopeless boy has counterparts in homes more stable and much more prosperous than his: many children of middle-class parents feel hopeless, too. More young people die by their own hands than die of illness in the United States, and by no means are all of them poor. As terrible as it is for a child to think that nobody cares and nothing matters, it can be just as deadly for him to think that his difficulties in life will always be solved by a strong and capable parent. If he never has to solve a problem himself, he may be unable to trust in a future whose shape is largely up to him. Along with confidence in us, children need confidence in themselves. Just as it is cruel to allow a child to grow without love and guidance, so it can also be cruel not to allow him to learn from his mistakes. Most of us need to fall on our faces a few times. It's one of the ways we learn best. We suffer if mis-guided love denies us that chance.

JANUARY 10

They say in their heart, "God has forgotten; he hides his face;
he will never notice."
PSALM 10:11

✦✦

The Jews of Jesus' time were very interested in the idea of a messiah who would come in some miraculous way—they pictured a dramatic descent from the clouds and a big army. He would right all the wrongs that had been visited on the people. This messianic hope made it possible for people to endure their suffering. *It may look like God isn't paying attention to us,* they would tell each other, *but just you wait until the messiah comes and the bad guys will get what's coming to them. Everything will be made right.*

It often does look as though God's attention has wandered. Innocent people suffer terribly, while perfectly dreadful people prosper. A mudslide carries away a whole town. Earthquakes swallow people's houses. If God is so good, why are all these bad things happening?

In this particular psalm, this very modern-seeming note of doubt is sounded by people the psalmist refers to as "the wicked"—people who want to do evil for the sheer fun of it. They are reassured by the idea that God isn't looking: *The coast is clear,* they tell each other gleefully, *and we can do all the mean things we want without fear of punishment.* The psalmist knows better. *Oh, yeah?* he says to the wicked. *Just you wait!*

I confess that both the psalmist and the wicked puzzle me a little. Is fear of punishment the only reason for being good? If I admit that joy and suffering are unevenly distributed in the world—and how anybody could think otherwise is beyond me—then must I conclude that God is inactive?

I guess I just don't buy the idea that God causes everything. Lots of things happen that are not God's will. What God does is lead us to find meaning in life, offer us the opportunity to grow as a result of the things that happen, good and bad things. That's not at all the same thing as saying that God "sends" us terrible things to teach us or punish us or test us, like a sadistic schoolteacher. Only that there is nothing—and I do mean nothing—on earth from which we cannot grow in wisdom and compassion. Whether or not we choose to do so is not up to God. It is up to us.

How long will you hide your face from me?
PSALM 13:1

＞＜

*M*y daughter Anna had a tremendous need to save face when she was little. She couldn't bear to be shamed. When she did something wrong and was scolded, she would go to her room and find her special blanket. Then she would reappear, the blanket completely covering her head, and stand silently in our midst, a penitent ghost. She would stand there like that until we began to say things like, *Where is Anna? She's such a nice girl. I wish she would come back.* And then the blanket would come down and the little face would appear, flushed with embarrassment but sure, now, of an enthusiastic welcome.

The psalmist is talking about a rupture in communication with God. It seems to him that God is silent; he's not getting any clues about God's heart from the bad things that are happening around him. When someone hides his face from someone else, he is signaling a complete unwillingness to talk. Anna felt cut off from us by the shame of being scolded—cut off from us, angry at our having put her in her place, a weak child against powerful adults—and so she hid her face. When we can see each other's faces, we see so much: we read love, anger, humor, desire in the eyes, in the set of the mouth, the furrows of the brow.

I notice that many people wear sunglasses these days, even when it isn't sunny; I often wonder if they are not a means of hiding our hearts from one another. Anna knew how to do that, little as she was; she would not let her heart show in her face until she was sure it was safe to show it. For she knew that once we could look into each other's eyes, we would not be able any longer to resist our bond. We would not be able to maintain our estrangement. We would have to move from separation into forgiveness, from isolation into community.

One of the first games a child learns is "peekaboo." Babies as young as six months old respond to the delicious tension of the game: mommy's beloved face is hidden by her hands in a simulation of the terrible possibility of abandonment, and then—peekaboo!—her hands open and she returns. And a look of pure delight suffuses the little face as eyes meet loving eyes.

JANUARY 12

The fool has said in his heart, "There is no God."
PSALM 14:1

✦✦

A lot of people say that. Not all of them are fools.

What's interesting about this particular atheistic manifesto, though, is its age: apparently there were people when this psalm was written who did not believe there was a God. That was a long time ago. We tend to associate unbelief with modernity, and to think that everybody was religious and observant in the old days. Apparently, that wasn't the case.

Since I'm one of the people who do believe, I welcome the news that unbelief goes way back. So many people think religion is what you do if you're too dumb to do science or history, and that once you know about the Big Bang, there's no further reason to explore the possibility of God. But I have never thought that my faith was primarily an intellectual, fact-finding enterprise. I have never thought that knowledge was the enemy of faith. For me, faith has been made of other things: of decision about how I want to live my life, of awareness that there is a reality larger than the one I and my fellow humans have created, of keen respect for the power of love and equal respect for the frightening power of hate.

How can you believe if you don't know anything about God? You explore the spirit of God the same way you explore the spirit of another person: you spend time in God's presence, you examine your own heart and mind with respect to God. You watch the world for signs of the spirit. You read what people in the past have felt and thought about it, and talk to people in the present who are also seeking. You sit quietly in meditation and see what comes up.

Being able physically to see or hear God wouldn't actually help us all that much, anyway: a person's spirit generally is largely hidden from others. We do not know one another well except after long acquaintance and shared history. The disciples, who ate and talked and walked with Jesus every day, were forever getting it wrong about who he was, but they all ended up thinking he was the messiah eventually. So it wasn't something they learned, the way you learn multiplication tables. It was something into which they allowed themselves to grow.

JANUARY 13

He does not give his money in hope of gain.

PSALM 15:6

→←

*A*nother come-on from a bank somewhere in the Midwest arrived with this morning's mail. I should take the high-interest credit card I use and transfer its balance to their card, where I will be charged five percent less interest. I get three or four of these a week.

I used to pay the credit card bill in our family. That was before my husband caught me making the minimum payment and carrying a high balance from month to month at a crippling rate of interest because I was ashamed to have him see how much I spent. Embarrassing, but true. After my arrest, I was barred from the privilege of paying that bill, probably permanently. I enjoy not doing it, but now I live with the terror of the conquered: he will set a limit to my spending, I'm afraid, or he will yell at me about something I've bought. So far, that hasn't happened. I may not be as extravagant as I think I am.

Our economic culture is so entangled with borrowing money that the idea that it's really not a very good idea is a hard sell these days. I know we all do it, but there is something spiritually weakening about borrowing money: it encourages the abdication of responsibility. You get to thinking that there really is such a thing as a free lunch. One of my tasks as a maritime chaplain was to lend seafarers money for room and board while they were looking for a ship. We didn't charge interest on these loans, and the seafarer could pay them back on his own schedule. You couldn't ask for a better deal. Guess what percentage of my debtors paid back their loans? Only about thirty percent.

That's not very good. The ease of obtaining the loan seemed to communicate to them that repayment is an option, not an obligation. Then, sometimes, they come in years later to borrow again. No dice, we had to say; you didn't handle this very responsibly last time. And sometimes I think we were being more respectful of their humanity in the second instance than we were in the first.

"You are my Lord, my good above all other."

PSALM 16:1

➤❤

*T*he thing that you hold most important is your God. The theologian Paul Tillich called this the "ultimate concern": the thing you know is above everything else in its claim on you.

Now, most people would probably say that the thing they hold most important is their family. For most people, that is the thing they can least imagine living without. This is true of religious people as well as of those who are not; ask somebody to answer quickly what is the most important thing in life and you'll probably hear "my family" or "my kids."

I don't think God is in competition with our families for our hearts. I'm not sure that the "most important thing in the world" test is exactly the right one for determining what it is you have as your God. I even think this can be a debilitating idea: I know a man who thinks his only son died because God saw that he loved him too much and took him away. I don't know about you, but I wouldn't work for a God who would be so cruel.

No, the reason your family cannot be your God is not that you must somehow learn to put your family second in your life. The reason your family cannot be your God is that you are going to lose your family. Fact: you're going to die or they are. You will lose each other in this life. And if your family is your God—that which makes it possible for you to live—you will have lost your God.

I propose another idea: God is that which you can never lose. Put anything else—family, wealth, bodily health, beauty—in the place of God and life will destroy your faith. You are certain to lose all these things. Everybody does. God is what remains after you have lost everything else.

And it's not nothing. Talk to someone whose child has died, who has sustained that loss of which most people can hardly bear to think. For a while—and it can be quite a while—life has no meaning. But many of them manage to find their way to meaning again. Many do it in fellowship with other bereaved parents. I don't mean life is again what it was before—nothing is the same after such a loss. But life can have meaning again.

That which gives life meaning, even when everything else is gone. That's what God is.

JANUARY 15

Hear my plea of innocence, O Lord.
PSALM 17:1

➤✦

You shouldn't talk about sin with that woman, the psychotherapist tells me. We've been discussing my pastoral care of a young woman who was sexually abused as a child. *She's lived in shame all these years about what happened to her. The last thing she needs to do is confess her sins.*

I am not so sure. For starters, sin and shame are not the same thing. Shame is taking the whole of the evil in an event and locating it within oneself. This is a sign of disease, and needs to be clinically addressed by a therapist. Acknowledging my sins, however, is just admitting to a specific behavior or pattern of behavior which has gotten in the way of my spiritual wholeness. I can confess my sins precisely because I am not in a state of shame: I am someone made in God's image who has chosen to act in a way unworthy of myself. I may be too weak or too stubborn to stop, but I can learn how if I am willing to learn. And life is tough; if I am out of harmony with myself and others, it is sure to teach me just how and where that is true.

Because the disease of shame has imprisoned so many people, the confession of sin has gotten a bad rap as well. In freeing ourselves from the culture of shame, which did so much harm to so many, we have gone from thinking almost everything a sin to thinking almost nothing is. And even in the case of our unambiguously sinful actions, everything is now someone else's fault. Lawyers make a lot of money demonstrating to juries just how this is so. It is very difficult for modern people simply to say, about anything, *I did this and it was wrong. I wish with all my heart I hadn't done it and am heartily sorry that I did.*

That is really not such a hard thing to say. It presupposes health and personal freedom. It is a line spoken by a grownup, not by a guilty and petulant child. It is much more dignified, it seems to me, than the usual flurry of reasons why I was actually the victim and thus cannot really be blamed for what I did. What is my fault is my fault. What's yours is yours.

JANUARY 16

The earth reeled and rocked; the roots of the mountains shook; they reeled because of his anger.

PSALM 18:8

➤◄

The ancient Near East, where these psalms were sung so many years ago, is earthquake country. This line is probably a description of one of many frightening tremors the psalmist had experienced over the course of a lifetime: the very ground itself shaking underfoot, revealed to be anything but secure. No wonder it seemed as if God must be angry.

People get killed in earthquakes. By the thousands, sometimes.

Why does this happen, we ask one another when we read of another tragedy in which whole villages are swallowed up. If God is good, how can he allow it? Earthquakes are not among those things we can chalk up to human sin, either: nothing we do causes them, so we can't blame the suffering they cause on ourselves and thereby get God off the hook.

I don't believe God sends us bad things. The anguished "why?"—which we cannot help but ask—is actually a question about the wrong end of a tragedy. We cannot know why; as far as I am concerned, there often is no "why" at the beginning of an event. But there is always a "what?" at the end of it, and in the midst of it as well: what can I do with what has happened? What do I learn about myself and about life?

That's not to say that this is what tragedies are for. Only that this is what happens as a result of them, if we permit it: we grow in wisdom and stamina. I know it has been true in my own life: I have learned much more and grown much stronger from the painful moments than from the sweet ones. I may wish with all my heart that something had not occurred, but I must also honor the strength I have gained from surviving it.

My stepson was killed at twenty-seven by a drunken driver. I met his father as a result of that tragedy: I heard about it and sent a condolence note, and he wrote back. Our marriage has been a blessing beyond anything for which I could have hoped. Even so, would we give it up if it would bring Ross back? You bet. In a heartbeat.

But we don't get to make those kinds of deals with history. We have the losses we have. They are grievous and they are undeniable. But the love that has come to my husband and me from this one is undeniable, too. It is what it is, and it is not what it is not.

One day tells its tale to another, and one night imparts knowledge to another.
Although they have no words or language, and their voices are not heard, their
sound has gone into all lands, and their message to the ends of the world.

PSALM 19:2–4

✣

What time is it where you are? my daughter asks me when I call her from Italy. I am already up past my bedtime; it is midnight here. But she is just now getting home from work; it's only dinnertime. Tomorrow, I will have been up and out for hours by the time she awakens.

The time difference didn't matter before the invention of the telegraph. You approached a foreign country slowly, by water; by the time you arrived, you no longer noticed the time difference that makes modern travelers so tired halfway through the second day after an ocean crossing by airplane. Now I can talk on the phone to somebody who is not yet living in the same day as I am. That's a little unsettling.

Some days seem so important that they cannot end. I think of the days on which I have lost someone I loved: my mother and then my father, or the day on which I lost my tiny baby, too small to live in this world. On the day after each of these sad days, it didn't seem quite possible that a new day could just dawn, same as always, as if these things had not occurred. But it did. That's what days do; they just follow one another, no matter what. They take their places in the past. Most of the marking of them that matters so much to us, the anniversaries of things, matters only to us. The days do not notice their own importance.

But they do communicate to one another. They mark the time of the earth. They shorten after one pivotal day in midsummer, a few minutes each day, bringing briefer and briefer spans of daylight until the very shortest day, going quietly to sleep in the cold winter, secretly pregnant with the hidden green shoot of summer to come.

As I grow older, their passage seems so fast. A month of them is a moment. A year is short now, not the eternity I remember from childhood. Throughout the days, I love and lose and love again, laugh and cry, remember other days, look forward to the day when my days will end. And, in an odd way, I am comforted by the inexorable passing of the days. They pass whether I want them to or not. Whether or not I can imagine them passing. Whether or not I am here at all. I am here for such a short time, even if I should live to be very old. But that's okay: the world is bigger and older than I am. It will go on without me.

JANUARY 18

We will shout for joy at your victory.
PSALM 20:5

>+<

*I*t takes a generous heart to rejoice at someone else's good fortune. Most of us have trouble doing that on occasion. I often fight a jealousy of which I am ashamed but which I must acknowledge, at least to myself. I know I should be glad when someone I genuinely care about has a stroke of uncommonly good luck, or achieves a smashing success after lots of hard work. And I am. But I also find myself wondering why I didn't win that victory, why my work wasn't recognized in quite the same way. Never mind the hundred-and-one great things that have happened to me: I lust after the one that has happened to someone else.

Well, the devil expresses his spiteful self in us chiefly by means of setting us against one another, and he has no more effective means of doing this than an appeal to our insatiable egos. I will not cooperate. I will acknowledge this jealousy, but I will name it for what it is: inappropriate and small-minded. Good things don't happen to others at my expense. They just happen.

Most of us are civilized enough to know that we should rejoice in one another's good fortune and self-possessed enough at least to pretend that we do. I think of the Miss America pageant, the way all forty-nine beauty queens hug the one winner when you know they are crying inside and, many of them, outside as well. And the training civilization imparts is a good thing: it molds us from the little egotists we all are at birth into people who often can do what we know we should do, whether we want to or not. We can still hear our old enemy whispering in our ear, trying to work us up into a jealousy that spills out of our hearts and into our actions. We can hear him. But we don't have to listen.

JANUARY 19

For you meet him with blessings of prosperity.
PSALM 21:3

→←

Whatever is wrong with the car will cost six hundred dollars and inconvenience me for a week. Trust me.

On the same day I receive an unexpected check from a person I forgot owed me money, the water heater will break and cost about the same amount. Depend on it.

I dream of prosperity, and I have more than most people in the world have—many times over. But I never seem to get ahead. Why is that, I wonder. It used to make me depressed. That was before I began to look at money that comes in unexpectedly as the great gift it is. *What if I hadn't gotten that check,* I ask myself, *and the water heater broke?* I'd be in a bad way. So unexpected money is probably sent my way by some guardian angel accountant, who knows that I have an expense coming up before I know it. I should expect an unforeseen expense when I open the envelope. That's what it's for.

I wonder if the very rich also feel this way. Is it possible that Donald Trump is anxious about money? I'll bet he is. His billion-dollar deals probably feel like emergencies to him. He probably worries about not having enough, just as I do, poor guy. And since he defines himself primarily by means of his money-making, these worries must be a lot closer to home than my fuming about the water heater. His worth stands or falls in accordance with how much money he has. That's a very dangerous way to live.

In my church, we have a potluck supper after the worship service each week. Everybody who can afford to brings something. Nobody goes around with a yellow pad and asks people what they're bringing next week; we just trust in God and one another and do the best we can. And every week there is a wonderful meal—a little lopsided once in a while, maybe, but wonderful nonetheless. A good model of the way life is: worrying about what you may not have in the future—or what you do not have now—will not add a red cent to what you have. Do your best and step out in trust and you will get what you need—or you will find a way to manage without it.

Those who delight in violence he abhors.

PSALM 11:6

>‹

*A*nother child shooting a child in the newspaper this morning: people clamor for gun control every time this happens. For reasons that I've honestly tried to understand and simply cannot, though, there are many Americans who view gun control as dangerous. *If two or three people had carried guns on that Long Island railroad car when Colin Ferguson opened up on all those commuters,* one man from the National Rifle Association said, *they could have taken him out easily.* I try to imagine such a shootout on my evening train, and I think he's seen one too many Charles Bronson movies.

An earnest news commentator says that violence is part of American self-definition. He says we all still think we're on the frontier. It's true that I spent much of the 1950s watching cowboys kill one another on TV and noboby stopped me, while I would not have been similarly at liberty to watch movies about people making love. Death was okay; sex was not.

And now? Sex is clearly okay, too, as anybody who can sit through five minutes of MTV will tell you. In fact, the sensibility of recent years appears to have married the two: the sex that sells best in the nineties is violent sex, full of whips and chains and degrading images of women. This is alarming enough in itself, when I stop and think that it is targeted specifically at young people, I fear for the future.

Well, violence is part of human nature, says a psychotherapist friend. *We all have the capacity for it.* True enough. But admitting that fact about ourselves is not the same as celebrating it. Not everything that is in us needs to be given free rein; you don't warp yourself psychologically by learning how to say no to your baser instincts. We are not like the animals: we don't have to act on all our impulses, as they do. We are a mixture of good and evil, and the main goal of growing up in human society is learning to tell the difference between the two so that we can enlarge the one and control the other.

JANUARY 21

You were my God when I was still in my mother's womb.
PSALM 22:10

I have read the following amazing thing: if you take two cells from the hearts of two different animals and place them in the same laboratory dish, they will continue to pulsate, to "beat" as they did when they were part of the entire heart. At first, each will beat with the rhythm it brought with it. After a while, though, they will begin to beat together, in the same rhythm. Think of it: these two tiny specks of life, the most basic building blocks of even the most complex life form, communicate with each other when they are close together. Together, they face the strange new world into which they have been thrust. They talk to each other.

Even at the most basic level of life, we are talking. Our natural tendency is to be connected with one another. Even inanimate things talk to each other, attracted by magnetic force and electrical force and chemical force, rearranging themselves in response to realities beyond themselves. The interrelatedness of things is the order of the universe.

This is God's way for us. Only by acknowledging our connectedness to one another do we live in peace; one of the most damaging human sins is the ugly suspicion that we are not all related, that we are each alone, that the universe is fragmented and meaningless. *No,* say the tiny cells, the particles of metal, the atoms of elements, *that is not how it is. We're not little unrelated pieces. We are all one body.*

A love that recognizes the truth of our oneness is a love that can find the courage to face anything. Ultimately, we are not lost, even in death. We continue in another way, part of the Everything that is God. In one another's faces, we see God. In touching one another, we are touching God. This is relatedness as God intended it from the beginning, as it has always really been. The order of the universe hasn't changed. We have always been one body. Our faith lies in knowing and embracing this truth.

JANUARY 22

Your rod and your staff, they comfort me.
PSALM 23:4

✦✦

$\mathcal{T}$his is the psalm that many people who may not know any other psalm by heart can recite; when I perform a wedding or a funeral and there are dozens of people in attendance whose religious traditions are unknown to me, I can count on at least half of them being able to say the twenty-third psalm with me from memory. I once heard a man who could no longer remember his own daughter's first name repeat it without a single error. Most people find it profoundly comforting. I know it has gotten me through more than one heartache.

So I almost hate to bring it up, but I think you should know: most scholars believe that the word "comfort" in this psalm doesn't mean what we normally associate with the word. When we think of comfort, we are apt to think of somebody nice gently stroking our hair, or of settling into a lovely hot bath, or of being consoled by a best friend when we are sad. Sort of a "there, there" thing.

Nope. Look at the verse again, what is it that "comforts" the psalmist? A rod and a staff. A big stick. Think about it for a minute; you don't stroke somebody gently with a big stick. You prod with a stick. A shepherd uses his staff to prod and push the sheep, to keep them going where they're supposed to go and prevent them from going where they shouldn't.

The word "comfort" is used here with an old meaning that modern English has forgotten; *com-* (with) + *fortis* (strong). To strengthen. To make strong. Not to stroke gently, but to push forward toward a destination, to empower in order to reach a goal.

I remember crying in school once, in the second grade. My teacher spoke firmly to me: *Stop right now!* she said, and I did, whispering silently to myself about how mean she was. She called me to her later to explain: *If I had spoken gently to you, you would have cried harder and found it harder to stop yourself. I didn't mean to be sharp. I only wanted to help you strengthen yourself.*

Little as I was, I appreciated that explanation. She was right; her tone did help me pull myself together in a situation where crying was not appropriate. Comfort isn't always a gentle "there, there." Sometimes it's a sharp "here, here."

"Those who have clean hands and a pure heart."
PSALM 24:4

✦✦

Turning into our driveway every afternoon on my way home from school, I would reach into the paper box and pull out the newspaper. When you were a kid you probably dived eagerly into the same thing I did every evening: the funny papers. Winnie Winkle. Dondi. The Jackson Twins, who had ponytails and boyfriends and a Model T Ford named "T for Two." Little Orphan Annie. Gasoline Alley. Then I would turn to Ann Landers. Then the horoscope. Hints from Heloise and the recipe column. Finally, I would do the scrambled word puzzle and then the crossword, quickly, before it occurred to my brothers to look for it.

Usually I consumed the newspaper lying on my stomach on the living room rug. I would open it out on the floor and begin, head in hands. This meant that my elbows rested on the newspaper. *Why are your elbows always dirty?* somebody in school asked me once. What? Shock and shame choked off my answer. I had never really looked at my elbows before—it's not that easy a part of one's own anatomy to examine, you know. But I stood in front of the bathroom mirror that night and twisted and turned until I could see them: black as the ace of spades. I set out on a campaign to restore them to their original beauty, scrubbing them almost raw with a nailbrush and then applying some of my mother's cold cream. It took several treatments to get them clean. From that day to this one, I have never leaned my elbows on any newspaper, and I don't expect I ever will again.

In biblical times, people used to pour ashes on their heads as a public admission of guilt—their faces and bodies dirtied to symbolize the sorry state of their souls. We respond to physical dirtiness as a symptom of moral degeneracy. People who are racially prejudiced usually ascribe physical dirtiness to the minority group they hate, and people who have confessed a sin and feel forgiven often refer to themselves as having been cleansed. It was moral shame I felt about my black elbows, not only embarrassment: actual guilt.

Be careful, though: it is not always the case that cleanliness is next to godliness. I've known pretty cruel people who never, ever got their hands dirty. We sometimes mistake beauty for goodness, but they are two different things, and they are not always found in each other's company.

JANUARY 24

Let integrity and uprightness preserve me, for my hope has been in you.
PSALM 25:20
✣

*I*t's pretty clear to me that the psalmist is hoping to strike a bargain with God familiar to all of us: *I will be very, very good, and you will protect me from harm. Deal?* But we all know that integrity and righteousness often don't protect people from harm; nor does misbehavior always issue in punishment.

The expectation that virtue will be rewarded and wickedness punished in some fairly immediate way dies hard in us. We learn it as children, and we do not forget. *Why me?* the woman with cancer asks piteously, searching her memory for a sin commensurate with her current suffering. *What did I do to deserve this?* As hard as it is for us to accept it, the evidence of our lives just does not support the belief that joy and suffering in this life are assigned on the basis of good or bad behavior. Sometimes the bad guys get what's coming to them. Sometimes they don't. It varies.

So in what sense can it be said that integrity and uprightness will preserve me? Certainly not in the literal one, whatever the psalmist (or we ourselves) may have hoped. After all, look how much is made in the Christian tradition of the sinlessness of Jesus, whose dreadful death is so painstakingly detailed in the gospels. The early Christians dwelt on those stories for a reason: even he did not escape, and the simple equation between sin and punishment was not at work in that suffering. Perhaps our reasonable hope is not that we will be excused from pain and sorrow; perhaps it is, instead, that we will experience them with integrity and uprightness. Perhaps our hope is that the hard times will not defeat our personhood, even if they may kill our bodies. I cannot, after all, choose whether or not I will die. All I can choose is how I will live.

JANUARY 25

Though an army should encamp against me, yet my heart shall not be afraid.
PSALM 27:3

❧❧

*E*ugene and his buddies are talking to a reporter about their experiences during the Second World War. *Were you afraid?* the reporter asks. He is about thirty years old. Gene breaks into his big, slow smile and shakes his head. *Naw, I wasn't scared,* he says, *I was just excited.* He says it several times, as the younger man presses him. *I was young back then, you know.*

There's a reason why eighteen is the age at which young American men have to register for military service. Young people make good soldiers. They are the ones who will experience fear as "excitement" and keep right on going into danger. They are the ones who sense their own strength so powerfully that they cannot really believe it could ever be bested. And so they are the ones needed—thousands of them at the ready—by those who decide when and where the armies will fight. They will go readily where an older and wiser person might hesitate. And, every time, many of them go and do not return. They remain, eternally young and brave in the memories of their comrades and the people who love them. Nineteen years old forever. Gone before life has really begun.

In a way I cannot explain, even to myself, the entry of young women into this world—their inclusion, now, in combat situations—has heightened the horror of war for me. A lovely young wife is shot down in Operation Desert Storm. A young woman talks about her love of military service on TV, and in a few months we hear that she has been killed in a helicopter crash. I look at their smiling faces and think of the loss of those lives, of the babies they will never have, the things they did not live to see, the years of love they will miss. Then I ask myself if the loss is any less grievous when it is a young man's face on the television. And, of course, it is not. I see that it is the same. Male or female—an early death is always a wrongful death.

Fear keeps the human race alive, for to love life is also to fear its loss. We find out how fragile a thing life is as we go along its path, but we don't know this early on. And so young people feel excited. It is up to their elders to feel the fear.

*. . . the evildoers, who speak peaceably with their neighbors,
while strife is in their hearts . . .*

PSALM 28:3

➤◄

*S*he said that about me?

More than one friendship has ended with just those words. It's a terrible feeling, to think that someone you thought was your friend is saying terrible things about you behind your back. Nothing stings in quite the same way.

You should never just accept a report like this without investigating further. Why, to begin with, is your informer telling you this? Some people enjoy starting trouble—don't be a pawn in someone else's sick game. And don't ask around to all your other friends about it, either: this is between you and the person alleged to have spoken against you. Find her and check it out, and listen to what she has to say with your heart, as well as with your ears. The instruction it gives may surprise you.

If she was misquoted, she will hasten to repair the breach in your friendship caused by the error. She will be furious at your informant, and even a little peeved at you for believing him. All these things are easy to fake, of course, and you must listen to your own insides while you're listening to her. Is this something you believe, or not?

Or maybe she did say that awful thing about you, and you can tell that she did by the way she is behaving toward you now. Maybe she admits it; maybe not. But you can tell if there is something unspoken between you that needs to get out in the open, and this awkward and painful interview is an opportunity to get it out. If there's a friendship left to save, this is the only way it's going to survive.

Let's say the worst is true: she did say it, she's not sorry, and, while she's at it, there are a few other things wrong with you that she thinks you should know about. How do you handle your pain, and how do you handle what remains of your relationship with her? This may shock you, but sometimes there is nothing left to do when someone has wronged you but forgive her. She may not deserve it and justice may not even be served by it, but there are times when there is no other approach to an injury you have suffered but to forgive it. The relationship is too important to you to do otherwise. In this behavior, you model a generosity from which your friend may learn. You do not, in forgiving, set yourself up for life as her doormat; if this is her habitual behavior, you'll be wanting to ask yourself just why you stick around for it year after year. But deciding to forgive, from a position of moral strength and honest love, can change both you and your friend in ways that neither of you could imagine.

JANUARY 27

The voice of the Lord is upon the waters.
PSALM 29:3

><

A few years ago, I came upon a remarkable man of prayer in a surprising place: the engine room of an enormous ship. Usually I don't pay a call in the engine room—it's a busy and potentially dangerous place—but this particular time I had a message for one of the engineers, who was overseeing repairs that morning. A very dirty fellow in serious need of a shave escorted me down a couple of ladders to the place where the engineer and one of the oilers were gazing intently at a gauge; I delivered my message and my guide took me carefully back up the ladders the way we had come. Thus far, all of our conversation had been conducted in hand signals and nods; you can't hear yourself think next to the big pistons. We left the noise and the heat and emerged into the hallway.

Ship is praying, he said to me with a grin, pointing over his shoulder at the closed engine room door behind us and then at my collar.

Say again? I thought he meant "paying"—his English wasn't the best, and I don't speak Greek—and that he was talking to me about a problem with his wages. But why would he be smiling about a problem with his pay?

Ship is praying to the God, he said, making a piston-like motion with his arm. *Engine praying all the time. Boom, boom, boom.*

What a remarkable thing: instead of being dehumanized by his many months in the belly of the great ship, he had transformed the constant noise of the engine into prayer. The engine never ceased. It propelled the vessel forward, and it generated the power for life support—heat, lights, refrigeration—for everyone on board.

That's also what prayer does for a person. It is the spirit that makes us live and move, that makes our bodies more than machines, and the sound the spirit makes is always prayer. Prayer is its language, no matter where or why: prayer about a problem, prayer deep within the soul, even the wordless exclamation at the sight of great beauty or overwhelming sorrow. Your soul is always praying; it has hummed beneath your consciousness every day of your life and will continue its song long after you have died. Sometimes your intellect and your will join its sound; sometimes it hums on alone, inaudible above the noise of the day. But, like the engine of the great ship, it is always there.

For his wrath endures but the twinkling of an eye.

PSALM 30:5

➤◀

We got kind of a late start this morning, so we had to dash tensely around the house getting ready for work. With only five minutes to make my train—the station is nearby, but five minutes is a little *too* tight—Richard speeds along the street and jerks to a stop at the light. He is fuming about the mess one of the kids left in the bathroom, and he barks at me when I ask him why he's bothering with that right now.

Because they don't have any consideration for others at all! he roars.

So why are you yelling at me?

Who else am I going to yell at? he demands, still furious, until what he said has dawned on both of us and we begin to laugh: me first, of course, but then even he cannot stop the grin from stealing across his face. He shakes his head, and we part with a laugh and a kiss.

Well, who else *is* he going to yell at? People shouldn't take out their frustrations on the ones they love, of course, but once in a while it doesn't hurt me to take a hit that by rights belongs to somebody else. Especially if it can end up like it did this time: with both of us laughing and feeling glad to be loving someone who can handle our less-than-attractive moments. This time it was Richard, but God and he both know about my occasional tirade in our kitchen that's really about something that happened far from there. Richard is remarkably wise when I do this: he is quiet, content to wait it out without trying to argue me back into lucidity. It passes. I remember my irrational behavior and am sorry and ashamed. He says it's okay, and I know it genuinely is.

There is a thin line—but one which must be strictly observed—

between the occasional tolerant decision to absorb someone's misdirected anger and a consistent acceptance of the whipping boy's role. One is an accommodation to a normally loving partnership; the other is masochism. In one case, wrath is brief: "the twinkling of an eye." In the other, it is a dispiriting daily reality, one that love does not demand. Love demands equality in power and in freedom of expression—even the expression of things about which we feel silly or ashamed later on.

JANUARY 29

When they see me in the street they avoid me.
PSALM 31:11

✴

Sometimes people respond to the suffering of others as if it were a contagious disease. They don't call. They don't ever mention it should they chance to meet the sufferer. *How're ya doin'?* they ask brightly, and the person can tell by the resolute cheeriness of the inquiry that any reply besides *Great!* would be most unwelcome. Divorcing? *Great!* Mastectomy? *Just fine, thanks!* Lost your job? *Terrific, thanks, and you?*

Why is this? We don't really think we'll catch tragedy from one another. But someone else's misfortune reminds us of our own vulnerability: you may have breast cancer, but I don't know for sure that I don't. Sorrow can strike so capriciously. There is so often no relationship between virtue and well-being, sin and suffering. *It could so easily have been me,* you think uneasily, and next time it just *may* be you.

And you are right. The sorrows of others do remind us that there are few guarantees in life, and that we'd just as soon do without the ones that do exist. Can you sit with other people in their sorrows?

You're better off if you do. Facing other people's trials with them has taught me a lot that came in very handy when it was my turn to cry. And they are better off if you do, too: one of the worst things about sorrow and pain is the loneliness. You can ease that for someone else without even saying a word.

Do you cross the street to avoid someone who's dealing with something you'd rather not face? Don't. You'll deprive yourself of a chance to grow. And a chance to serve.

JANUARY 30

"I will guide you with my eye."
PSALM 32:9

>+<

I am not a night person. I have slept through the final acts of most of the major operas and many, many Broadway hits. I have fallen asleep in the face of more than one dinner date—not all the guys I dated were as exciting in conversation as my husband is. I used to fall asleep every New Year's Eve, right after the countdown to midnight, in the middle of a party we hosted. I have excused myself from a fair number of dinner tables on the pretext of using the restroom. I used it, all right: as a nice, quiet place to stretch out on the floor and doze for ten minutes. I used to wilt during the night shift at the seafarers' center sometimes; I'd turn off the chapel lights and curl up behind the altar, using my Eucharistic vestments as blankets. Disgraceful.

This is an embarrassing problem for an adult to have. You're supposed to be able to stay awake at night when you're grown up; you spent your whole childhood looking forward to it. I'm not really eager for the whole world to know about this childish trait, so I don't like to just come out and tell my husband I'm falling asleep when we're out together with other people. Accordingly, we've devised a warning system: if I look steadily at him without speaking, that means I need to leave right away or I'll fall over.

To guide someone with my eye: it must be someone I know well, if I can speak my thoughts to him without words. I have often known something of another's heart through the eyes: my daughters', sometimes, or a friend's. I suppose that is why many people have trouble meeting other people's eyes: they are afraid they will be revealed beyond what is safe, or that they themselves will see something unwanted in that gaze. So they talk earnestly and long, looking all the while at a point somewhere over the left shoulder of the person with whom they are conversing.

Someone who takes the trouble to look into your soul through your eyes probably cares about you too much to abuse what he finds there—and if you know that's not true, ask yourself why in the world you're talking to this person in the first place! So look straight into his eyes when you talk together. Our time together is too short to avoid the truth to be found in one another's gaze.

JANUARY 31

For he spoke, and it came to pass.
PSALM 33:9

✦

The origins of the universe continue to be a loaded topic in American life. The ongoing crusade against recent theories about it is peculiarly ours: the issue does not command the same attention in other countries that it does here. Why is that? I think it is because Americans are very religious.

Don't laugh: I know that ours is easily the most materialistic society on the planet. But we do self-identify as religious to a greater extent than is true of people in many other countries: more of us go to church, more of us identify religion as important in our lives. And we also have a high degree of respect for science; faith in American technical wizardry is an important part of the American self-understanding. No wonder we get nervous about apparent contradictions between the two. We have appropriated the scientific criteria for truth as the only valid ones; no wonder we panic when the Bible fails to meet them.

And so people struggle mightily to explain the exact biographical journey of Adam and Eve, the historical mother and father of the human race. They run the numbers again and again, trying to make the biblical chronology come out right. They puzzle over how it was that people in the Bible lived to be hundreds of years old. They approach these writings with the literalism they would apply to a store inventory. They are handicapped by a conviction that these things can only be true if they are historical fact, when in fact humankind knows and uses many different kinds of truth and knowing, of which historical fact is only one.

Did the Genesis account of creation "really happen"? Depends: is it a literal historical document, or a piece of storytelling that is primarily moral in intent? The truth it conveys—that creation has meaning, that it is grounded in the love of God, that human beings bear a special responsibility to it—does not depend on its being historical fact.

We do not need to subject God to scientific tests. God has many more truths than just scientific ones to show us. God spoke, and the world came to be. What did that "coming to be" look like? The Bible just doesn't say.

Come, children, and listen to me.
PSALM 34:11

➤◄

Forty-five minutes I was trying to get her to find her jacket and her home-work, and she just wouldn't listen. The young mother's voice on the phone sounds flat and discouraged. *She goes out of her way to avoid minding me. Finally I smacked her.*

The powerful and peculiar chemistry of the mother-child bond is never neutral. Our children unleash so much that is primitive in us: primitive love, so strong it takes our breath away, but also primitive anger that we are much less willing to acknowledge. Few among us have not felt this anger; fewer still are willing to talk about it. But it's very dangerous not to: it is the polite conspiracy of silence around the violence in a mother's or father's soul that makes child abuse happen. If you strike your child in anger, you need to talk about it to someone you can trust.

We want everything to be so perfect for them. *She will not endure what I did,* we promise ourselves, betraying as we do so that some of our longing on our children's behalf is really sorrow about our own past. Danger, again: your child is not you all over again. You cannot get that which you lacked through your child, or avoid through her what you suffered. She is a new person, separate from you, and cannot re-fight your old battles. It is our struggle with our own child-hood sorrows and fears, our continuing vulnerability to them, that makes us feel angriest at our children about the things we most hate in ourselves.

The young woman on the telephone was furious at her daughter for her messiness and lack of planning. Yet the mother herself is messy, and frequently does not plan ahead. Burdened by her own shortcomings, she erupted in rage at her child's. For a moment, she *was* her daughter. And, in the midst of this dangerous illusion, a child was humiliatingly struck in the face. Now the mother is ashamed, and angry at herself as well as at her child. The violence did not improve the situation; it made it worse.

Talk to your children. Help them to go slowly, to pay attention. Be liberal with the affection they need, and matter-of-fact about the limits they need. But when you feel the thin ice of your own vulnerabilities beneath your feet in dealing with your child, be very careful. You both could end up in deep and dangerous water.

FEBRUARY 2

Fight those who fight me, O Lord.
PSALM 35:1

✢✣

The people who heard these words probably understood them quite literally: they believed that winning battles meant that God was on their side. They used to carry the Ark of the Covenant—it looked something like a bread box mounted on long poles, and contained the scrolls of the law by which the Hebrew people identified themselves as God's chosen—into battle with them: the physical token of the divine presence, an added bit of insurance for victory. From a modern point of view, theirs was a decidedly tribal understanding of what it meant to be the chosen people: God would kill some of his other children in order to let the children of Israel triumph.

It wasn't long before they had to adjust their expectations. There were high points and low points in their history, just as there are in the history of any nation, or any individual. You don't have the presence of God only when you're winning; you have it all the time. We all win and we all lose, and God's love for us does not stack the deck in our favor. You can't tell much one way or another about someone's walk with God just by looking at the level of his prosperity.

Standing at the door of St. Paul's Chapel one noonday, I was helping with the distribution of bag lunches to the hungry who gathered there every day. There were always 150 lunches to give, never more, never fewer. The one-hundred-fiftieth man in the line reached out and took his lunch; I told Number 151 that I was sorry. Number 150 opened his bag and pulled out the sandwich in it; he held out half to 151, who took it. The two of them walked off together. They had nothing, and they split it. The presence of God.

FEBRUARY 3

There is a voice of rebellion deep in the heart of the wicked.
PSALM 36:1

➤❖

*I'*d expand on that statement a bit: there's a voice of rebellion deep within the heart of everyone. Something about being asked to comply makes us want *not* to. We just don't like to be told what to do. I recently had to confront this very thing in myself, as follows:

I had fallen into a pattern of making fairly substantial purchases and investments without telling my husband until after I had done so. Such as a beautiful pearl necklace—I used some money my father had left me, and told myself that he would have wanted me to have it. Such as a sizable memorial contribution to my parish in my dad's memory—tax deductible, I told myself. Such as Waterford wineglasses—I'd always wanted some, and my sister-in-law had recently acquired a set. Such as painting our apartment a rich, dark green—a color I did not discuss with Richard, as I had not discussed the two-thousand-dollar price tag or even, come to think of it, painting the place at all. So he was pretty surprised to come in one Saturday afternoon to find the place half green and half white and festooned with plastic drop cloths. *I need a beautiful environment in which to write,* I offered lamely, when he expressed the wish that I had talked about it with him beforehand.

Why didn't I talk these things over with him before I did them? It was my own money, I told myself defensively, although I never hear Richard talk about his "own money" when he writes out a hefty check for our mortgage. I wanted my autonomy. I didn't want to have to ask permission. I was, after all, an adult. But how adult is it, really, to commit significant sums from the family treasury without any consultation with the person who shares the leadership with me? How confident was I of the appropriateness of these investments if I felt I had to carry them out in secret? My secretive spirit became more than a little greedy. I could have used some direction, but I didn't want it. There was a voice of rebellion deep in my heart.

FEBRUARY 4

Do not fret yourself because of evildoers.
PSALM 37:1

✦

A young man comes to see me. He is preparing to be baptized, and we are to discuss some matters of the faith that are unfamiliar to him. Among the things we talk about are sin and guilt and how they relate to heaven and hell. He is very certain of the existence of heaven and hell—he is, perhaps, a little more geographical about them than I am, as if they were places, which I suspect they may not be.

As we talk on, it becomes clear that he is very concerned about this: how can we know if we are saved? What about Buddhists? What about Hindus? Are they going to hell for sure, no matter how good they may be? What if certain relatives of his who are not believers die—will they be among the damned? What if *he* is not saved, and ends up in hell for eternity? What if, in his confession, he leaves something out, and then dies—will he go to hell?

We talk a little about the difference between salvation and transformation. I'm not much on salvation, actually: it seems to me that the concept invites people to focus on themselves in a way that is essentially unhealthy. Human spiritual growth is not just about whether I myself am okay. It is about transformation from the loneliness of self-absorption to the self-giving joy of community. I can't imagine that God's action in us is so limited by our pathetic selfishness. To me, the life of faith is a response to God's generous invitation to a life of spiritual wholeness, not the simple fear of punishment. Or, to put it more crassly, if you're behaving yourself only so that you'll make it into heaven, don't bother. There are better reasons to act lovingly than that one.

Of course, you already know this. So does the young man, actually: all of our lives contain moments of what can only be called righteousness, called forth in us by love. Think of the willingness with which you put your children's needs ahead of your own, so much a human reflex that we are stunned with horror when it fails. Think of how love survives in marriage long after youth and beauty and health are gone. You already know something of what it looks like to love unselfishly.

The spiritual life is a paradox: it answers the needs and anxieties of the self through a process that leads beyond the self. The young man begins his formal religious life worried about the state of his own soul. My guess is that he won't stay that way.

*My friends and companions draw back from my affliction;
my neighbors stand afar off.*

PSALM 38:11

➤❦

Of course, the housing arrangement would be temporary, we told them. The able-bodied seaman and his wife could stay in our house for retired seafarers while he was looking for a ship. Then, when he got one and some money started coming in, they could get their own place. Fair enough.

Her hand shook, I noticed, as she held her cup of coffee. She was thin and pale, and her eyes were red. Her ID had been stolen, she said, and my antennae went up. No place to live, thin and jumpy, no ID: *This lady has a drug problem,* I said to myself. It was against my better judgment to allow them to stay, but I did. After all, I told myself hopefully, I could be mistaken.

But I wasn't. At first, she bustled happily around the house, talking brightly about "a woman's touch" as she stirred canned spaghetti on the stove. Then he got a ship and went off to Spain, and she was alone in their room. *Something's just not right,* one of their housemates said to me a couple of weeks later. *Something funny's goin' on in there.* She was receiving late-night phone calls and rushing out immediately upon hanging up. She was borrowing small change from the neighbors. *The other night, there was a strange man in the room.* His faded blue eyes blazed indignantly.

She had to go. Of course she cried, and said something about some money arriving from her husband soon. On the day she was to leave, she was nowhere to be found. Her room was littered with candy wrappers and dirty clothes. *Put it in bags and hold it for a week,* I said.

A day or two after the sanitation men come and haul the bags away, she calls about her things. *They're gone,* the old oiler tells her. *Oh,* she says without anger, and then she says good-bye. *Probably done this before,* he says, *just walked away from all her stuff. It ain't the first time, I know that much.*

I should never have let her stay. I let her frailty and her homelessness blind me to her unsuitability for that living arrangement. I was trying to be kind. I didn't want to "draw back from her affliction." But it was wrong to provide support for her self-destruction. So did I help her, then, by putting her out? Who knows? But I certainly wasn't helping her by letting her stay.

FEBRUARY 6

I will put a muzzle on my mouth.
PSALM 39:2

✦✦

$\mathcal{M}$y husband and I are having a little discussion. This one was my idea, and I chose the venue: the restaurant in town we used to go to sometimes when we were courting. I thought it would be good to have this—er, talk—at the Cornerstone for a variety of reasons. This was the place where, years ago, he first came right out and said that we ought to go someplace where we could be alone; I had just touched his hand lightly with one finger and offered him a *quarter* for his thoughts, in what I hoped was an unmistakable way—brazen hussy that I was in those days. He got the point.

Also, they have live music at the Cornerstone. This is a plus: people won't hear me when I swear.

The waitress keeps trying to bring us things, trying to see if we want to order dinner. Finally she notices my body language—head forward, chin out; hands in my lap, drumming furiously on my thighs; talking nonstop without smiling, my eyes boring into his eyes; occasionally breaking into an exaggerated animation, the venom of which would not have been lost on Forrest Gump—and leaves us alone. I am so angry. It feels so good to speak it: to feel those great, hard tumors of rage dislodged from places in my soul where they do not belong. I swear a little during this confrontation—no, actually, I swear a lot. My husband does not swear. This is a generational difference: he is quite a bit older than I am. I'm so glad I landed in the age group that gets to cuss.

Again, he gets the point. We reconcile in a gingerly way. We pay for our drinks and walk out of the Cornerstone. In the street he takes my hand; I hesitate before giving it. I am not over this yet.

The next day I say something about it again and he tells me to shut up and not beat the thing to death. "Shut up" is progress for him: he usually doesn't allow himself such coarseness, and I take it as a good sign. I can see immediately that I have misjudged; we needed to have that fight, but now I *have* beaten it to death. I need to stop talking and wait for what I have said to sink in, and then we need to deal with it together. I don't always know when to stop: I feel so liberated by the expression of pent-up feeling that I usually go overboard. Too vehement for too long. Maybe a muzzle on my mouth wouldn't be such a bad idea.

He lifted me out of the desolate pit, out of the mire and clay.
PSALM 40:2

✦✦

$\mathcal{T}$he story you are about to read is absolutely true:

A former colleague was officiating at a funeral. All of the liturgy that was to be in the church was finished, and now everyone was gathered at the graveside for the committal: the widow, the children of the dead man and their children and in-laws, all of their friends and neighbors. My friend went to take his place beside the coffin at what he thought was the head; the undertaker plunged forward to stop him, but it was too late: the lurid green carpet undertakers use to hide all the dirt also conceals the grave opening itself, and Walt disappeared from sight in a swoosh of brocade and AstroTurf. The undertaker's beefy assistant and the even beefier grave digger hauled him out immediately; caked with earth but otherwise intact, he continued the service. The shaken widow was all solicitude afterward. *Never mind,* Walt said cheerily, *I've always said I'd never send my people anywhere I wasn't willing to go myself.*

I wonder what it was like in the grave. Walt was back on the surface before he had time to meditate on it, and I've never heard him say. I would think it might be disturbing, though: a grave is a very small room in which to spend eternity. He joked about being willing to go where his people went, but he really is accustomed to accompanying people to their fearful places: besides being a priest, he is a psychotherapist. I once watched him lead a woman who was in the midst of a terrifying psychotic break back into our world. He sat quietly on the edge of her bed, listening as she described the frightening things she saw and heard. After a time she was silent, and then she began to weep, like an exhausted child. *Can you tell me where you are,* he asked her gently, *and who I am?* She looked at him for a long time, and then she said, quietly, *I don't know where I am, but you're Walt Zelley,* and a long sigh came out of Walt, right from the soles of his feet.

It was as if he had gone into her own grave with her. Then he clambered back out and, caked with earth, reached back a hand to help her out.

FEBRUARY 8

Happy are they who consider the poor and needy!
PSALM 41:1

✦✦

My friend was laughing as she talked about last week at the homeless shelter. *I shouldn't laugh, though,* she said. *It wasn't funny.* A Brownie troop came to help serve the dinner. One of the mothers just couldn't seem to stop talking about the renovations she was having done on her house: they were putting a skylight in, and redoing the kitchen floor. *It was just unbelievable, the mess,* she said, shaking her head and looking around her for sympathy. An odd thing to talk about in a room full of homeless people, huh? There was more. Later on, while the Brownies busily scraped plates and washed dishes, the woman was full of righteous indignation: why didn't the homeless people help with the dishes?

We wondered what the woman thought she was doing at the shelter. *Getting her daughter another patch, I guess,* my friend said. The Girl Scouts require that the girls perform one community service project each month. Girl Scouts have had a service requirement right from scouting's beginning in the early years of our century. It is intended to allow the girls to learn about the satisfaction helping others can bring into their lives. Many lifelong volunteers first acquired their taste for service in their scouting days; they know that it is not about getting another patch to sew on your uniform. Somehow the Brownie mother at the homeless shelter didn't get it: she brought her world into the shelter, all right, but she didn't let the shelter enter her world.

Almost always, volunteering brings people out of self-absorption and into community. We're not intended to hole up in our new kitchens with their new skylights and leave it at that. Decorating your home should make you happy: it's lovely to make your nest beautiful and comfortable for yourself and for those you love. But we do not live with our families on little islands, unrelated to the community around us. My home is only a haven for me if I allow the outside world to challenge me. If I don't, I have no need of a haven.

FEBRUARY 9

Why are you so full of heaviness, O my soul? and why are you so disquieted within me?
PSALM 42:14

→←

Some days are just like that: everybody I've run into today has been feeling just a little dispirited. A lawyer friend lost a case that he cared a lot about; he's not sure he's up to this any more, he tells me. A teacher thinks she may have to resign: *I just feel so burnt-out. I don't think I do these kids a bit of good.* Another friend's worried sick about her mother: she's just been given a cancer diagnosis. *The crazy thing is that ever since we found out about Mom, I've felt that something terrible is wrong with me, too. Wonder what that's all about?*

Odd: it was a gorgeous day today, one of those bright days in early spring when the potential of everything is so very obvious. Does the hopefulness of the little green shoots of plants reaching for the sun after their winter's entombment remind us too clearly of our own weariness? Have we seen too much to recognize anything of ourselves in their hope?

Go for a walk outside. Now. I don't care if you're busy: it will all still be here when you get back. And never mind if it's drizzling: take an umbrella. I want you to go and find some of those little green plants. There are some things I want you to notice about them:

1. They're not young and stupid. They're just hopeful. Some of them have been coming up every spring since before you were born. So they've seen a fair amount, too.

2. They've been in the ground. What happened to them last year was a part of their lives gardeners call "dying back." They have to die back if they're going to come up again the following year: their leaves turn yellow and then white, and they go limp. Sound familiar? Thought so. But listen: you know all the nutrients that were in the leaves? They get sucked back into the bulb, where they are stored until it's time to come up again in the spring. Their dying back fuels their new life. So can yours.

3. This blossoming thing is a completely new job description for them. Being a flower in the sun is nothing like being a bulb in the ground. But both are stages in the same life. Plants pretty much take things as they come, which is what we all have to do.

Bring me to your holy hill and to your dwelling.
PSALM 43:3

➣➣

*T*he people of ancient Israel, in common with other people in the ancient Near East, often connected the experience of God with being on a mountain. I can imagine why: people noticed nature a lot more in those days. They noticed that rain came from the sky, that great clouds sometimes descended to earth from it and hung magically over the ground, that sometimes arcs of fire flashed across it, great rolls of thunder. The night sky was wondrous to them, as it still is to us when we bother to notice it. In places where they don't light up the night with a lot of neon, the stars lean right out of the sky like fat, bright, glowing fruit, so close you think you can reach your hand up and pick one. *If we climb to the highest place,* the people reasoned, *we will be among those stars, right in the midst of those clouds, close to that rain, that mysterious fire.* Closer, therefore, to the one who made them.

This ancient conviction remains part of our consciousness today: we call a moment of keen wonder a "mountaintop" experience. The spiritual power of such a moment is undeniable: *That was the real thing,* we think after such a moment, *I wish I could have that all the time.* But such experiences are rare: most of us don't live on the mountaintop. We live in the valley below. And, as appealing as was the ancients' idea of the geographical closeness to God one might achieve by climbing up high, God doesn't really live in the sky. The entire earth is God's creation, not just the high places. Long after Moses, when the people of Israel began to change their political organization from the nomadic society he had led and to live in cities, the location of the holy place moved down from the mountain. Solomon didn't build the temple on a lonely mountain. He built it in Jerusalem, right in the middle of daily life.

Too busy to have a spiritual life? Can't pray because you don't have a quiet place away from the demands and enticements of your world? The presence of the spirit is breathtaking in a high, lonely place full of stars. But that's not the only place it can be found. The spirit is present everywhere.

FEBRUARY 11

Will not God find it out? for he knows the secrets of the heart.
PSALM 44:21

➤✦

People are often nervous about the idea of confession. Some of them remember mumbling their sins to a hidden priest and then scuttling away, hoping he hadn't been able to identify them from the other side of the screen in the confessional. The screen was very important: it was supposed to remove the penitent's human partner in the confession from view in order to enhance the experience of God's presence and diminish the distracting effect of personality on that experience. These days, it is increasingly common for confession to be handled differently: not in a big wooden booth with a screen, but face to face, the priest and the penitent sitting down together like two adults.

It does take some guts to do this—on both sides. The penitent may know very well that God's love is bigger than any of the ways in which he or she may fall short, and that God has always known what these things are and why they are, but to sit there and let another human being in on them is a tall order. It's just plain embarrassing. But it is also embarrassing in a different way for the priest: she knows full well just which pieces are lost in the puzzle of her own soul and she knows that her brokenness is visible, written in a fairly legible hand on her own life for anybody to see. She knows herself to be in no position to judge another. *Go in peace and pray for me, a sinner* are the final words in the confessional rite I use most often. That's the truth, I usually add inwardly. And in someone else's office, I sit in the other chair and get honest about things I wish weren't true about me. And so it goes.

Two people who fall short. We help each other in this sacrament of reconciliation: the priest helps the penitent speak his painful truths, and the penitent reminds the priest of her own. God has always known about both of them.

FEBRUARY 12

He takes up the weak out of the dust and lifts up the poor from the ashes.

PSALM 113:6

➢➢

*I*t was bitterly cold on one of those very bright winter days. My first child was still a baby. We were poor—we had no car, for instance, and there were a lot of other things we didn't have, either. I had bundled up the baby and taken her on a city bus to the doctor for a checkup and was on my way home again, having written the doctor a painful check for her inoculations, a check that completely wiped out my grocery money for the next week. We waited for the bus. I stamped my feet in the cold and tried not to think about what I was going to do for food. The bus didn't come and then it didn't come some more. The wind grew colder and colder. I bent down and hugged Corinna in her stroller, trying to keep the cold from her. More than a half hour

I had crouched there. She was crying now, and I was trying not to. Where the hell was the bus?

A truck driver stopped and offered us a ride. I looked up into his face and said yes. We got in. *It's too cold to be out there with a baby,* he said. *I know,* I told him. *I really appreciate the ride. Please let me pay you the bus fare. Nah,* he said. *Can you let me out at the grocery store?* I asked. I had three dollars, maybe, which was more in 1968 than it is now but still wasn't very much. *Might as well buy what I can now with what I've got,* I thought, *and just make it last.*

As I got out of the cab, I sneaked the thirty cents onto his dashboard where he'd find it later and thanked him. Wheeling Corinna through the grocery aisles in a shopping cart ten minutes later, though, I came face to face with him. He looked angry. Shoving my thirty cents into my hand, he said, *I could kill you for doing that.* And he turned on his heel and walked away, leaving my *thank you* trailing uselessly along after him.

He was genuinely angry, I believe. I've thought of him often. After all these years, I still don't know why he reacted that way. *I could kill you for doing that.* Doing what? Depriving him of the privilege of doing a good deed? Treating him like a cabdriver instead of like the Good Samaritan he was? It seemed an extreme thing to say. And I don't really know why I insisted on paying him the thirty cents. I think it was because I was ashamed of being so down-and-out, and paying my way in that little exchange helped somehow. Maybe he felt the same about himself.

It's a terrible thing to feel so powerless. Terrible that thirty cents should assume an importance so beyond its worth. The main thing about being poor is that something you know is very small to most people becomes very big for you, and there's not a thing you can do about it. Very hard on the spirit. I've never forgotten how it was to live that way, although my circumstances eventually improved and I am now one of the most fortunate people I know. Prosperous people already know they matter. They are already so secure in their human dignity that they usually don't give it much thought. It is the poor whose attempts to claim their own dignity—small, but often so costly—need affirming.

FEBRUARY 13

Clap your hands, all you peoples; shout to God with cry of joy.
PSALM 47:1

><

How was it? I ask my friend who has just returned from a weekend retreat. *It was good,* he says, and then he hesitates and corrects himself. *I mean, it ended up good. Actually, I just about went nuts in the middle of it.* He goes on to tell me about the retreat. The leadership wanted people to get in touch with the joy that comes with acknowledging God's great goodness in their lives. To that end, the tone of the weekend was relentlessly cheerful: people were constantly smiling, enthusiastically thanking one another for sharing. People were hugging each other and singing strummy songs about praising God. *I shared some painful things in my life and immediately felt like I'd rained on their parade,* my friend said. *I just felt uncomfortable and angry after a while—all that smiling got to me, I guess.*

That's an embarrassing thing for a religious person to admit: that sometimes faith in God doesn't fill him with joy and happiness. That sometimes he just feels sad, and sometimes he just feels quiet and introspective and doesn't *want* to sing a happy clappy song. That he might feel a very warm regard for another person and yet not wish to give him a great big hug. But we are not all alike. There is more than one way to express joy and more than one way to feel it. The soul has many moods and God knows about all of them.

It's important to acknowledge the soul's many moods, primarily because we should be honest when we focus on spiritual things. Does God want me to run through a list of amiable thoughts that I learned from somebody else's good mood, or does God want to hear from *me*? Is God's ego so slender that he can't bear to hear my negative things? I don't think so.

FEBRUARY 14

God gives the solitary a home.
PSALM 68:6
➻

Maybe you could ride down to visit my mother with me, my friend says. Her mom lives about an hour away. *We could talk on the way. It's been so long since we had any time.* I am torn: I have a deadline to meet. But I've done pretty well today. I'll get it done. *Sounds good,* I tell her. She'll pick me up after work.

Her mother is old and sad—eager, I think, to die, but unable to do so. This is a hard time for my friend—there is nobody to share the emotional burden of her mother's obvious sadness. She dreads the visit—not just now, but every time. *Somehow, I've never been a source of joy to her,* she says, her voice trembling a little. This is incredible to hear: my friend is beautiful, brilliant, successful, funny. Go figure.

Families sure are strange. That's why so many people make their own, I suppose: circles of friends who see each other often, share a lot and take care of each other and don't carry the huge amount of emotional baggage around with them that families of origin sometimes pack. Groups in which a certain distance is understood and expected. There is something very appealing about this easier form of community—Family Lite, you might call it.

Is this marriage? another friend once asked me about six months after her second wedding. *It doesn't hurt!* People are always bemoaning the state of the family and predicting the end of society because of its disintegration. And there is no pain greater than that sometimes inflicted upon people by those who are supposed to love them. But people can revisit the ruins of families more murderous than nurturing and build something new on them. Not every family of origin can be saved. Not all of them should. But no one has to be utterly alone.

FEBRUARY 15

Trembling seized them there; they writhed like a woman in childbirth.
PSALM 48:6

➤❈

I don't remember actually writhing, but maybe I did. It's been twenty years since my last baby, and you do forget. These days, parents are so well schooled in the ins and outs of giving birth: they go to their classes, they watch videos, they read manuals. I'll bet the fathers could have the babies themselves if they had to. I don't know when it started, but there has even been a grammatical change that sums up the new team approach to parenting; most of the couples I know who are expecting refer to their status in this way: *we're pregnant,* they say.

It's easy for a mom of yesteryear to smirk at such earnest coupleness: do *we* have ankles that puff up like balloons? Do *we* throw up at the smell of food cooking in the morning? Are *we* so tired at night that we fall into bed in *our* clothes? I resist the easy entrance of men into women's mysteries. Hey, guys: you don't have babies. We do that part.

But, actually, I am not completely right about this. Years ago, my husband had to go to Lamaze classes by himself, a lone unaccompanied man among all the couples. I was bedridden throughout most of that pregnancy, so he went to the classes and taught me what he'd learned when he got home. We would read in our little book about the stages, and he would demonstrate the panting he had observed the women doing in class. And when the time came for me to be delivered, as they say in the Bible, it worked just fine. Women's mysteries are all very well. But fathers are not incapable of entering into them.

FEBRUARY 16

For we see that the wise die also; like the dull and stupid they perish and leave their wealth to those who come after them.

PSALM 49:9

✧

We are spending our children's inheritance says the bumper sticker on the car in front of me at the toll booth. I've seen this one before and still don't quite get its intent: is it supposed to be a serious-minded rebuke about the enormous federal deficit, or is it a happy-go-lucky commentary on how much fun you can have once the kids are grown? Maybe it's the latter: I often see it on recreational vehicles.

It had been years since I had seen Loretta. *How's Herb?* I asked her at the church door, and her hesitation and stricken look told me before she did that her husband had died since I had last visited St. Luke's. It had been about two years, she said. Heart attack. We reminisced about what a great guy he was. She had sold the house, she said, and moved into a little apartment. She was thinking of doing some traveling. *I'm spending my kids' inheritance,* she said, and we both laughed. I thought of how she and Herb had sacrificed for their children. They worked so hard for so long. If anyone deserved a little fun, it was Loretta, and I told her so. We hugged good-bye. *Guess I'll go say hello to Herb,* she said cheerfully, and strolled over to the memorial garden. Fifteen minutes later, as I left the church, she was still standing there in the garden, her hands pushed down in her raincoat pockets, looking at the place where all that remained of her husband's body lay buried.

It wasn't six months after that moment at the church door that I chanced to see a parish newsletter from Loretta's church that listed hers among recent funerals. She didn't spend much of her kids' inheritance; she didn't live long enough. I don't know if she got to go on any trips.

FEBRUARY 17

Do you think I eat the flesh of bulls, or drink the blood of goats?
PSALM 50:13

➻

*U*ntil the temple in Jerusalem was destroyed by the Romans in 70 C.E., it was the spiritual center of Jewish life. Animal sacrifice happened there every day during the life of Jesus of Nazareth; it was the primary act of the Jewish religious life into which he was born, and had been so for centuries. Animals were killed in prescribed ways by certain temple functionaries, and their flesh and blood was burned, the rising smoke understood to be the means by which God partook of this food. That was why Mary and Joseph brought their baby all the way from their home in Galilee in the north to Jerusalem in the south:

to offer a pair of doves to be sacrificed in the temple as a thank-offering to God, as the law required. The money changers whose tables Jesus upset were part of this system; they provided the means by which animals could be purchased for temple sacrifice. They weren't trespassing upon the holy precincts of the temple; they were supposed to be there.

Yet this psalm, dating from a period some five hundred years before Jesus was born and presupposing the practice of animal sacrifice as part of the normal scheme of devout life, also asserts an insight just as ancient in the Jewish tradition: the act of religious observance is not by itself pleasing to God. Animal sacrifice had never been a matter of fixing God a tasty meal in order to get on his good side. The practice was a symbolic act. Grisly? Yes—to us, anyway—although the use of animals in this manner represents the gentling of an earlier Near Eastern practice of human sacrifice. So it sure could have been worse. But the tradition has always known that it is in the human heart and mind that the sacrifice pleasing to God really happens. If religious observance is not an outward sign of this spiritual reality, it is useless.

FEBRUARY 18

The sacrifice of God is a troubled spirit; a broken and contrite heart,
O God, you will not despise.
PSALM 51:18

❧

Yesterday's discussion of animal sacrifice may have shed some modest light on the history of the practice, but it didn't give us much in the way of reflection on how the spiritual life of a modern man or woman can be connected with this ancient and—to us—bizarre custom. Or, for that matter, why on earth any normal person would *want* to be connected with it. This verse does: our tradition, which began so long ago, which incorporated into itself so many practices whose original meaning we have long forgotten, is at bottom a matter of presenting the truth about ourselves to a God who loves us. We long to tell someone the truth about ourselves, but we are afraid that our truth will drive the one we love away, and so we are silent. The God of this psalm is not driven away by our truth.

I had a secret for thirty years. Didn't tell a soul. This was my secret: when I was thirteen, I was caught shoplifting with two other girls. I'd slipped a pair of nylon stockings into my school notebook. Don't ask me why. The chief of police called my mother—it was a small town, and the law enforcement business was a little slow—who came to get me in the car. I was humiliated and ashamed. And although I have since committed worse sins than that one, I was somehow unable to share my youthful brush with crime with any living person for thirty years. I didn't even tell my daughter when she and her girlfriend were caught red-handed in just the same circumstances, and I imagine it would have done her some good if I had. But just the other day, I was giving a reflective meditation about being fully open to the spiritual meaning of everyday life, and it just seemed natural to talk about that experience. Out it came, easy as pie. A couple of other people shared similar experiences, and that was that. At lunch afterward, I told them that they were the first people I'd *ever told*, and we all laughed.

People who love you are not driven away by your truth, even if it is a truth of which you are ashamed. They can take it—they know nobody's perfect. They usually value the trust you have shown them. So also the God of whose love all our loves speak.

I shall teach your ways to the wicked, and sinners shall return to you.
PSALM 51:14

✦

In our house we have a very valuable oil painting. It is abstract in style, so it doesn't "look like anything" to the people who come in and out every day. It hangs at eye level. One day, stopping to look at it for no particular reason, I saw with horror that someone had written a word we don't need to discuss in these pages in the lower right-hand corner. Oh, no. The printing was in a childish hand, and I ran through the list of children who had visited recently. Hmmn. I called the mother of one of them, who promised to have a talk with her that evening. Then I bought an artist's eraser and carefully removed the graffito. No permanent damage done. Sometime later, the phone rang.

I'm so glad you called, I said to the treble voice at the other end of the telephone line, *there's something I've been wanting to talk over with you.*

I did it.

You wrote on the painting?

Yeah.

I told the child how expensive the painting was. She was shocked. *But it doesn't look like anything,* she said, and I told her I knew that. Then she was silent for a while, having suddenly realized that her tough spot was even tougher than she thought: vandalism is bad enough, but how was she going to explain her use of a word she's not supposed to know? She thought fast.

I was trying to write "frog" and I spelled it wrong.

I don't think so.

Smelling defeat: *Well, I did get "frog" wrong on my spelling test once.*

We hear a lot about "the wicked" in these ancient songs—how

deceitful they are, how self-centered. This psalm, though, seems to suggest that the only real problem the wicked have is lack of information. Teach them the right way and back they'll come.

In my experience, people usually aren't stuck in some destructive form of behavior just because they don't know any better. They usually know, all right. Their disorder is not in the intellect but in the will. Get 'em while they're young, I suppose: I don't think my young artist friend will ever deface a painting again.

I'm going to leave the painting to you when I die so you can always remember what happened.

Okay. Quiet.

That'll be a long time from now. By then, you'll know why a painting can be important even if it doesn't look like anything.

Okay. Very quiet: it hadn't occurred to her before that I won't live forever.

We hung up.

FEBRUARY 20

Your tongue is like a sharpened razor. . . . You love all words that hurt.
PSALM 52:2,4

➤←

I have to watch myself when I am angry, which happens more often than most people think it does. I am not tempted to physical violence, but I do possess a quick and sharp tongue. It doesn't take much to get me going, given the right level of bottled-up annoyance, and before I know it I have devised a real zinger, aimed right between the eyes of whomever I'm annoyed at. Usually it's something elegant, like *Oh, don't be silly! What's a little cruelty between friends?* (Think about it.) I hardly ever actually fire the dart. I just savor it in my mind. I always half wish I had actually said it, and imagine the deliciously stricken look on the face of my adversary if I had. But on those occasions when the zinger has actually escaped my lips, the look on the face of my adversary—who is usually my husband—doesn't give me the satisfaction that it did in my imagination. He looks surprised and hurt. I feel unexpectedly childish. I always wish I'd kept it to myself.

But how *do* you express anger? Disemboweling someone you love with your tongue isn't the answer. Family therapists say that if you keep your complaints focused on the issue at hand that won't happen, and you won't find yourself dredging up things that happened in 1968 before you know it. They also say you're supposed to talk only about yourself: not as in *You never listen to me,* but as in *I really want to talk about this at a time when you can concentrate on what we're saying.* I try, but that is so much easier said than done, especially if you're the kind of person who doesn't come forward with anger right away. My first impulse, and my usual practice, is just to swallow it and make myself sick with it—literally. By the time I do get up enough steam to express it, I'm already over the top and ready to do some serious damage. Embarrassing to me and hurtful to others. I hate it.

Lately I've taken to asking for help with it: from God and from those who live with me. I know that I am not very good at pacing myself in expressing anger, and so I need a power greater than my own to help me. And the fellowship of someone who loves me enough to tell me the truth when I'm acting like an idiot. I pray for sense enough to hear it.

God looks down from heaven upon us all, to see if there is any who is wise.
PSALM 53:2

*B*eam me up, Scotty; there's no intelligent life down here. You see that on a lot of tee shirts and coffee mugs these days—trekkies recognize it as Captain Kirk talking to the *Enterprise* on his communicator, a device that seemed miraculous in the 1960s, before every third person you saw on the street was shouting into a cellular phone.

A man comes to see me. He is full of indignation at the stupidity of other people and what it costs him. He even gets mad about other people's errors when it *doesn't* cost him anything; one day last week he spent a full ten minutes inveighing against a woman who, he thought, read the Bible in a simplistic and literal way. *Why don't you just interpret it your way and let her do it her way?* I asked. *It doesn't sound to me like she's doing anybody any harm. Maybe she has a thing or two to teach you.* He looked at me incredulously. He knows that I am not a fundamentalist, either, and he thought he could count on me. *It doesn't make any sense! It's a waste of time and energy,* he almost shouted.

But I have learned a great deal from people who were not as sophisticated as I am, or who hadn't had nearly as much formal schooling. There is more to wisdom than the accumulation of knowledge. Wisdom is much more than the combined weight of what we know. Facts and logic are only two ways of knowing; there are more. Ours is a culture that values education and intellectual development, and rightly so. But we also try to limit our experience to that which can be rationally explained, and this means we have to leave a lot of life outside our field of inquiry. Things like love, loyalty, wonder. All the things, in short, that make life most worth living—none of them dependent on how bright you are.

Save me, O God, by your name; in your might, defend my cause.

PSALM 54:1

➤←

People at the time this psalm was written thought the very name of God was powerful. They wouldn't speak it, devising instead an unpronounceable anagram, YHWH, to stand for God. *Yahweh,* we sometimes say today when we translate. Orthodox Jews won't say it even today: *The Holy One, blessed be He* is what they say, a respectful ring of words around the unspeakable holiness of God. *Oh, my God,* I have been known to say about something surprising or horrifying or delightful or funny. I have been known to say things a lot worse than that, in fact. My mother would be shocked if she could hear me: she didn't like to hear the Lord's name taken in vain. Actually, I agree with her. I do trivialize this mystery in which I believe when I say that. I must try harder not to do it lightly.

What, precisely, is wrong with it? Why is it rude to swear? We don't believe in magic words anymore—at least, I don't. But I am good for a string of expletives that would make a longshoreman blush when something doesn't go my way. Something about being angry just makes me want to trespass against something. To break a rule. Maybe that's it: I swear a blue streak when I feel powerless. Step on God's toes when I feel impotent or frustrated. Step on polite society's toes, too, if I feel like it.

I'm not recommending this, you understand. Just owning up to it.

Anybody who can see and hear knows that the culture itself has a much higher tolerance for profanity than it used to. Newspapers print things and radio personalities say things that would have landed them in court even twenty years ago, and nobody bats an eye. I wonder—if it's true that I swear out of frustration with my own powerlessness, could it be that the same is true of society? Are we profane because we know we're weak?

The other new thing about swearing is that it was formerly done only by men in the company of one another. *There are ladies present,* one man used to say warningly to another, when the language got a little too graphic. Few such warnings are heard these days, and few are necessary. I've used some words I'm sure my father never used, and so do a lot of women I know. Swearing has become an equal opportunity vice.

Is this good or bad? Sometimes I think letting loose with an oath clears the air, vents my frustration in a useful way. Other times I'm not so sure: maybe I've capitulated to my own powerlessness, uselessly giving up some of my self-control at the very time when I need all my resources close at hand. Maybe my curses don't just arise from my awareness of my own weakness: maybe they make me even more weak.

FEBRUARY 23

And I said, "Oh, that I had wings like a dove! I would fly away and be at rest."

PSALM 55:7

❧❧

A friend lent me a copy of a children's book of African American tales that had been part of the oral tradition during slavery. It's called *The People Could Fly,* after one of the stories in it, and its cover illustration is glorious: six or seven people of different ages—men, women, children—dressed in faded work clothing and *flying,* serious and dignified, all in a group, high above the cotton fields where formerly they had bent under the heavy sacks. When the African people first came to these shores, the story goes, they could fly, anytime they wanted to. But here they forgot how to fly, and thus were unable to escape from bondage until they remembered. It is a story about the powerful memory of freedom.

In Salt Lake City, you can use the genealogical archives of the Mormon Church to look up your ancestors. The Mormons maintain these archives because of their belief that the living can be baptized into the Church on behalf of the dead and thus procure salvation for their forebears, but you don't have to be a Mormon to avail yourself of the records. A few entrepreneurial folk have set up shop near the Mormon headquarters to sell paraphernalia related to what people find out about their roots while their genealogical enthusiasm is still high: wool plaid skirts and mufflers in the tartan of the clan to which you've just discovered you belong, coffee mugs with dubious coats-of-arms on them, dolls dressed in the national costume of your ancestors.

I didn't see much merchandise aimed at African Americans. There's not much in the way of records. The memory was almost completely wiped out: no names, no villages, no kingdoms, no languages remain. Other names, another tongue was imposed on them. The people almost forgot how to fly.

The same friend who lent me the book went to Kenya once, to find his roots. I think his researches yielded something, but he returned home aware that his personal roots were much more in the state of Delaware than in the continent of Africa. He is certainly a person who's figured out how to fly: he's a highly regarded church leader and community organizer with a couple of advanced degrees. There was some sense of loss in his admission, but also a feeling of living in the present: he knows where he comes from, but he also knows where he is.

You have noted my lamentation; put my tears into your bottle.
PSALM 56:8

✣

A Greek sea captain was digging in his garden when he unearthed some old pottery—three little bone-colored vases, each no more than three inches tall. He kept two of them and brought one to me as a gift. *Do you know what this is for?* he asked. I turned it over in my hand. Its bottom was rounded, so it couldn't stand up by itself. It had a little hole in the rim, and a black design of animals and wavy lines going around its middle. I couldn't guess what use such a tiny thing that couldn't even stand up could be. *It is for tears,* he told me. When somebody died, the mourners put their tears into these bottles and wore them around their necks. So the little vase isn't really a vase—it's a bottle for mourners' tears, a sign of bereavement like the black arm-bands people wore up until the third or fourth decade of this century. Perhaps they buried the bottles with the deceased—maybe that's why my friend found three of them in the same place. I don't know.

Mine is old, really old, dry as a bone. The tears it once held—if it ever really held any—dried up long ago. The dead one they mourned has been forgotten. The mourners have been forgotten. Just this little symbol of love and loss remains, and the memory of its function is so much a thing of the past that I didn't even know what it was until I was told.

The psalmist is addressing God here: *You know my sorrow,* he says, *you have my tears in your bottle.* He is saying that God feels our sorrows as we feel them, as if God had one of these little clay bottles full of our tears around his neck—a far cry from the "Why is God doing this to me?" wail that we usually come up with when we are stricken with pain. Considered this way, God is not the detached dispenser of joys and sorrows to defenseless human beings, but the one who joins us in our lives no matter what happens. Why do we love and lose? I don't know. But I do know that we are not alone in our losses.

They have dug a pit for me, but have fallen into it themselves.
PSALM 57:5

➤<

*T*he people responsible for the terrible bombing in Oklahoma City, in which more than two hundred men, women, and children lost their lives, turn out to have been right-wing fanatics who took the current widespread suspicion of government to a horrible and insane extreme. They viewed the government as the enemy, but the people they chose to punish were people like themselves.

There is a lesson for us in this tragedy. It is this: we cannot live apart from our communities and do as we please. Freedom has never meant that. We each bear some responsibility for one another. It has never been true that the unlimited, self-centered exercise of the individual will automatically works for the general good. We hear a lot these days about how terrible government is; in Oklahoma City, we see just where that belief can end up.

Hoping to embody the rugged spirit of the American frontier in their fierce independence, hoping to inspire others to resist their obligations to our country, the terrorists are likely to see the opposite occur instead. Most of us do not want to live selfishly. Most of us know that you can't get something for nothing. Most of us know that a free society must have laws to which everyone is subject, and most of us are willing to sacrifice absolute freedom for the chance to live and work in peace.

The first accused terrorist to be apprehended was caught because he didn't think he had to have a driver's license like other people do. He dug his own pit, and then he fell into it. He and his friends are about to learn that the rules apply to them, as they apply to all of us.

FEBRUARY 26

"Surely there is a reward for the righteous."
PSALM 58:11

➤﹤

Υ*eah, right,* as my kids would have said when they were teenagers— they were excellent at expressing scorn, my kids. If there is a reward, it's sure not immediate and it's sure not obvious. Most of us long ago gave up the idea that there would be a dependable relationship between behavior and blessings. That leaves us with two choices: either there is no reward or we must reframe our idea of what a reward might look like.

I like the second option. There's a reward for righteousness: it is an inner ease that makes a hard life a whole lot easier to bear. I may not be able to control many of the things that happen to me, but I can control myself. Others may be cruel, but I need not be. I can cast my lot in with people, living or dead, whose compassion and fortitude I admire, and I can be one of them. I may not get a reward from the world for my behavior, but one reward I have: I am a member of the fellowship of those who strove for the good.

There is an interesting fringe benefit: membership in this society makes small mercies seem large. When I am not focused primarily on myself, I am less obsessed with my own well-being. I have more energy at my disposal to appreciate what I have when I'm not using it up complaining about what I don't have. The world no longer stands or falls according to whether or not I'm okay. This is a reward that is real—unlike the demonstrably false idea that good things are meted out to righteous people. It is a good and honest way to live in a world that is often neither good nor honest.

FEBRUARY 27

You have given us wine that makes us stagger.
PSALM 60:3

➜⬅

We can walk to freedom, Martin Luther King once said, *and we can run to freedom. We can even crawl to freedom. But we cannot stagger to freedom.* I saw this quotation on a poster in a room where a number of Alcoholics Anonymous groups meet and it stuck in my mind. I meet with a friend who has been struggling to stop smoking ever since I've known him. The last time I saw him, he had logged forty-odd days without a smoke. *How goes the battle?* I ask, and he shakes his head. *I'm too freaked about the job and money,* he says, *I just couldn't deal with not smoking on top of it.*

I was so sorry to hear that. I've been there. But addiction isn't *on top of* the events and tasks of life; it is *beneath* them. It is a malignant stream running just underneath the surface. Staying clean isn't just one more thing on a long list of annoying jobs to do; it's the one thing necessary to make all the other jobs *possible.* I may have a lot to accomplish, but I can't accomplish any of them until I am free of that shackle: I am passive, a victim, the resentful target of all manner of slings and arrows from any number of places. I can't manage anything else if I can't manage my life; I may look as though I do, but I am actually hanging on by my fingernails.

Life happens. It unfolds as we go along. And heavy burdens come our way and settle on our shoulders—some of these burdens we seek out and accept joyfully, like a demanding job, and others that are imposed on us, like the burden of racial prejudice. But, no matter which kind of burden we bear, a just one or an unjust one, we can't carry it if our arms are so full of our own brokenness that there is no strength left to carry anything else. First things first: my own spirit in order, so that my arms are free to embrace my life.

FEBRUARY 28

Set me upon the rock that is higher than I.
PSALM 61:2

➔⬅

I grew up to be six feet tall, but I remember how annoying it was to be shorter than other people when I was little. I remember hoping somebody tall wouldn't sit in front of me at the movies. I remember looking around for something to climb up on at parades, so I could see something besides a forest of adult legs. When Nelson Mandela came to New York shortly after his release, we gathered on the porch of St. Paul's Chapel, on lower Broadway, to watch him go by in a ticker-tape parade. The sidewalks were twenty people deep; even on the porch it wasn't easy to see the street. Several nuns were with us, including one tiny older sister, not even five feet tall. Somebody ran and got a sturdy chair and Sister Felicitas ascended, a little grey figure standing above all our heads, her steel spectacles glinting in the sun, waving with all her might. When Mandela passed, he looked right at her and nodded his head in a small bow, smiling his beautiful big smile.

Sometimes people treat short people as if they had deliberately chosen to be short, just decided to be unable to reach things easily or to have a hard time making the first step on the bus. And sometimes short people are treated as if they were children: *People are always patting me on the head,* a diminutive friend once complained, *I get so tired of being cute.* The disregard of boundaries that makes adults think they can pinch a toddler's chubby cheek without a proper introduction also affects short adults.

I think of Mandela's respectful bow to Sister Felicitas: there were many things about her that he might have treated dismissively: her small stature, her age, even her nun's habit. Mandela is famous, and very tall. But he, too, knows what it is to be dismissed. And so he bowed to her age and to her faith, seeing in her vigorous wave a strength like his own.

FEBRUARY 29

Why should the heathen say, "Where is their God?"
PSALM 79:10

✣

It has always been difficult to have faith. Even for people whom we now revere as saints, it has always involved some work. We know this because many of them wrote about their struggles with doubt. So it's not just we cynical modern folk: people have always found it hard to believe. The world has always tugged at our sleeves and whispered its cynical discouragements in our ears. Life has always taught things other than faith in a God who holds its disappointments in a loving and powerful hand. From the beginning, people have had to decide whether to walk along the road with that God or by themselves.

Nothing could be more useless than for people of faith to turn their backs on the present age and try to live in an earlier one because we think it was a better time. History moves only forward, and human beings live in history.

And God contains all of human history. Each era provides its own ways of drawing closer to God. You will do that like the modern person you are. You may read the words of someone who has been dead for centuries and find yourself tremendously moved and strengthened by them. "I could have written that myself," you may exclaim, wondering how someone writing so long ago could sound so much like you. But you will act on his words in your way, about your issues, in your language.

If we are faithful and attentive, we will know God in our way, in our day. Our task is to find the way for our age, not that of another.

MARCH 1

For God alone my soul in silence waits.
PSALM 62:1
→←

How can you study with that awful music on? I must have asked Anna a thousand times. She always swears it doesn't interfere with her concentration. She has a hard time, though, with roommate Rosemary, who is a night owl, playing loud music until six in the morning. *I can't sleep,* says Anna. *I need it quiet.* Something's happening to *me* lately, too, I notice: I used to love to write to music; I'd be annoyed with Richard when we worked in the living room together because he couldn't have it on. Now I can't seem to concentrate with music on. *I'll play this new medieval plainsong CD while I say evening prayer,* I tell myself. *That'll be cool.* But halfway into the first band I turn it off: too distracting. *Maybe I'll listen to something nice while I'm falling asleep,* I think on a night when my husband is away. *It'll be like the old single days, when I used to fall asleep with the radio on every night.* I end up turning it off, though, and listening instead to the soft wind in the trees outside my window.

Maybe it's because I'm getting older, less able and less willing to do sixty things at one time. Maybe it has to do with being a little more serene these days than I used to be. Whatever it is, silence has come to feel sweet to me, sweet and expectant; something will come to me in the quiet, it seems: a thought, a word, maybe just a gentle sleep. Some sweet gift. At the end of a day which has involved my listening hard to many, many people, maybe I don't need music. Maybe I just need some serious quiet.

MARCH 2

. . . for the mouth of those who speak lies shall be stopped . . .
PSALM 63:11

✦✦

I have a suspicion that, in the end, it is impossible to lie successfully. I have a feeling that all lies are eventually exposed. Certainly those who live a portion of their lives within a lie know how anxious a way to live it can be: at any moment, your house of cards may come tumbling down, with results ranging from embarrassment at best to tragedy for you and others at worst.

Sometimes a person comes to me with a lie that has been a burden for years. To come out with the truth now after all this time seems silly; still, he can't seem to shake the lie loose from his mind. *Should I set the record straight?* the person asks. Depends: what will happen if you do? Will you transfer the guilt off your plate and load it onto someone else's in the form of pain? Maybe so. You alone know whether or not the relationship can bear the shock of a sudden truth. If it can, tell it: it is always better for things to be as they seem.

Often, a sudden truth-teller is surprised: it turns out that the one to whom he has lied knew all along. Maybe she didn't know the specifics, but she knew that things were not as they appeared, and the knowledge was troubling. Something was wrong and she didn't know what it was. When she receives the truth, certain things fall into place. There is some relief in that, even if the truth is bad news. Then the two of you can begin. Serious work together needs to happen in order to restore trust, as well as serious self-monitoring on the part of the former liar: the lie served a purpose, and people usually find it fairly easy, once they've done something once, to do it again in similar circumstances. But the lightheartedness of living in the truth instead of in the lie is well worth the trouble.

MARCH 3

Hear my voice, O God, when I complain.
PSALM 64:1

❧❦

I tell my husband about something that irritates me. Right away, he begins making suggestions about what I might do to change the situation. *As if I didn't know,* I tell him silently. I wasn't asking for advice: I just wanted him to listen to my complaining for a little while. A signal difference between men and women: *they* think they're supposed to be able to fix things, and *we* think they should just be able to share things. *What's the point of that?* they wonder. *You've got a problem, let's solve it. Let's stop complaining and do something.*

Complaining is *doing something,* I mutter to myself. But I know I have lost the battle.

So, what *is* the point? Why *does* it feel so good to have somebody listen to my complaints? I think it's because it allows me to recapture something of the magical safety of my childhood while still retaining the adult responsibility—and privilege—of solving my own problems. When I really feel heard, it is as if another pair of shoulders joins mine in carrying whatever it is I'm carrying. I am not alone with my problem; I can bring it to somebody, as I used to bring things to my mother. When someone truly understands my frustration, I feel stronger: now I *can* get cracking and do something about it. I feel accompanied.

Of course, you can get carried away. It feels so good to complain that some of us get so we do it most of the time. Not good. It's not supposed to be an indoor sport. It's supposed to be something you share with someone who cares enough about you just to listen.

MARCH 4

You still the roaring . . .
PSALM 65:7

➤✦◄

We are all on the train home on this Sunday afternoon. I am returning from a retreat at a monastery upstate. Fully half of my traveling companions are children, many more than I usually see on this train during the week. The circus is in town; they clutch balloons and colored pennants. Some of them have their faces painted up like clowns' faces. Their parents are with them, sometimes a grandmother.

One little girl is crying inconsolably. I saw her with her mother and grandmother before we got on the train: she sitting on the stairs howling, the perplexed women who love her sitting with her, trying their best to cheer her up. Just too much circus, I guess. Her best dress is rumpled and the sash has come untied; one white sock is uncuffed. The adults are disappointed; she's been talking about the circus all week, they've been looking forward to her enjoyment, and now, these tears.

I remember crying at the end of my own birthday parties. I remember bursting into tears when my grandmother asked me if I'd enjoyed myself at the school Halloween party, and leaving more than one slumber party in the middle of the night. I remember my children doing all of these things, too. Sometimes you just overload and don't know it, when you're little, and you go into major meltdown. And the grownups who are knocking themselves out trying to show you a good time find themselves wiping your eyes and helping you blow your nose. Don't take it personally. Just remember what it was to be little.

Now two or three more are crying—the original has stopped and is asleep in her mother's arms. She *did* enjoy the circus. It's just time to go home.

You have tried us just as silver is tried.

PSALM 66:9

><

*M*y grandmother had an amazing spoon: an old metal mixing spoon that she used for mixing all the different things she baked. She'd used it for years, and here is what was amazing about it: she'd used it for so long that one edge of the bowl of it was not curved, but straight—she'd worn the metal clean away. I was deeply impressed, and one day I resolved that I would erode a spoon of my own. I went to the kitchen drawer and chose a large spoon, and then I embarked upon an orgy of cooking: every kind of cake mix Pillsbury made, every kind of Saturday afternoon fudge in the cookbook. Sometime during that period I began to make cakes from scratch, too, with a little advice from my grandmother, just for a change from what came in the boxes. I made oatmeal cookies. I made peanut butter cookies. My brothers were in hog heaven, but my spoon remained discouragingly symmetrical.

I don't remember how long I worked on the spoon before I came to the end of my attention span and moved on to something else. My spoon was 1950s stainless steel, while my grandmother's was probably 1890s silver-plated tin—a much softer metal. But that wasn't really why hers wore down. It was the time that did it, the decades of hard use. Years of love expressed through the medium of food for the family. Imagine: love is strong enough to bend metal to its sweet will.

But let the righteous be glad and rejoice before God; let them also be merry and joyful.

PSALM 68:3

➤✦

*T*hree women—no, make that four women—approach me with concerned expressions on their faces. *Are you all right?* This is because they saw me wiping away tears during the eleven o'clock service. *I could see that you were upset,* one says, touching my arm lightly. I explain that I wasn't upset, really, that a certain hymn just makes me cry more often than it does not—reminds me of my dad, I guess. This is one of the drawbacks of my calling: you are on display up there in front of people. You can't hide. And you'd better not mist up, either. It worries people.

But I do. I am easily moved, by all kinds of things: I cry when I am sad, of course, but I also cry when something is beautiful or noble. I try not to, but eventually a tear sneaks down my cheek, and then another one follows in its tracks. I whisk them away with my hand, but I don't always get them all. I don't make any noise or sob or anything like that. I just have a few tears.

I wish people weren't scared by this. There's nothing wrong with an occasional tear in a leader. It's not a sign of impending chaos. I was not "upset," in the sense that a carefully arranged pile of apples would be "upset" if somebody pulled one out from the bottom, sending them all rolling all over the floor. I have no desire to go through life that carefully arranged. I'd hate to be someone who never felt something enough to shed a tear, or to be so self-conscious in public that my own emotions were unavailable to me.

Let those who take pleasure in my misfortune draw back and be disgraced.

PSALM 70:2

➺

You may have heard about this: in the spring of 1995, the national treasurer of my church was discovered to have embezzled more than two million dollars. It came to light after she had already been asked to resign because of her abrasive working style. In the course of packing up her things, she made out a check to herself for ninety thousand dollars in back pay and vacation pay. Whew.

Little love had been lost between her and her former co-workers. People were furious, but for some there was also a certain satisfaction. Stories of her high-handedness were traded, always ending with some version of *Well, I guess what goes around, comes around, huh?* News of the embezzlement spread like poison ivy throughout the Church and crossed over into the secular press. *The Washington Post* ran an editorial on it. *The New York Times* gave it almost a full page of investigative reporting. People couldn't believe it at first—how had she gotten away with it for so long? Was it really deliberate? And did her husband—a priest in the Episcopal Church—know about it? How much was missing? And, most of all: what would happen to her now?

Mail and fax messages flooded the Episcopal Church Center in New York. She and her attorneys deeded over her two opulent homes to the Church, and plans were made to sell them to make up some of the stolen money. She hoped she would be permitted to make such restitution until it was all paid off and escape going to jail. She wrote a rambling letter in which she claimed that she had suffered a rare kind of mental breakdown and didn't remember any of her transactions. She also said that the breakdown happened because she was under stress as a woman in a male-dominated church.

Far be it from me to criticize other people's breakdowns. I've got more than enough to keep me busy managing my own life. I have no idea why she did what she did. But there is a lesson to be learned here about forgiveness.

This person must be forgiven—whoa, Nellie, let me finish: that doesn't mean that she will get away with her crime. It doesn't mean that it's okay to do what she did—it's not okay. It doesn't mean she won't have to pay for it; we pay for everything we do in this life. She'll have to make restitution. She may serve time in prison. Forgiveness doesn't erase history. This thing will always have happened. But life will go on, and she will still be here. She may be our fallen sister, but she is still our sister.

MARCH 8

Be my strong rock, a castle to keep me safe.
PSALM 71:3

➸➺

I will never forget the way my father's house looked and sounded after we had taken everything out of it. The rooms echoed, it seemed, although that's really quite unlikely—they were too small to echo, somewhat smaller than I had remembered their being. The long, elegant draperies that my mother had been so proud of looked limp and a little apologetic. The wallpaper looked tired, and there were rectangles of fresher paper that had been under pictures. I finally admitted to no one in particular that I had never thought the wallpaper went particularly well with the furniture.

But I didn't go there for decorating ideas. How many times did I arrive late at night with two sleeping children to be carried upstairs to sleep in my old bed? How many early evenings did I stand in the backyard by the clothesline and look across the field to the houses on the hill beyond? The field is gone now, I see: rows of new houses come right up to our back fence. How many dogs and cats are buried in that yard? A lot. May they rest in peace.

When my marriage came apart my toddler and I went back there to live for a year. I'd resisted doing it, hadn't wanted to lose my independence. But my folks were glad to have us. Glad to help. Always there. And that first night after my mother died, when I heard my father mumbling in their bedroom: the same evening prayers I used to hear in two voices now in one. Now both voices are gone. It was a good school in which to learn about the dependability of God's love, that house. Good teachers, the two of them. But a sad little place without all our things. The lady who bought it wants to know if I'd like to see what she's done: a new walk, I see, and a new entrance on the side. I look through the open door at her furniture, the new wallpaper, her purse left open on the dining table. *No, thanks, I'd better get on the road,* I say.

MARCH 9

May there be abundance of grain on the earth.
PSALM 72:16

✥

*T*here is actually plenty of food, I am told; it's just not always in the right places. American farmers are paid not to grow wheat while African children die for want of bread. Well-meaning people send a shipload of food to a starving country and it rots on the dock while local factions jockey for power over it. And the so-called acts of

God—flooded rivers, mudslides, droughts—that result in massive starvation in many parts of the world sometimes have their beginnings in bad decisions about where to build villages and how to harvest timber.

So when a person of faith prays for an end to world hunger, he's not just crossing his fingers and hoping for the best. Such a prayer also involves an ethical challenge to human selfishness. Basing any decision solely on "what's best for me" is always significantly less than the best a moral being or a society can do, and sometimes it does serious harm. And praying for an end to hunger is more than thinking vague, kind thoughts about poor people with your hands folded and your eyes closed; it also means rejecting the human actions that cause hunger. It can make people uncomfortable, that kind of talk, for you and I have been the beneficiaries of the current arrangement of the world's resources, and privilege doesn't renounce itself without a fight. Talk about the sinfulness of unequal distribution of the world's wealth and they'll say you just don't understand modern political realities. I say we understand them all too well.

MARCH 10

When my mind became embittered, I was sorely wounded in my heart.
PSALM 73:21

✛

You probably know people who haven't spoken to one another in years. Somebody said or did something ages ago, and the rift has never been healed. I remember a pair of feuding ladies in the church where I grew up—each would step stiffly into her pew on Sunday, head held high, refusing to allow the other to enter her field of vision. It was a small church, and that behavior stuck out like a sore thumb. Finally the minister intervened, drawing their attention to a seldom-used provision in the prayer book that allowed him to refuse communion to anyone living at enmity with another. *This is it,* he told each woman separately: *no communion until you two begin talking.* The next Sunday, the same stiff entrance, the same studied lack of eye contact, and one new thing:

Good morning, Mrs. Johnson.
Good morning, Mrs. Brown.
Amen.

Well, that wasn't what he had in mind, but it was a beginning, I guess. They did heal whatever it was eventually, and the cold war came to an end. I don't know whether either of those two women felt wounded by the years of enmity; if you had asked, they probably each would have reported being wounded instead by the other's long-ago offense. But that wasn't really so: you may do something to offend me, but I alone decide how long I'm going to hold on to my anger about it. And if I elect to keep it on the front burner, that means I've got one less burner to work with. And whom does that hurt?

MARCH 11

They set fire to your holy place; they defiled the dwelling-place of your Name.
PSALM 74:6

✣

Everyone knows that the Church has sometimes walked hand in glove with some secular power people from whom it would have been better to be a little more distant. The wonderful Gothic cathedrals people love to visit in Europe, for instance, were built by societies that had kings and queens and nobles and peasants, in that order, and the kings and queens and nobles depended on the church to help make sure that the peasants remained in their proper place. The German Christian Church of the Third Reich developed a whole theological discipline designed to give a religious context for the Nazi program. And in America every president knows that it doesn't hurt to be seen, at least occasionally, asking a well-known clergyman for advice, separation of church and state or no.

So it's no wonder people who fight against political oppression sometimes consider religion part of the problem. Visit some of those Gothic cathedrals, especially in France, and look at the statues: somebody has lopped the heads clean off a fair number of them. Just as they did to Marie Antoinette, and for much the same reason: they were sick and tired of being walked on by rich people, and the church hadn't done much of anything to make it stop. I guess the saints portrayed by those statues looked like just so many more rich people to them.

What a shame, when the strongest continuous thread in the common Jewish, Christian, and Muslim tradition is the love of God for the humble. When the One to whom those churches were built was poor. Power corrupts memory: the worst thing that could have been done to those saints was to dress them up like rich people, and that's just what happened. You still meet highly moral people who are convinced that religious belief carries with it a callous indifference to the plight of the poor, and who will have none of it.

In every age, the Church has done things it should not have done. The same is true of every institution, every nation, and also of every person. You're not going to find anything perfect in this world, so to turn away from something or someone because you have made the astonishing discovery that there is sin there means either that you will search all your life for an association with something that doesn't exist or that you will live alone. And you will deprive yourself of much of the good that is to be found in this profoundly mixed world.

That Martin Luther was a brilliant theologian was a good thing. That he was also an anti-Semite was not. That Thomas Jefferson believed in the freedom and dignity of every person was a good thing. That he was a slaveholder was not. These distinctions shouldn't be too hard for a smart person to grasp. We can treat the people and institutions we encounter with the same discernment we wish to be accorded ourselves: honestly celebrate the virtue and honestly name the other stuff.

MARCH 12

We give you thanks, O God, we give you thanks.

PSALM 75:1

＞＜

I visit a lot of churches, and so I have a chance to see how things are different from one to another and how they're the same. One thing I often notice: when there is an opportunity in the prayers for people to make their own intercessions, lots of folks do so. *Let us pray for our own needs and for those of others,* the leader might say, and everyone has a list of names: Bill who has AIDS, Terry who lost his job, Mary who has cancer and Victor who cares for her, Steven who has died and Henry who mourns, and so forth. The buzz of special intentions might go on for a minute or two, or even longer. But when the leader says, *Let us give thanks to God for all our blessings,* there is a slightly embarrassed silence. Someone may mutter a name or two. A few sensitive souls look uncomfortable; they know they have a lot to be thankful for, but they don't know quite how to begin. The leader gives it a beat and adds a few vague ones of her own, like "this day" or "this place" or "this congregation."

I wonder why it's so easy to be explicit about the things that hurt us and so hard to be similarly clear about our joys. Not that we *aren't* thankful for the congregation or the weather, of course; it's just that the urgency of our thanksgivings seems never to equal the urgency of our need. Or maybe it's something else: maybe we're embarrassed to say out loud how utter a gift the good things in our lives really are. We may work very hard, and we may be very good, but neither our work nor our goodness makes our blessings inevitable. We do not earn those blessings. They are gifts. That's hard to hear. We want there to be an immediate and dependable connection between our good behavior and our good fortune. But we stop and think, for even five seconds, of all the people we've known who were good and suffered anyway, and of the times that this has happened to us, and we know that all our good news is pure blessing.

MARCH 13

They sink into sleep.
PSALM 76:5

I must have slept in the wrong position again: I was dreaming about a sinister figure digging into the small of my back with a supernatural fingertip that conferred unbearable pain on everything it touched, and in the middle of begging him to stop, I awakened with a sob—is there anything more eerie than waking up crying? This dream happens sometimes when my back hurts, as if the nerves were trying to send a message to the brain by showing the same cheap horror movie again and again. I look at the clock. Too late to take one of my Mickey Finn pain pills; I'd never make it out of bed in the morning. Damn.

There are exercises I can do when this happens; they will stretch the ligaments and relax the muscles and after a while I'll feel a little better. I creep out of bed and lie down on the floor to begin. I think about the nature of pain as I go through the stretches and flexes. What is awful about that recurrent dream is not just the physical pain: it's the idea that a frightening being is deliberately causing it. It is fear, as much as pain. The main difference between chronic pain and acute pain, in fact, *is* the ingredient of fear: acute pain is designed to make you pay attention to whatever is happening to your body and do whatever you have to do to make it stop. Chronic pain is not about that—it's just my familiar old enemy dropping by for a visit, like an unwelcome in-law.

My dream takes my chronic pain and adds fear to it, transforms it into acute pain, so I'll wake up and do something about my sleeping position. Pretty smart. Not the most pleasant method of alerting me to a problem, but it works: I never sleep through *those* dreams. The ancients thought God spoke to them in dreams, and they consulted dream interpreters for guidance. I agree, and add: the word of God is not always a word of comfort. Sometimes it's an alarm.

MARCH 14

I will cry aloud, and He will hear me.
PSALM 77:1

➤←

Sometimes one grandchild or another will hurt herself slightly— scrape a knee, bang a funnybone, shut a finger in a drawer. She will pause, absorbing the shock of a sudden pain, and then, if I am in the room, she will look at me. Sometimes that look will determine whether she goes on to wail at the top of her lungs and end up on my lap for five minutes or else just laughs and says *ouch*. If I seem receptive, a small injury becomes a good opportunity for her to soak up some serious sympathy. If not, there are better things to do. Interesting: crying is not just a private response to grief or pain. It is also a form of communication, and a most effective tool for influencing the behavior of others.

This is so often true, in fact, that a lot of us come to believe—unconsciously—that the people we care about will know we are crying even if they can't hear us. I remember luxuriating often in solitary tears in some obscure hiding place when I was little; I was able to get quite worked up about the fact that nobody was coming to see what was wrong with me, even though I was hidden from sight and nobody knew where I *was! Nobody loves me,* I would tell myself—a patent untruth, dubiously documented by the isolation I myself had sought. But it was seductively sad, a little glamorous, this lonely sorrow of mine, for nothing quite equals the dark pleasure of being an innocent victim, and many of us are prepared to go to considerable lengths and ignore a fair amount of history in order to savor it. Sometimes we use our tears to get us a comforting lap to sit on; sometimes, perversely, we use them to insure that there will be no lap. Sorrow joins us to others or it isolates us; we are the ones who choose which it will be.

Oh, God, the heathen have come . . .
PSALM 79:1

➤◄

Two days in a row working and writing on spiritual concerns at home—this is what life is supposed to be like every day for me, the failed telecommuter. But I'm always running into the office when I shouldn't, getting involved in meetings I ought to have delegated to others. This time, though, I've done it right: I've scheduled the meeting I can't delegate at a time I can attend by speakerphone, and have arranged for the person who needs to see me to come to me here at home. And so I sit in a chair with my laptop and my cordless phone, an afghan covering my legs because I'm still trying to get over the flu, and the hours stretch invitingly before me. I will be extremely productive today, and even on into the night—my husband is away at a conference.

But the phone chirps. Can Rosie and Madeline come over this evening while their mommy goes to dinner? Far be it from me to sabotage a dinner date—of course they can. They can play with the new marble run I bought them to enjoy when they come over. Another chirp—friend Norah. What am I doing tonight? Do I want to have dinner? Well, sure—I can bring the kids and the marble run over to her house, I guess. And another: do I want to bring anything to the church flea market across the street? Well, there *are* some things I need to get out from underfoot. I'll go up and sort through them and bring them over.

This is what happens: I get things all arranged and then life happens all over everything. The heathens have invaded my domain—but after all, they only get in because I let them in. And maybe I don't want to *have* a domain. Maybe my lumpy, crowded life is good enough for me.

Give us life that we may call upon your name.

PSALM 80:17

➸←

You do get the sense of this, right? The psalmist is proposing a deal: God will do whatever it is that's needed and, in return, get a lot of nice public praise. Many of the psalms contain this kind of promise at the end: *Grant my request and I'll tell everybody I know how great you are, Lord, okay?*

More than a little amusing, but so very human. We've all been there, I think: finding ourselves in a very tight spot and promising God all kinds of things if we can just get out of this. I have seen it, sometimes, in people who know themselves to be dying: sudden attendance at church after years of backsliding, or a sudden reversal of bad behavior toward a spouse. It is so common in this particular situation that those who work with the terminally ill have given it a name: it is called the "bargaining" stage in dying.

Well, it's understandable. Something terrible happens and you ask the eternal human question: *Why me?* And then you remember two or three things in your character that are not as you know they should be, and you wonder if this misfortune might not have something to do with them. *You never know,* you tell yourself. So you resolve to fix them right now, so that you can make the terrible thing go away. In most cases, of course, your prognosis is not greatly affected by your sudden good behavior. Many people call it off after a while, moving into the eminently understandable next stages: depression and anger.

But even if one is dying, there are reasons to mend the torn places in your soul that don't have anything to do with warding off illness and death. If my days are numbered—and whose aren't?—maybe I want to end my life sober instead of addicted. Maybe I want to achieve some resolution of the cold war that has been my marriage before I die. Maybe I want to explore the mystery of God in the faith tradition in which I was raised, to ponder the meaning of my life and the possibility of the also-life, that reality which contains this one and does not know its sad limits. Those are important things to do at any time in life, but especially at its end, when one is forced to confront the meaning of one's own history.

MARCH 17

And yet my people did not hear my voice, and Israel would not obey me. So I gave them over to the stubbornness of their hearts, to follow their own devices.
PSALM 81:11–12

✣

Not even God, according to this psalm, can compel obedience and attention. We can always choose not to listen. And so we see God doing what some of us have had to do with our grown children: giving up. What a painful thing that is: to try and try to get through to your child, until you've tried everything, and then to reach that point where you can do no more and just have to stop.

More than once, I have had to abandon ship. Time after time, my advice and warnings would evoke a bored heavenward glance. Time after time, my careful arrangements for the future would fall through. Nothing I tried worked. It was only when I gave up in despair that they—almost magically, calmly, of their own accord—began to act in their own best interest. My warnings didn't do it. My advice didn't do it. My arrangements didn't do it.

I remember talking to a wise older friend while I was still trying to manage a knotty period in one of my daughters' lives. *You know, she has a God, too,* my friend said gently. That was a stunning thing for me to hear right then, one of those dozen or so lines you remember for the rest of your life. The one you love has a God, too. You are not in charge of her life. Her life is between her and her God, just as yours is between you and your God. Letting her discover her own destiny is not abandoning her. We all must discover our destinies on our own.

MARCH 18

"How long will you judge unjustly, and show favor to the wicked?"
PSALM 82:2

>+<

As I write this, the O. J. Simpson murder trial is in its fourth tedious month. Publication of a book usually takes about nine months after the manuscript is completed, so I assume that we will know by the time you read this whether or not the football star sliced his pretty wife's throat from ear to ear. Or maybe we won't; maybe the super–soap opera will still be playing every day on Court TV. I wouldn't be totally surprised.

Unlike lawyer dramas, this kind of television has brought millions of Americans into contact with the real thing—or do I mean the sur-real thing? Some people shake their heads at the intricate scenario pieced together by a defense lawyer; others listen and wonder, *Do I know for sure he's not right?* And, as angry-making as it is, it's essential that each side's case be completely made, whether it's a glamorous case with million-dollar attorneys like this one or a case involving an unknown defendant with a court-appointed lawyer. Or a defendant whose guilt is already widely assumed, like the man accused of planting a bomb that blew up the federal building in Oklahoma City and killed 164 men, women, and children. People shouted at Timothy McVeigh about the death penalty they hoped he would suffer as he was led from his jail cell to his arraignment. *They should just kill him now and save us all the bother,* a taxi driver told me that morning as we listened to his car radio.

Well, no, they shouldn't. All citizens are entitled to a competent defense, not just good citizens. If Timothy McVeigh can get a fair trial, then I can trust that I will, if I am ever accused of a crime. The extreme cases, handled well, ensure that the vast middle ground is protected. And yes, that means taxpayers' money will be spent defending criminals. It's a system, and we must apply it fairly to everyone. It may exasperate us, but it also protects us.

MARCH 19

*The sparrow has found her a house and the swallow a nest
where she may lay her young.*

PSALM 84:2

✣

*T*his was my mother's favorite psalm. Its coziness has always reminded me of her. We used to play a game, in the morning when we kids would invade her bed, about being lost and then found—two different games, actually: one about a mother cat who had lost her three kittens (my brothers and me) and another one about a mother peanut who had lost her three little peanuts and ended up in a peanut butter factory looking for them. Both games ended in a joyful reunion: kittens—or peanuts—popping up from under the bedclothes to a delighted and eternally surprised mother cat—or peanut. My mom always reminded me of a nest; long after I was grown up, I still loved to lie beside her for a little while at night when I visited, or in the morning while she drank her coffee.

Modern life is pretty rootless. We grow up and scatter. The years at home, when I look back on them now, were very few. I left home very young—too young, really—and so much more of my life has been spent contending with the world than was spent in the nest. No wonder I long for it sometimes, and no wonder I turn to this psalm when I miss my mother. She is gone; there is now no nest to which I can return. But I am still here, and my imagination remains my own. Having known the safety of the nest, I can make use of my memory of it. I can make a nest for others who need to know of safety and love: my children, my grandchildren. And here is something I've noticed: when I am making such a nest for them, I feel safe and cozy myself. So the palpable comfort didn't just come from my mother, nor does it come from me. It comes through us, not from us. It comes from God.

MARCH 20

Mercy and truth have met together; righteousness and peace have kissed each other.

PSALM 85:10

✣

This image: mercy and truth meeting, maybe shaking hands, and two allegorical figures representing righteousness and peace exchanging a kiss—it is so sweet that it almost doesn't matter to the reader what it means. But it's not just a string of pretty words: it is a careful description of a particular way of thinking morally about life. Mercy and peace are things we all want in the world; we want as much as we can get, as soon as possible. But this ancient line of poetry imposes conditions on how much mercy and peace we are likely to see: these good things don't just happen at random. We will have mercy and peace to the extent that we behave honestly and righteously.

That's true. There's not much we can do about those wrong-place-at-the-wrong-time events of human existence: the tornado swooping in from nowhere, the freak accident, the virus that happens to find you and decides to stay. But those sorrows are not things that rule out mercy and peace: everyone lives with troubles, but not everyone is embittered by them. A gentle nature is not something you have to be born with. It's something you can cultivate. My headaches aren't really infinitely worse than other peoples'. My misfortunes are not personal affronts; they are merely part of life. I am not supposed to get special treatment from life. Being honest about my troubles can help me weather my sorrows without wasting time and energy resenting everyone else who doesn't have them. Thus unburdened by an armload of old scores to settle, I can be free to act lovingly and reap the rewards that come from doing so: when you behave lovingly toward others, a fair number of them usually love you back. That sweetens any number of bitter cups you may be called upon to drain.

MARCH 21

Save your servant who puts his trust in you.

PSALM 86:2

➤←

So many references in scripture to servanthood—and so few instances of it in modern life. Servanthood reminds us so vividly of the shameful heritage of slavery that the image of the servant is no longer very useful. I may contract with someone to clean my house if I am too busy to do it myself, but I don't consider that person my servant: she's an independent contractor whose services I am purchasing. The time when human beings bought and sold other human beings in America is too recent for us to feel very open to the idea of servanthood. And it raises questions for us about the nature of God: is God someone whose primary interest is in his own authority? Are we bound to God by power, or are we bound by love?

In this question—the question of whether the signal divine attribute is power or love—modern sensibilities usually come down on the side of love. Talk of a God who may on occasion send his people suffering in order to punish, test, or instruct them made more sense in a world like the one the psalmists lived in: a world of absolute monarchs and hierarchies based upon the capacity for physical coercion. We don't inhabit that world anymore. How, then, do we relate to these three-thousand-year-old hymns?

In this, as in all instances when the fact of my modernity puts me in an untenable position with regard to my tradition, my job is not to find a way to believe as the biblical writers believed, but to find a way to allow the experience of God they record to come also to me. In other words, I don't try to talk myself into a slave-holding mentality, but ask, instead, *what will do for me what the concept of servanthood did for this ancient poet?* Let me give it a try:

This verse does talk of a servant, but it also talks of trust. The totality of the master's impact on a servant's life made the servant utterly dependent: there was no power in his life outside of the master's will. So the master is, in a sense, the servant's world. Now we're getting somewhere, for I know what it is to live in my world, to be bound by its realities rather than free to just make up my own. The psalmist lives in God; there is no greater reality. I can live like that, if I choose to, or more accurately, I can acknowledge that God is, in fact, where I live. You, who encompass and contain my life and the life of the world: *I put my trust in you.*

Glorious things are spoken of you, O city of our God.
PSALM 87:2

✦✦

Private prayer is habit-forming: make it part of your life and you will not want to live without it anytime soon. But it would be a mistake to think that it exhausts the possibilities of living the spiritual life. Besides praying by yourself on a train or in your bathtub, there is much, much more. The aspect of spiritual life involving you in community is equally necessary: it feeds that part of you that needs other people, and it also helps to shape your interpretation of the almost-uncommunicable contemplative experience. The essentially irrational character of contemplative prayer makes us nervous, social animals that we are: part of being human is communicating with one another about things that matter, and now here we are with this very important yet quite indescribable experience, groping for words to share it and failing to do so adequately. We don't like that. We know that there are people in state hospitals who also think they talk to God. It is no accident that the mentally ill often experience and communicate their illness in religious terms: the man who has been instructed by God to kill someone, the woman chosen by God to prophesy paranoically on the street corner, the schizophrenic convinced that he *is* God. However various the exotic manifestations of their illness, such people all have one tragic fact in common: they are profoundly isolated. They are extreme examples of something that is true for everyone: the spiritual life lived in isolation is unhealthy. Its ultimate extension is madness. We need other people with whom to walk on our spiritual journey.

From its earliest expression, the Judeo-Christian understanding of God's action in human life has been a corporate one. Famous individuals arose in the history of Israel, but God chose the people as a whole, and raised up famous figures for the sake of the whole of Israel. The Christian understanding of Jesus as Messiah would be meaningless if there were no people of whom he was to *be* the messiah: his life is not lived for himself, but for us, and it is poured out in death for us as well. It is not too much to say that there is no such thing as a Christian alone, and the same is true of a Jew. Neither my worth nor my happiness rests entirely with me; they can only be complete in the company and service of others. We may encourage, support, annoy, or bore one another, but we cannot be without one another. Our souls are in danger if we try.

MARCH 23

I have grown weary with my crying; my throat is inflamed.
PSALM 69:4

❯❮

I thought it was from crying, at first—I had been listening to Samuel Barber's *Adagio for Strings*, which always does me in—but my scratchy throat and runny nose are worse this morning, even after I've moved on from the music and had a good night's sleep. I must have a cold. The telephone rings: can I watch Rosie, who also has a sore throat today? I greet a very pink little girl and feel her forehead: a bit hot. We curl up on my big bed together and play computer solitaire. She drifts off to sleep, unusual behavior for our Rose; I can see she really needs to be right where she is today. I take advantage of her silence to work on a few things—luckily, I don't have to go in today, either. All afternoon to write.

But although I have a nice big block of uninterrupted time, I don't really get much done. Just not concentrating very well, I'm afraid. I doze a little myself, and find myself idly turning to computer solitaire instead of to the story I really need to finish. I listen to the radio and read a magazine. By the time Rosie's mother comes for her, I'm exhausted. And I've hardly done anything all day.

It's funny about this cold virus, how little a person can really do about its considerable effects. You can slog through them, of course, if your really have to, and you can take something for your stuffy head, so people can at least understand you when you speak, but idleness and rest feel especially well deserved when the throat scratches and the eyelids are heavy. Besides, there is a reason to stay in that has nothing at all to do with how *you* feel: being out among people means you're bringing the virus into their lives. Do you really have the right to do that to others? Is that really such a brave and wonderful thing to do? Time was, I would have thought so. Not anymore. Do yourself and others a favor when you're contagious: rest at home. And feel better.

MARCH 24

Let my prayer enter into your presence.
PSALM 88:2

➤✦

A woman comes to see me. She wants to begin praying regularly, but isn't sure how to begin. *I remember prayers from when I was little,* she says. *You know, "Now I lay me down to sleep," but I feel silly saying something so childish. I want to center myself, to be in a peaceful place, but when I try, I think of a million things I should be doing.*

People have been thinking and writing about prayer for centuries now. You can read what they have said about finding the presence of

God in prayer, and that's interesting and helpful. Many of them, though, were monastics whose lives revolved around opportunities for corporate prayer and long stretches of uninterrupted time. For those of us who aren't nuns or monks, the challenges of prayer are different from the ones they faced.

Distractions are what discourage most of the people I talk to about prayer. *I think the devil must wait for me to begin and then reminds me about tonight's meat loaf or the dry cleaning,* says a woman I know. The same thing happens to me. I've learned from experience not to fight it. Here is what I do:

When I'm trying to be still and hear the voice of God, I invariably think of some practical matter I have left undone. I don't try to shove it down or drown it out. I welcome it into my mind, invite it into my prayer. It becomes part of the words to my prayer—the distraction itself, and what it means, something like: *As you know, Lord, I am anxious because I can't remember if I have enough sour cream to make chicken paprika tonight. I remember how good it tastes, and how much everybody likes it. I remember how good it felt to make it for my children when they were little, and to see them eat. I remember how blessed I am to have had them, and how different it is now that they are grown. I didn't know our time would be so short. I remember the ways in which I am worried about them now, and the things I wish I'd done differently back then. I get nervous about them, as you know, Lord, and I forget that you love them, too, and will care for them as you care for me. That even when I die, you will be with them, and I, too, will be with them in my new life in you. . . .*

It's a kind of stream-of-consciousness, one-thing-leading-to-another sort of prayer. It takes a distraction and makes it holy. I don't know in advance where it will lead me, and that's fine—when I meet a friend and strike up a conversation, I don't control where that talk will go, either. I let my thoughts carry me into the presence of God, and they do . . . because there is nothing in my life, no matter how mundane, that is meaningless in the sight of God.

You have crushed Rahab of the deep with a deadly wound.
PSALM 89:10

➵➴

Who is Rahab? She is a terrible sea monster who was legendary in ancient Israel. She lived in the sea, but she symbolized chaos of any kind to the people who sang this song. Rahab was probably a familiar figure long before the psalms were written, perhaps even before the Hebrew people thought of themselves as a distinct group. They had probably been scaring each other with stories about Rahab for generations.

The sea has often been a symbol of chaos in stories and songs passed from generation to generation. It's big and unpredictable, and human beings don't control it. It's such a good metaphor for the frightening unpredictability of life that many of the important literary figures of human culture have been people who sailed the sea: Gilgamesh, the mythical hero of the Babylonians; Odysseus, the wandering Greek hero; Aeneas, the seafaring survivor of Troy who ended up in Italy. And Noah. And Jonah. And Ishmael, the narrator of the American epic *Moby-Dick*. And when we feel uncertain and lost, don't we sometimes say that we are "all at sea"?

I've spent years around ships and the people who sail them. I never met one of them who lacked a healthy respect for what the sea can do or who took its dangers lightly. They know that human beings are not very powerful creatures. They know that the best way to deal with a storm at sea is to get away from it: you're no match for it. And so these various myths from various places sound a lot alike: heroes who, against all odds, escape with their lives from the perils of the deep. There are a lot of close calls in life, and you don't have to be a sailor to have experienced a few. The powers that God called into being are awesome. And we are all so small.

Teach us to number our days.

PSALM 90:12

✦

$\mathcal{M}$y friend's father has ALS—Lou Gehrig's disease. People who have it usually die within three years of diagnosis, and it looks like he's right on schedule: a year into it, he can no longer talk, and he is losing the ability to walk.

He has a laptop computer with which to communicate. He sits at dinner with his large family as he always has. His wife makes the wonderful food she's always made for them. It is noisy and normal—too normal. He taps out an occasional message on his keyboard, but the easy give-and-take of the normal dinner conversation is too fast for him to keep up with, and he stops trying. After a while he leaves the table and goes to the living room to lie down.

I wish they'd all shut up for once and acknowledge that he's dying, says my friend. *It's so weird: everybody chattering away as they always do and him dying by degrees in the middle of it all. Nobody is saying anything about what's happening to him, never. And it's almost too late—I don't know how much longer he can type. His hands are starting to go now, too.*

Why do so many people refuse to talk about life's ending, as if they would bring it on by bringing it up? Why do they fight so hard to keep everything "normal"? We have nothing to fear from the truth. The honest expression of sorrow and fear doesn't make things sadder or more fearful. So you're clumsy and emotional when you talk about these things—so what? Do you think the one you love wants you to be "normal" about your future parting? I doubt it.

He shall say to the Lord, "You are my refuge and my stronghold."
PSALM 91:2

Spiritually, I'm in a pretty good place, says a woman who has come to see me. *I've come through some tough times. But now I feel that as long as I have my husband, I'm okay.*

Actually, that doesn't sound like a very good place to me at all. It sounds to me like a pretty dangerous place. All that stands between her and chaos is the life and affection of one person, a person from whom she is absolutely certain to be separated eventually: he will die, or she will. I meet a lot of people like her: people whose lives depend on someone else. There are so many reasons why it happens. The idealization of romantic love in our culture is one: the prince and princess get married and the curtain falls. Our high divorce rate hasn't done much to shake the myth: you just get a new prince and, again, the curtain falls. Or, for a mother or a father, the shock of how fiercely a child is loved: the emotion and the responsibility are so awesome, so far beyond whatever else one has known of love. No wonder so many people feel that, in a sense, they *are* their children, that they have no existence apart from them that counts for much of anything.

When my father died, we went to California, where he had been living in retirement. We stayed with my stepmother at their house. One day, somewhere in the midst of the funeral home visits, the friends dropping off casseroles, and the choosing of hymns, we found ourselves in the garage. I was bringing a basket of laundry from the clothesline with my stepmother; my husband was getting something from the car. Somehow we all just stopped to pass the time of day a little, and she began to tell us about her experiences as a nurse during the war. She talked of the young men she had dated and the ones she'd cared for in the hospital. She talked of meeting her first husband, and how he had proposed. She talked, of course, of the happy years with my dad, so late in life. We must have stood in the garage for an hour, listening to this twice-widowed woman speak of her life. We marveled, afterward, at the powerful sense of her own responsibility for her self-worth that she conveyed in everything she said and everything she did. It was her life; she was a force within it, someone who walked with a purpose and a destiny of her own. Her love for each of her two husbands had been total and her grief at both their deaths profound, but she has always understood her separateness and uniqueness as a child of God. We are born into the human family, but we are each born alone and we will die alone. We each have a destiny of our own, and we each relate to God in our own way. If you're only okay because you have a husband, or a mother, or a child, you're not really okay. For none of us can be another's god.

MARCH 28

I shout for joy because of the work of your hands.
PSALM 92:4

➻❮

I met my friends near the Acropolis in Athens. Up the stone path we climbed, to poke around the ruins, to marvel at the Parthenon. The husband often takes visitors to see it; the wife admitted, laughing sheepishly, that she had never been there until that very day. *You live here and you've never seen it?* I asked, and she smiled and shook her head. *You must visit me in New York,* I told her. *We'll go to the Empire State Building. I've never been there, either.*

I hope you all never take the beautiful place in which you live for granted, I told an audience in New Hampshire while conducting a retreat there on a fall weekend. And it was breathtakingly beautiful: rolling hills drenched with fiery color, little jewels of ponds, old stone walls meandering through green meadows, plain white houses and churches from two hundred years ago. The people smiled the same sheepish smile. *We do forget how beautiful it is here,* a woman told me at the coffee hour. *You get so used to it, you just don't always think to look.*

The people of New York City walk along the sidewalk, staring at their feet. Visitors are always easy to spot, craning their necks to see the tops of the amazing buildings. The city is bounded on all sides by the water—Manhattan is an island. Ships move up and down the rivers, tugboats, barges, ferries. But almost nobody thinks much about the fact that New York is a port, that the harbor is, in fact, the reason why New York *is* New York: its enormous prosperity has its roots in that fact. The harbor is large and complex, and it is beautiful, and most people don't even know it's there. Sometimes, though, you ride along the waterside in a cab and look: takes your breath away, it's so lovely. Wherever you are right now, there is something lovely you have stopped noticing because you see it every day. Enjoy.

MARCH 29

He has made the whole world so sure that it cannot be moved.

PSALM 93:2

✦

Most of us have had a time in our lives when it seemed as if the ground were giving way under our feet. Maybe you've survived an actual earthquake, or maybe it was something else that seemed as eternal as the rocks suddenly giving way: the sudden revelation of betrayal, the end of a marriage, your parents' divorce. Your own, perhaps. Suddenly nothing is sure.

I used to go with my children's classes on field trips sometimes: the fire house, the American Museum of Natural History, a French restaurant once. We would travel in pairs, walking hand-in-hand when we crossed a street, and it was the parents' job to be sure everybody stayed together. One little girl always stayed glued to my side, every trip; no matter where we went, there she was, holding my hand. *This was how we walked in my country,* she whispered to me one day, *all together like this, holding hands.* She and her family had left Vietnam on foot; she had come to America from a refugee camp in Thailand. *We walked through a river holding hands,* she said as we walked, *and there were snakes in the water.*

When we went to the natural history museum, little Mary couldn't have been more than eight years old. The river of snakes was a very early memory for her. I think often of that family, clinging to one another as they walked away from their home forever. I think of the terrified little girl fording the river, seeing the snakes, holding on tight. No wonder Mary got so quiet walking in a group. No wonder she held my hand and wouldn't let go: it reminded her of the time her world ended. She and her sister Madeleine grew up to be beautiful and accomplished young women. They are now in college. Mary plays the cello. Her fearful early years are part of her life, but only one part. Her world collapsed. And another world began.

All evildoers are full of boasting.

PSALM 94:4

I know people who have absorbed this bit of ancient wisdom so well that they are completely unable to admit to doing anything well. I've always wondered what they're like when they apply for jobs and have to tell someone else about their strengths. Pretty quiet interview. The whole culture of Japan encourages people to be like this, I understand; it is considered very rude in Japan to allude to one's own excellence. I read somewhere about a study comparing Japanese high school students with American teens: the Japanese kids all evaluated their level of skill in math as poor, while the Yanks assessed themselves much more favorably. The actual level of math skill proved, humiliatingly for the Americans, to be the reverse: the Japanese students scored much higher than their self-confident Yankee counterparts. So much for self-esteem, the great American cure-all.

So whether or not you *think* you excel may have little objective relation to whether or not you actually do. I sometimes wonder if a more reliable indicator of excellence than self-assessment might not be the extent to which we enjoy our work. The product of a passionate worker is a holy thing, whether it's an oil painting or a chocolate cake. You work because you love your job, or because you love the people who benefit from it. Most household chores are like this, actually: I didn't actually enjoy transferring all the telephone numbers and addresses from our falling-apart address book to a pristine new one this morning, but I loved the thought of how easy it will be now for Richard to find things without having to guess whether or not the address before him is current. This made it *a good job, well done,* as my mother would have said.

Harden not your hearts, as your forebears did in the wilderness, at Meribah, and on that day at Massah, when they tempted me.

PSALM 95:8

✣

$\mathcal{A}$t Meribah and Massah—two oases that the Hebrew people stopped at in the course of their desert wanderings—the people "tempted" God. What does this mean? It means that they expressed doubts concerning God's ability and desire to take care of them, and demanded some proof of it. And so at Massah and Meribah, where they were grousing about the water supply, God caused water to gush out of a rock and they all drank. The people expressed doubt and God provided a miraculous positive answer as a sign of his presence. He didn't like it though; the story goes on to tell of various bad things that came about as signs of how annoyed God was at all the complaining.

If there's a God, a friend of mine always says when we arrive somewhere in her car, *there will be a parking place near the entrance.* Sometimes there is and sometimes there isn't, which either means that God passes very easily in and out of nonexistence, or else that parking availability is an inadequate index of the divine presence. A trivial test: my friend is joking. I have another friend, though, who has worked in Northern Ireland and in Somalia, and was a medic in Vietnam; he grows cold with fury when people talk about God's care for human beings, and he's anything but joking. The human prosperity test for the existence of God is the wrong road to travel if you're after an authentic spiritual life. Too many things are too terrible for too many people.

God is with those who live and prosper and God is with those who suffer and die. Sooner or later, we're all going to end up in the second group; whether we live or die, we are God's. The life of the spirit goes on in either case, and the solace of that life is available to all. People whose lives are going along splendidly may not be as aware of needing that solace, and people who suffer terribly may be too blinded by their pain. That is why it's important to develop your spiritual life *now*, to listen to what your soul has to say and try to hear what it hears *now*, while you can still read and think and ponder. Don't let the lack of a parking place limit your soul's wisdom. Someday you will need to withstand things a lot worse than that.

APRIL 1

Then shall all the trees of the wood shout for joy.
PSALM 96:12

>+<

I swear I am not making this up: the bamboo in our backyard put out a colony of four shoots about twenty feet from the main stand of it, and they grew three feet *in one night*. Honest. My husband fights an ongoing losing battle against the bamboo. He uproots four or five, and seven new ones greet him the next morning. They have been apprehended clear on the other side of an asphalt driveway, having traveled forty feet underground from the mother patch. They are determined.

Yes, we need to contain them so we can get to the tomato plants on the other side, but aren't they brave? And like the blood of the martyrs, the uprooting of the bamboo missionaries seems to make the bamboo nation stronger. That's generally true in the plant kingdom, and it is the principle behind the art of pruning: cut off the new growth at the top and the energy by which it was sustained will produce twice as much nearer the bottom. The plant will grow bushy and gorgeous instead of long and gangly.

Is this also true of humans? Do we also benefit from a little judicious pruning now and then? Ouch. But it is true: it *is* better for us to be bushy than gangly. We need lots of plump new leaves, close together, near the source of our life, rather than one or two skinny daredevils way out in front. It is better to be sure our spirits are rooted and strong before we run off on too many tangents, to have who we are well in hand before we take off after who we wish we were. Sometimes we learn this very painfully, and we can feel ourselves being pruned, feel things that inhibit our growth being taken away from us. Sometimes life tells us *Not yet. Wait awhile. It's not time for this yet.*

APRIL 2

His righteousness has he openly shown in the sight of the nations.

PSALM 98:3

✦

*I*t's not that easy to focus on goodness when everyone around you is focusing on power. When "the nations"—which is the group noun the Bible uses to refer to all the various people who are not Israel—talked about their gods, it was always in terms of their power. The purpose of the human race in relation to the gods of the ancient Near East was always either to serve them or to be pawns in their hands—themes we sometimes also see in the biblical Israel's view of humanity. But the nations did not, as the people of Israel did, think that they were also supposed to imitate their gods in righteousness. They didn't think of righteousness right away when they thought of their gods. They thought of power.

The Hebrew scriptures also speak often of the divine power. But the signal characteristic of the God the psalmists approach was not power: it was goodness. They may talk of God thundering around in the heavens, or of God ruling the sea, but the human approach to God is always through God's righteousness expressed—and this was also a new wrinkle—in fidelity to the law. The human moral code was God's imprint on society, the means by which we might imitate God. This is very different from something like the Code of Hammurabi, a Babylonian legal document, which locates the source of human moral obligation not in the gods, but in the king.

So we resemble God most closely when we are most righteous. You may have had a taste of that now and then, when you made a difficult moral choice that did not carry with it an immediate nice reward, or that may even have cost you more than you could comfortably pay. You may have discovered an unexpected feeling of power when you did that, a gratifying certainty of being in contact with something much greater than your own self-interest. We can't expect the world to reward such behavior—it is too busy hanging on to power and privilege to bother with these things. But *we* can act otherwise, and experience an unexpected freedom when we do.

APRIL 3

He spoke to them out of the pillar of cloud.
PSALM 99:7

❯❮

*T*here goes Richard Nixon. That's what my husband says every time we see a stretch limousine. I remind him that Mr. Nixon is dead. *You can never be sure with him,* my husband says, *and you can't look in the windows of those things to see who's in there. You don't know it's not Nixon.*

Well, I think I can be fairly certain. But it's true that you can't see who's in those ridiculous long automobiles—hiddenness is part of being rich and famous, and you can rent its mysterious allure along with the car. The well-known guard their privacy with a ferocity that occasionally adds unattractively to their notoriety, as when they slap a reporter or smash a camera that comes too near, and end up in court, pouting.

The pillar of cloud, from which God speaks to certain famous Israelites who then relay the divine message to the rank and file, is like that mysterious glass in the limousine windows: we can't see in, but we can be seen. Its purpose is not the same as that of the car windows of the rich and famous, though: in these old stories and poems, the hiddenness is to protect *us*, not God. The ancients believed that a person would die if exposed to the countenance of God, and they developed the idea of God thoughtfully shrouding himself in a cloud to protect mortal eyes from the full effect of his glory.

Both the Richard Nixons of the world and Creator of the Universe know that to see another is to share intimacy, and both understand the relationship which always follows upon being seen, whether you want it to or not. There are few things in life richer than the gaze of someone whose love matters intensely to us, and few things more impoverishing than the painful experience of trying to talk with someone who will not meet our eyes.

APRIL 4

Come before his presence with a song.
PSALM 100:1

✢

Be kind to your web-footed friends. . . . My husband and I belt out the silly verse and then roar with laughter, as if we'd just pulled off something brilliantly funny. Rosie and Madeline look at each other and roll their eyes—the song makes no sense at all, like most of the other things Mamo (that's me) and Q (my husband) do. Richard and I aren't close in age, but there is a body of American song that we share from childhood, songs everybody knows. *Used* to know, that is: there aren't as many venues for public singing these days as there once were. People just don't do it as much. Kids don't know the words to "Around Her Neck She Wore a Yellow Ribbon" or "Put On Your Old Grey Bonnet" or "White Coral Bells."

There is a tyranny of the useful among us, an unwillingness to live in the moment because of our responsibility to a future full of important achievement: let the baby point to a violin on television and gurgle, and we'll mortgage the house to make him a Suzuki fiddle prodigy. But the simple community of people singing silly songs together just for fun is not worth much in our eyes. We're losing an important vocabulary of humor and memory. These songs weren't important because they were so profound—they were anything but that. Most of them were decidedly dumb. They were important only because we all knew them and could sing them together.

If something's worth doing, it's worth doing well, they say. Oh, lighten up, for heaven's sake—there are lots of things worth doing that don't have to become sacred vocations, and singing is one. It is worthwhile no matter how well or how badly it's done. Is God only glorified by the oh-so-serious? Isn't the human family enjoying a bit of silliness together a pretty glorious thing as well?

At Q's college reunion, the men sing their school song: *Oh, Lord Geoffrey Amherst was a soldier of the king and he came from across the sea. . . .* Good Lord Geoffrey may have been the first person to use germ warfare—apparently he gave the Indians blankets deliberately infected with smallpox. Nice. Another icon of American virtue bites the dust. But these boys didn't know about Lord Geoffrey's dark side in 1946, when they first learned this song, and they are thinking of other things now, more innocent times. Forty-five years later, and the old harmonies return as if it were yesterday. I listen to my husband's tenor climb on the shoulders of his roommate's baritone. I look at the grey heads all around us. I imagine them all twenty years old. *We used to call Amherst "The Singing College,"* he tells a youthful waiter, and asks hopefully, *Do you still call it that?* The youth looks puzzled, shakes his head with a smile, and moves away with his tray of dinner plates. He has more important things on his mind. He's an opera student, and has no time for amateurs.

APRIL 5

I will strive to follow blameless course.
PSALM 101:2

⇥⇤

$\mathcal{B}$ill and I were walking back to my place after dinner at Bill's favorite restaurant. A bicycle passed us swiftly, its rider high on the seat and low over the handlebars, wearing a helmet and those black spandex shorts that people on bicycles wear today. *I really miss riding a bike,* Bill said, and I nodded and said, *Yeah, I'll bet you do,* as we continued our slow walk. We always walk slowly: Bill's right side is paralyzed, and he wears a heavy brace on his leg. He holds one arm bent against his chest, so his two arms don't swing when he walks, like other people's arms do. But I should put all these verbs in the past tense, I suppose, for Bill's walking days are over. He's lying in a hospital bed now, blood seeping into his brain from a tumor buried somewhere deep within it. His talking days are over, too. He can no longer see. At thirty-five, the powers of his body are walking out the door, one by one, and his death is now very near. *I gave him the last rites yesterday,* my colleague tells me on the phone. *I think he understood. I think he was making the responses. I mean, all he could do was groan.*

We have lots of thirty-five-year-olds dying at St. John's. But Bill isn't dying of AIDS, as all those others are. He got this brain tumor when he was fourteen—almost died then, but they pulled him through, with only the paralysis to show for a terrible year's ordeal. *That must have been tough,* I said, and he smiled. *I had just realized I was gay,* he said, *and when I got sick I thought God was punishing me.* I stirred my coffee and said nothing; he talked on about his self-loathing, his terror, and his pain. We talked, as always, about his recovery from the alcoholism and drug abuse in which he had buried that pain for a dozen years or so. We talked about what serenity means. What responsibility means. Bill's always beating himself up about his failures. I think about him struggling out of bed in the morning and strapping on his leg brace to go to work, and I tell him he sure doesn't look like a failure to me.

We talk a lot about healing. Eight years of sobriety is a powerful healing. Discovering a religious faith that isn't all about shame and guilt is another. I see him at the Eucharist, or at Morning Prayer, bowing from the waist in a solemn bow at the name of Jesus, and crossing himself very slowly and deliberately. He wears a cross around his neck—sometimes two or three crosses, and sometimes he wears a cross earring on one ear as well: Bill's a unique dresser. *I know that God doesn't hate me. It wasn't true that he made me sick because I was gay. That wasn't true.*

No, it wasn't, I tell him, and I feel myself shaking: I am so angry at whoever taught a young boy to believe in a God who would send him a brain tumor for being gay that I just don't trust myself to speak further.

Things are about the same, says his mother now when I call the hospital. *He's not really awake at all now. They say it won't be too much longer.* The body that now lies dying knows very well what it is to live with pain and weakness. But still his faith has made him well—he groans out the responses in the Church's last anointing of his body on this side of heaven, inarticulate groans that mean *And also with you* and *AMEN*, as he prepares to leave his maimed physical body for his perfect spiritual one. His soul has gotten strong. His soul is what will remain, and it is enough. So Bill was healed—of so many things. That fourteen-year-old never rode a bike again, but I think of him, the way he will be soon, and I send him this vision: *In glory, Bill: strong, both arms free and both legs pumping hard, riding a bike as fast as the wind, straight into the city of God.*

APRIL 6

Hide not your face from me in the day of my trouble.
PSALM 102:1

✢

$\mathcal{M}$ore times than I can count, a person in trouble has told me that he feels unable to call upon God in his distress because he never bothered much about matters of faith when things were going well. That's understandable. But the wry definition of home—when you have to go there, they have to take you in—is also true in a more positive way of God's love for us. Of course we pay more attention when we're hurting—human nature. God is not surprised by this. Our troubles are opportunities for us to tune in to spiritual realities we are apt to ignore in better times. The consistent love of God is always turned on us; it doesn't come and go. It's just that the times when you really need a friend are the times you'll pay attention to it.

Sometimes I look back on a hard time and marvel that I survived it. I examine my scars and see that I did not come through unscathed, but

I came through. And what about that final hard time in my future, the time when I will come right up to death's front door and then just go right on in? When I am *not* saved just in the nick of time? Am I to conclude that God is not with me if I don't win? That won't take me very far, spiritually. My own prosperity is not a good test for God's presence—I die and the world ends. My spiritual state in the midst of heartache and fearfulness is, though. Even when all hope is gone— hope as we all prefer to think of it, hope for health and healing and victory—serenity is possible if I am connected with a reality greater than my small self.

APRIL 7

As a father cares for his children, so does the Lord care for those who fear him.
PSALM 103:13

➤❮

*T*he image of God as father is difficult for many modern people. In the last couple of decades, people have been trying to find ways of speaking of God in a more inclusive way: as creator, say, or even as mother. Predictably, the reaction to this effort has ranged from applause to scorn. Is this an appropriate effort to speak to an age that struggles to understand gender in a new way, or is it a trendy tampering with a tradition better left alone? Depends on who you ask.

It would help if the notion of God as father were not so often connected with the idea of fear, as it is in this verse. We do have other things on which to draw: traditional fatherhood *has* been largely about power, but it has also been about love. The Bible contains both emphases: the God who inspires all this cowering is also the God who, in the book of Hosea, looks at his people with tenderness and asks himself, *How can I give you up?* Both these images emerged from the imaginations of writers who were human beings, like we are. They decided which aspects of the experience of God to emphasize, just as we do. Perhaps the era in which maleness is symbolized by an AK-47 and a bloody glove is the wrong era in which to dispense with male language about God altogether. There is no doubt that we need to enlarge our vision of what it means to be a man. Perhaps we need also to enlarge our vision of God in a way that doesn't subtract from its meaning, but adds to it.

APRIL 8

That they may bring forth food from the earth, and wine to gladden our hearts, oil to make a cheerful countenance, and bread to strengthen the heart.
PSALM 104:15–16

➤❖

Notice how neutral a thing wine is on this list of delightful things? Surely "gladdening our hearts" refers to that gentle buzz, when your jokes are extra funny and your self-confidence is high, and not to the soggy era of maudlin self-absorption that follows upon it if you keep drinking. Remember how Jackie Gleason and Dean Martin incorporated their heavy drinking into their comic personae? We have changed—people wouldn't laugh at that stuff today. Too many drunks have killed too many people for us to regard being smashed as a private matter.

Surely there were alcoholics when this psalm was written, although the concept of alcoholism as a disease was not one they knew. The psalms refer to drunkards—number 107, for instance, compares sailors struggling to remain standing during a storm at sea to drunkards—but one searches in vain for a reference to drinking as a social problem. St. Paul includes drunkenness in the list of things he doesn't want to hear of Christians doing, but it is clear that drinking to excess was one among many private sins and not a matter for the community to address beyond censuring it. More and more people have come to think otherwise.

Are we a group of unrelated beings who happen to occupy the same planet, or are we connected? The second must surely be the truth. My behavior matters to you, whether or not we ever meet. In so many ways—in the cruel relatedness forced upon multiple sexual partners of the HIV-infected, in the more devious relatedness between the Third World producer and the First World consumer, or in the hateful collision of metal and flesh when a drunken stranger at the wheel of a car singles out somebody's child for sudden death—we cannot help but relate.

APRIL 9

He gave his people the lands of the nations, and they took the fruit of others' toil.

PSALM 105:44

➤❖

*T*here's probably not a country anywhere in the world whose current inhabitants didn't take it from those who lived there before. Some of these transactions still fester—in Israel, in South Africa, in Northern Ireland. Some of them are theoretically over, like the transfer of land from Native Americans to newcomers of European ancestry, although the closing of that deal required the near-elimination of an entire culture. A line like the one above reflects history as seen by the winners:

we fought for this land and won, so God must want us to have it instead of the other guys.

Is everything that happens God's will? When I win, does it mean that God was on my side? And what does it mean when I lose? This scenario sounds a lot more like the gods and goddesses of ancient Greece, who manipulate human beings as pawns in their own rivalries and games, than like the actions of the creator and lover of the entire human race.

The human moral vision develops throughout scripture, and it still develops today. People used to think it was God's will for one human being to buy and sell another, and most people no longer think so. Some people think it's God's will for millions of people to starve while others throw away food. Others are not so sure.

The ancient Israelites took as their defining moment the time when God sustained their deliverance from the Egyptians, when they triumphed over a much stronger adversary. The Jewish people of the twentieth century saw millions of their number slaughtered—a terrible defeat. Yet those who sought meaning in the midst of this tragedy have managed to find it. The spirit of Judaism has not been killed. They learned from suffering as well as from triumph.

APRIL 10

They have said, "Come, let us wipe them out from among the nations;
let the name of Israel be remembered no more."

PSALM 83:4

➤‹

*W*ho *are the people in this picture?* Anna asks me as we are going through a family photo album. Some of them I know; others are nameless now. The people who knew their names are all dead. As we flip through the pictures and the costumes the subjects are wearing become more and more Victorian, I search the faces for hints of my father's eyes, his square chin. I think I see a few. I wish I had asked him. I want to remember what he remembered, and now, as the century whose first decade he saw comes to the end of its last decade, it is too late. They are all gone.

An occupying conqueror usually moves against the common memory of the conquered. The children are taught in the language of the conqueror, rather than in their own. Sometimes, a whole people have been made to change their family names, or to stop practicing their religion. There are friendlier ways of destroying history, though, that are just as thorough: my mother did not speak more than a few words of her family's Swedish tongue, for instance, and so I speak hardly any. They wanted to be American, and so now we are. My friend's father didn't want her to know anything about his terrible experiences as a Jew in occupied Poland, and so he changed his name to something WASP when he came here. She didn't know she was Jewish until she was in her twenties, and he was furious at the aunt who had told her, even then.

Our neighbors next door have a mixed marriage: he's Jewish, she's Catholic. They do it all: she's learned to cook all the Passover food, he sings the songs at their seder in Hebrew in his rich baritone. Their boys are acolytes at the cathedral and also loved to visit their grandfather in Israel when he was alive. On the coffee table during their recent seder was a photograph album, rather like mine. All the people in it are dead, like the ones in my pictures. My relatives died of natural causes, most of them at advanced ages. Their relatives all died at once, in the camps: aunts, uncles, little cousins. But he knows the names of every one, can name many more of his people than I can name of mine. The forces of evil tried to wipe out his memory and failed. The forces of complacency, in my case, were stronger.

And so they exchanged their Glory for the image of an ox that feeds on grass.
PSALM 106:20

➤✦

$\mathcal{M}$y daughter is so embarrassed: the second grade was discussing what the children would like to be when they grew up, and Rosie told her class that she wanted to be like Madonna. *I don't know what the teacher thought,* Corinna says, shaking her head. *And I don't know why she said that.*

You've grasped, of course, that my eldest granddaughter is not talking about a life in emulation of the Blessed Mother. The Madonna she's talking about is the one in the bullet bra. Or sometimes in even less.

I think Madonna's stardom is waning a bit—you don't stay on top forever in her business. Not having teenagers in the house anymore, I don't know who the new idol is. But I know there *is* one, and that he or she will make unimaginable sums of money over the next two or three years and then fade away. He'll turn up occasionally with a new date at the Academy Awards, or she'll make a movie to reinflate her sagging celebrity, but basically it'll be over.

Everything mortal comes to an end. It takes a certain amount of time for this truth to dawn on most of us, which is why lots of teenagers make idols of movie actresses and rock stars and not so many adults do, and why the adults we encounter who do live and breathe the life of this or that celebrity are always a little unsettling to be around. Enthusiastic appreciation is one thing; worship is another.

You can tell, though, how easy it is for any of us to make an idol out of something temporary every time a famous person dies. When Fred Astaire died, it felt to many people like the world had changed—even people who hadn't followed his career closely. And when Jackie O. died, the same—even for those people who hadn't haunted her apartment building every day, hoping for a glimpse. When John Lennon died, the same. Famous people look permanent. They embody the eras in which they live. We are shocked when they turn out to be mortal like us, shocked into unwelcome awareness that our time is passing whether we like it or not.

APRIL 12

They reeled and staggered like drunkards and were at their wits' end.
PSALM 107:27

➤❮

*T*he grandchildren have been begging me for several days to take them to Discovery Zone. *Some kind of science display?* I wondered. *Oh, no, Mamo*—Discovery Zone is a nationwide network of elaborate indoor playgrounds: tunnels and ladders and slides, enormous soft blocks to climb, and trapezes, all in strong primary colors, and rock 'n' roll coming at you through some serious speakers on the wall. The Mighty Morphin Power Rangers make a recorded speech in a continuous loop, admonishing the young guests to pursue righteousness and never act in the service of selfish goals, which is certainly good advice.

The floor in the play area is covered with a deep layer of thousands of plastic balls in bright colors—hard to walk on, so the children really *are* staggering around in there like little inebriates. They love it; they fall down and look at each other, laughing insanely. Or they swing out on the trapeze over a pile of balls and let go—down into the balls they fall, the way I remember falling from a tree branch into a pile of autumn leaves as a child.

This really is an amazing place, and it's wonderful for kids to have an exciting place to play. It's a little sad, though, that for many kids this is the only place they can really let loose, that adults have to make and then franchise a place for kids to play, something that used to just happen by itself. When I was little, it was safe for me to play alone or with a friend in the woods, and I did it all the time. I don't know anybody who would let her child do that today.

Naively, I have brought along my laptop on my maiden voyage to Discovery Zone—I thought I would get some writing done while they played. But I don't think I'll be able to concentrate on anything else while we're here: just the children playing while the mothers and fathers watch, just the memory of a carefree way of being a child that no longer exists.

APRIL 13

Happy are they who have not walked in the counsel of the wicked, nor lingered in the way of sinners, nor sat in the seats of the scornful!

PSALM 1:1

➤✦

When I was little, I wanted very much to be good. I had some vague ideas about what that meant: for the most part, it consisted of a list of things I would not do, like smoke, drink, steal, or have anything at all to do with sex. As long as I stayed in my tiny hometown, there was scant danger of my falling into any of these things—no one else in town did any of them except for a few notorious sinners, who misbehaved more or less on behalf of all the rest of us.

But when I was in the seventh grade, I went to junior high school in a larger town nearby. The kids there were more sophisticated; they stood in clusters before school began, their arms nonchalantly down by their sides, telltale plumes of smoke issuing from their cupped hands. I would hear them talking about going drinking on a Friday night. There were a few girls who were alleged to have gone practically all the way. My best friend and I criticized them soundly.

I resolved to remain virtuous. The badge of purity I chose was the fact that I continued to wear white ankle socks, instead of the nylon stockings that more and more of my schoolmates were adopting. The stockings came to symbolize acquiescence in sin to me. Imagine my devastation, then, when this very best friend began to appear in them in school, began to walk around in the hallways before school with other girls in nylons, girls we had whispered about only days before, other girls who were not me. *I don't see what's so terrible about it!* she snapped when I confronted her, and I was alone.

Just when I myself adopted the nylons is less clear in my memory—we do not retain our moral compromises nearly as well as we savor the recollection of the times we have stood firm. But by the time eighth grade was over, I wore nylons. And lipstick. I, too, walked around the halls with those girls. I didn't yet smoke or drink, but I was no longer horrified at those who did.

These days, I think there is a lot more to being good than merely refraining from doing things. I smile now at the memory of that young girl on the edge of womanhood, who embodied her anxiety about growing up in a drama of sin and virtue based on her choice of hosiery. But I have not forgotten how easy it was to adopt the ways of the people with whom I surrounded myself. I have not forgotten how very quickly I became willing to bend my idea of the good to my longing for acceptance.

> *When he is judged, let him be found guilty, and let his*
> *appeal be in vain.*
>
> PSALM 109:6

How did that case come out? I ask my daughter when she comes up the sidewalk. She works for the county prosecutor. Sometimes there's an especially grisly murder that grabs the headlines for days. This one involved a man who killed his girlfriend for her insurance policy and then threw himself on the mercy of the court because he has an eleven-year-old daughter. *He hardly ever sees his daughter,* Corinna says with a look of disgust.

The jury deliberated for two hours and came back with a death sentence. Now the appeals process will begin—it will take years to exhaust his appeals. We reinstated the death penalty in New Jersey in 1982. There are seven men—this guy will make eight—on death row. Nobody has been executed—not yet—though one man is nearing the end his appeals.

In some states, capital punishment is something on the order of a spectator sport. But those states don't enjoy a lower crime rate than do states that don't kill people. The death penalty isn't an effective deterrent to crime—criminals never believe they will be caught, and so the notion of punishment is a theoretical matter to them. Proponents of it usually express their support in terms of justice: a life for a life. And in terms of anger—some crimes are so heinous, many feel, that even hanging is too good for the perpetrator.

I know what it is to imagine the death of someone who has killed without mercy. I think all of us do. But I don't consider those imaginings to be my finest moments—they are among my most base. That they should be enshrined in law is to make us at our worst the measure of society's moral standards, rather than taking that measure from us at our very best.

APRIL 15

They stand fast for ever and ever.
PSALM 111:8

➤←

A young couple comes to see me—I'm going to officiate at their wedding in a couple of months. This is a little jarring to me, because I remember the bride when she was six. She's one of Anna's best friends. Now here she is, a young woman, bringing a man two or three years her senior with her to plan the ceremony that will make their private love a matter in which society has a formal stake.

There is so much to do—they're thinking of changing the time of the ceremony so the reception can be brunch instead of dinner. That means they'll have to put the invitation order on hold until they decide on the time. That will cost a little more, so they're weighing their options carefully. There are attendants' gifts to select yet, and the groom still hasn't quite settled on a best man.

If you're not careful, the logistical arrangements of a wedding can completely eclipse what it signifies—the marriage itself, which has next to nothing to do with matchbooks that say "Bill and Susie" on the cover. Divorce rates may be high or low, but the intention of couples who marry has not changed: they almost always mean for it to last forever. Long after the bridesmaids' dresses have gone out of style, even long after the young people who wore them are no longer young, even after they have all long since *died*, the spiritual community established in a good marriage endures and endures. It is a permanent part of the world's history, part of the precious and irreplaceable sum of human love.

And the other marriages? The ones that don't make it, that sputter to a discouraged end a few years later in a courtroom somewhere? At the very least, the intentions were good. There was love in some form at the beginning, and hope for a bright future. At the very least, something important can be learned from the pain of the marriages that fail in the end, and people can discover a personal strength they didn't know they had.

May Kate and Justin never have to learn about their strength in that painful way. May they learn together, instead, and live and love into long decades upon decades. The wedding will take about twenty minutes, maybe twenty-five. Anna is going to sing, and the couple's brothers and sisters are going to read the prayers. It will be lovely. But that day is not the end. It is only the beginning.

APRIL 16

They will not be afraid of any evil rumors.
PSALM 112:7

✦

What do you suppose it's like to be one of the people who write for supermarket tabloids? The one this week has a photograph—*UNRETOUCHED!*—of a luscious blonde cozying up to a man in a very obvious lime-green alien costume, and planting a pouty kiss on his metallic cheek. The headline says that she wants to have alien babies.

Alien babies are pretty standard in the tabloids, usually alien babies born to human women—although sometimes the aliens borrow one of us for their science experiments and then let the specimen go when they're finished. Celebrities' cliffhanger marital separations are good material, too—you can go for months with the same couple's unravellings and sudden camera-ready recouplings before one or the other finally decamps for greener pastures somewhere else. You haven't been able to find a tabloid without O. J. in it for more than a year now—the public has gotten so accustomed to legal news and clearly enjoys it so heartily that we will probably always have to have a major courtroom drama going from now on, even when O. J. is finally through.

The writers are just writers, though, like me. They're probably even good writers—it's not easy to get a job as a writer, and the tabloids probably have their pick of bright young college grads willing to write about alien babies, if they have to, to get started in their journalistic careers. They're making a living. They probably love words, as I do, and wish they were writing for *The New Yorker*. I wish *I* were writing for *The New Yorker*. They probably look at the finished product when it comes out, at the tales they've spun about voluptuous alien-lovers and the son-of-the-son-of-the-bloody-glove and feel depressed about the distance between what they thought they would do when they were in school and what they're actually doing now that they're out on their own. *I spent five hours on this?*

Or maybe they don't feel that way at all. Tall tales are a very American literary form. Mark Twain wrote them. Walt Whitman wrote them. Abraham Lincoln delighted in telling them. Americans have always loved them. Maybe the tabloid writers *are* proud of their work, even if they know it's not going to get the Pulitzer this year. Maybe it's just fun to make up crazy stories and think that somebody somewhere might actually believe them.

You are the fairest of men; grace flows from your lips.
PSALM 45:2

➤❖

Our friend the fashion photographer wants to take Q's picture for his portfolio. My husband, the model. He is shocked at the request: he has never liked photographs of himself, never looks in mirrors except to shave or comb his hair. The idea that his appearance is interesting is a new one; he doesn't quite believe it, even though I tell him how handsome he is about sixty times a day. What do I know?

He agrees to sit, though. What shirt should he wear? We select a striped one—he almost never wears a shirt that isn't striped—and a nubby-textured tie to go with it. The shoot is in Barry's studio, and it takes a couple of hours—also a shock. When the contact sheet comes back, there he is: a hundred or so extremely chic photographs, some dramatically lit so that half of his face is in shadows, some with arms folded, some not. Most are steely-serious, Major Intellectual Figure photographs. Q doesn't like that: *I kept trying to smile, but he wouldn't let me.* That was true: an ironic half-smile was the most Barry allowed. *You don't smile for photographs these days,* I tell him. *You're supposed to look grim.*

Actually, smiling for portraits is pretty new, in the scheme of things. Hardly any subjects in old paintings are shown smiling. The only people you see smiling are peasants, children, and fools, people of inferior status who are by definition too dumb to know any better. All the power people face the painter with seriousness. *This is not fun and games,* their sober gaze says as they look back at us from the canvas. *This is the record of my life.*

*When Israel came out of Egypt, the house of Jacob from a people
of strange speech . . .*
PSALM 114:1

✢

One of the remarkable things about the worldwide spread of Christianity, Judaism, and Islam is the way the scriptures remind us that the beginnings of these great faiths were very parochial; they were all about the doings of a tiny group of people who didn't count for much in the power politics of their world and who were very concerned with their own affairs. Here, for instance, they refer to the Egyptians as "people of strange speech"—as if their own little language were the definition of normal and you went from there. That's actually the way spirituality starts as well, for all of us; we begin out of a very local concern with our own affairs and our own needs. We experience a spiritual relationship with the larger world only later on. At first, the Israelites talked about the God of Israel, just as the Philistines talked of their gods and the Canaanites talked of theirs. It was not until later on that the idea of a universal spiritual basis for the life of the world seemed of much interest.

So you start with yourself and your own issues. In prayer, it's usually the same: the things I come up with first are the problems I've been stewing about during the day, as if they were the most urgent matters imaginable. It's only after I've gotten them out of my system that I find the spiritual energy for other things: to pray for other people, to rest in thankfulness for another day of life, to approach the still point in my soul where God speaks. Then the whole world seems related to me, as if I knew everyone in it by name, as if I could see it. As if I loved it. As God does.

Not to us, O Lord, not to us, but to your Name give glory.
PSALM 115:1

✦

Now and then you come across a very devout person who simply will not let you pay him or her a compliment. *I don't do a thing,* she says, *it all belongs to God.* Which is certainly true, of course, as far as it goes: every good endowment *does* come from God. But people either do or do not choose to make good use of the gifts God gives them, and it seems to me not completely out of bounds to commend them when they do. I can't think that God's ego is so slender that the occasional recognition of human excellence feels to him as if it were somehow at his expense. There is surely more than enough of the divine goodness to supply us all.

I remember having trouble understanding how to relate to the things I did well when I was little. At first, I bragged artlessly about them, until my best friend told me that it wasn't nice to talk about how great I was all the time. I then decided that the right thing to do was to pretend that I was having trouble doing things that were really very easy for me, and to make much of the things I couldn't do. I pretended to be worried sick about whether or not I would be promoted to fourth grade, for instance. There was a falseness about that, though, that soon wearied even me.

I concluded that the best thing to do was just not talk about whether I was good at anything at all—just do it, and let other people be the judge if any judgment were necessary. That's basically what I do to this day: in a job interview or some other forum in which someone asks me about my strengths, I find it difficult to come up with something to say. I think many people do.

For the creation, to be beautiful or fruitful or intelligent or kind or any other good thing gives glory to the creator. We are part of the creation. The spiritual value of all our individual excellence, of whatever kind, works together to increase the amount of good in a world that needs all the good it can get.

APRIL 20

In my distress I said, "No one can be trusted."
PSALM 116:9

✦

I know a young woman whose parents separated when she was still a baby. In a pattern unfortunately quite common, her father visited and paid child support for a few years and then stopped. She grew to adulthood without him.

She has come close to getting married a couple of times, but each time she has stopped short of the final, legal commitment. She is very beautiful and has had many suitors; she always ends relationships, though, when they become serious. No one has ever left her: she is the one who does the leaving. Sometimes she concocts a reason, although she is not aware that this is what she's doing. Or sometimes she behaves in such a way as to make *him* behave in such a way that leaving is the only possible action for her. But she is never left; she always leaves.

It is obvious that she does not trust men. And, I think, it is obvious *why*.

In one of life's more difficult paradoxes, it is only possible to find trustworthiness if you first trust. There is simply no way to know if another can be trusted if you are unwilling to go out on the limb of trusting someone with your heart first, without knowing for sure if your trust will be rewarded. That's just the way it is.

So what happens if you open yourself up like that and you're mistaken, if the one you trust with your heart betrays you? You get hurt, that's what happens. And you grieve. And then you get better. And you've learned a lot, probably. But you have actually lost nothing: you had no one before and you again have no one. You were alone before and you're alone again. You are still *you*. And you know how to do that, and it's not so bad, just being you.

But there is no way to be *you* in loving *relationship* without taking a chance.

APRIL 21

Praise the Lord, all nations, laud him, all you peoples; for his loving-kindness toward us is great, and the faithfulness of the Lord endures forever.
Hallelujah!
PSALM 117

✥

*T*hat's the whole thing you just read—117 is the shortest of all one hundred fifty psalms. Short enough so that even a small child could learn it by heart. These psalms, most of them, were sung by people of ancient Israel in their worship. I wonder just where in the service they sang this little cutie. They probably used it a lot, because they could count on everybody knowing the words—like "Jesus Loves Me" from my own childhood.

This psalm is twenty-five words long. The Lord's Prayer is less than fifty. The *Shema Yisrael*—"Hear, O Israel, the Lord our God, the Lord is One"—is the central affirmation of Jewish belief, and in English it's only eleven words. The Serenity Prayer—"God, grant me the serenity to accept the things I cannot change, courage to change the things I can, and wisdom to know the difference"—is a daily source of sanity for millions of people in recovery from addiction, and it's twenty-five words long.

Take a look, by contrast, at any bill that comes up before the Congress of the United States. Bills about state flowers or hog futures, whatever. Or any legal contract. By the time every jot has been titled, you're talking *a lot* of words. Complex human interchanges generate a lot of blah-de-blah. The things of God are much more direct.

Human beings complexify. We are builders; by nature, we cannot resist adding on to things. There would be no civilization if we were not this way. But we are apt to forget the simplicities of the soul in our avalanches of words, or to undervalue it because its voice is so small and quiet.

One thing a number of people do to slow themselves down in this regard is to use one of these little gems—the Shema, for instance, or the Serenity Prayer—as an ongoing refrain, a key to turn to so that they can get themselves centered enough to hear their souls speak. Just find a place where you can sit still—or a task that doesn't require concentration, like peeling potatoes or taking a shower—and repeat your key over and over to yourself. There will be plenty of time for complicated ideas later on; for now, the mere repetition of a simple truth will remind me of the image of God I bear within me. If there is something more important for me to remember, I don't know what it is.

They hem me in, they hem me in on every side.

PSALM 118:11

✠

*A*ll day, Rosie and Madeline have been very, very good. They cleared away their lunch dishes after being asked only once. They asked permission before watering with the watering can. They played a quiet game of chess and nobody cried. Nobody cried all day, in fact, which is why it's a little puzzling that, when their mother comes to pick them up, they begin to argue about who will sit in the front seat, and somebody pinches somebody else, who retaliates with a pinch of her own, until, pretty soon, both girls are in tears.

They were fine all day, I say helpfully, *until you came home.* Corinna shakes her head. She sits down on the couch, little girls clinging to her like barnacles. It isn't long before they are quiet again, but they continue to stick like glue. She drives them home—both in the backseat to forestall trouble. They will have dinner and maybe a story, and then to bed.

I was an aide in their mother's nursery school when she was little. I noticed that a lot of the children were like Rosie and Madeline: they'd wail inconsolably and cling to their mother's skirts as the women tried to leave, then turn matter-of-factly to their play as soon as they were out of sight. Often, the crying would resume when the moms reappeared, as if to convey the impression that the entire time apart had been unbroken misery, when in fact it had been a very pleasant day.

What they're trying to say is that Mommy is wonderful and important to them, that she is the great love of their lives at this point in them, that they value her immeasurably and would be devastated by losing her. They don't express this well—there are better ways of saying *I love you, Mommy* than by hitting your sister and screaming. But that's what it means.

I will sing and make melody.

PSALM 108:1

➤❖

A deep groaning noise from the bathroom wakes me out of a sound sleep—it sounds like the growl of a grizzly bear. I realize after a moment that it is my husband singing his Russian song, the one he's sung in the shower ever since he learned it in high school glee club. His voice is rumbly and low, quite unlike his usual rich tenor. I can tell it feels good to sing in that rumbly range. I remember that our grandchildren liked it, too; when they were babies, they would lie on his chest and listen to his rumbly voice—a welcome change after a day of women's trebles.

I remember waking in the morning at home to another low voice singing—my father making his breakfast down in the kitchen, singing a hymn without words, just low, rumbly syllables. I would lie under the covers and listen before getting up to join him, and I would feel completely safe. Until the end of his life he was famous among his acquaintances for his fine speaking and singing voice. I remember the first time I heard my husband singing his Russian song in the shower—after I realized it wasn't a bear. I was pleased to have a rumbly voice in my mornings again, after all those years.

Early sounds of home, sounds of a life cheerful enough to begin the day singing. I lie under the covers of my grownup bed, far from my childhood in years and in miles, but feeling the same safety. I know a man who hates the sound of a vacuum cleaner—his mother would be vacuuming when he came home each day, and he felt ignored. I know a woman who hates the sound of her espresso maker—it reminds her of the machine used in a medical procedure she endured twenty years ago. I know many people who would just as soon never again hear anything by Wagner—it's background music for a pogrom to them, and it can never be anything else. Sounds stick around and connect us, sometimes with startling power, with the past.

APRIL 24

Happy are they whose way is blameless.
PSALM 119:1

➵➶

A friend, whose father beat him cruelly and often when he was little, grew up to be a man who was always terribly distressed by the suggestion that he might have done something incorrectly, or made a wrong choice. He reacted anxiously to criticism, protesting his innocence examining his actions again and again. It wasn't hard to understand why: making a mistake was a dangerous thing to do when he was little. Long after he left home, his soul remembered the terrible consequences of an error.

Two things happened to change this painful way of living. The first was his entry into a recovery program that helped him gain control over some self-destructive ways of behaving that had come to dominate his life. And the second was a professional change: a promotion into a leadership role in which he was a primary decision-maker. Through his recovery, he acquired an important measure of self-love, contradicting years of self-hatred. And the duties of leadership gave him many opportunities to govern with wisdom and compassion, rather than with the brutality his father had used on him. He no longer panics when he makes a mistake. Although thanks to the careful nature instilled in him by his years of fear, he doesn't make many.

The things that happen when we are young do shape us. But we are not doomed to live in their shadow forever, nor to inflict on others the pain they occasioned in us. We can learn and we can change, if we want to, and we will be stronger—often, in the very spot in our souls where we ourselves were damaged.

APRIL 25

I am on the side of peace, but when I speak of it, they are for war.
PSALM 120:7

➤➤

There is no bond between people quite like the delicious one of intensely disliking the same person. It is furtive, at first, conspiratorial, as the two of you carefully explore just how pungent you can be with each other in the zingers you exchange about the object of your derision. Soon, though, you've thrown caution to the winds. No insult is too terrible. The mere innocent mention by someone else of the hated name evokes an exquisite secret exchange of significant glances.

To my shame, I have been involved in more than one such relationship. I've noticed each time, though, that the forbidden pleasure of these exchanges fades after a time. I began to feel guilty about them, to wish that my friendship with my partner in disdain were based on something more worthy than just disliking the same person. I became aware, in fact, of having overlooked some good qualities in the one we scorned. In fact, as luck would have it, I'd be thrown together with him right about then, and remember all the things I'd said about him behind his back.

Trying to stop the malice game with your friend, though, is easier said than done. It was fun, that gossip, and she doesn't want to stop. It turns out that it was as you feared: nothing of substance—nothing that's any good, anyway—unites you. The way you have conducted your relationship has brought out the worst in both of you.

The game may be fun, but the price is too high. *If you can't say anything nice about someone, don't say anything at all,* my mom used to say. *What a goody-goody,* I would say to myself. But she was right.

APRIL 26

I lift up my eyes to the hills; from where is my help to come?
PSALM 121:1

❯❮

Sooner or later, everyone finds himself in a place where all hope is gone. Illness, often, or unemployment that stretches on and on, through month after discouraging month. Divorce, maybe, or the terrifying waywardness of a beloved child. You've tried everything you or anyone else can think of, many times, but you've finally reached the end of your rope.

God is at the end of that rope, as God has been at every point along it. When you've done all you can, all that remains is to turn it over to God. Does this mean that you'll get your heart's desire? No—if that were so, the millions of people whose families prayed with everything that was in them for a healing and didn't get one would all still be alive. You don't know in advance what your help will be, or from which direction it will come. But, in unexpected deliverances and in anguished defeat, that which comforts and stays with us is God. Perhaps God will join your rejoicing. Perhaps God will share your sorrow. In your life, you will surely know both of these ways of feeling God's presence.

I think the question we can best explore with God is not so much

"What will happen?" as it is "What *can* happen in this situation?" God is not an appropriate subject for fortune-telling; God is a God of prophecy, of discerning meaning and the potential for good in everything that happens, the good and the bad. Viewing life's ups and downs in this way opens my eyes to possibilities I would never see if I located God only in those moments in which I got my way.

APRIL 27

As for those who turn aside to crooked ways, the Lord will lead them away with the evildoers.

PSALM 125:5

✦

Modern people often wonder about the place of punishment in religious belief. Does God really send people to hell if they're bad? We no longer have much of a consensus about this: for some people, the literal truth of a fiery place of eternal punishment still makes sense. For others, it is difficult to swallow.

Rather than spend time and ink defending this or that vision of hell and damnation—since none of us has firsthand knowledge about these things—I find it much more useful to think about how a person *gets to* whatever hell is; it's not so much what it is as how a person might become a part of it. This verse talks about those who "turn aside" being lumped together with evildoers, away from the company of the righteous. Now, whatever I may or may not know about hell, I do have some experience of this phenomenon: people who behave badly come to enjoy the company of other people who behave badly. They feel affirmed by one another, and so they seek each other out. If they persist in a self-destructive or cruel way of life, they eventually lose all contact with whatever goodness they once knew. For good or ill, our companions help determine who we will be.

People beginning the road to recovery from alcoholism must give up the people and places that encouraged them to drink. For many, those people and those places have become their whole world. *But I won't have any friends,* they protest, already half knowing that a person who helps you get plastered night after night really isn't much of a friend.

In Dante's Hell, the people are grouped together according to their offenses, living forever in a perverse version of the life they chose while they were alive. Thus, illicit lovers are bound together, front to front, and must spend eternity that way. That would put a strain on any relationship. In Dante's Hell you get what you order. We don't have to buy the medieval worldview in its entirety to realize that there's a fair amount of truth to that right here on earth.

APRIL 28

Restore our fortunes, O Lord, like the watercourses of the Negev.
PSALM 126:5

❯❮

Like what?

The Negev is a desert area in the southern part of Palestine: hot, dry, and barren. But once a year the rainy season arrives abruptly, filling the dusty gulches with streams of water. As if by magic, the desert blooms and bears fruit.

It really was a desert before the rains came. But it was not *only* a desert. Hidden within the parched husk of the land, seeds of life waited for the gift of water, so that they might do what seeds do: spring forth and change the landscape from brown and grey to a sudden, juicy green.

This psalm is often used at funerals. I officiate at all too many funerals these days, as the AIDS pandemic rages on and on—the funerals of young people, often, people who should have had many decades more than they got. I want very much for those who mourn to hear the promise this ancient song offers: *You will not always be as you are now. There is a life after loss. It is not the same life, but it can hold a different joy.*

I want them to hear the hope, but I go slowly. I remember too well that sometimes, when I have suffered, I have been angered by well-intentioned assurances that, one day, all will be well. I don't want to deny the reality of the desert, bullying people into a healing of grief that has not yet taken place. The return of happiness to a life that has been bruised takes time. The dry season lasts a long time.

It really *is* a desert. But there are seeds.

APRIL 29

Sons are a heritage from the Lord.
PSALM 127:1

➻❮

*A*nd what, pray, are daughters?

This is the kind of Bible quote that has sent more than one good woman right into orbit and right out of organized religion. Sometimes devout people try to explain these little gems away, to say that the ancient writers didn't really mean to imply that women were second-rate. But of course they did. We don't have to pretend they were better than they were. In common with virtually all traditional cultures, the various voices in scripture take the inferiority of women to men in society as a given, and no amount of tidying up on our part can change that.

But very few things we value have been unchanged from the beginning. You yourself are not—there are many things you did as a child that you'd be embarrassed to do now. Our country is not—people used to buy and sell other people in America, and women could not vote. Medical science in the twentieth century is not invalidated because doctors bled their patients with leeches in the eighteenth. God may stay the same—or God may not; how would I know?—but the human family definitely changes. If we are alive and living in it, we have no choice but to live with change.

Only the most determined of pessimists would say that the Judeo-Christian understanding of women is a done deal—it's definitely a work in progress. To be a part of that tradition is to participate in the unfolding of that understanding. That is not a prison. It's a privilege to help the world change for the better. It is holy work.

APRIL 30

May you live to see your children's children.
PSALM 128:6
➤❖

*A*lthough you hear people say so all the time, it isn't really just because you can give grandchildren back to their parents when they start to cry that makes having them so wonderful. It's something much deeper, and harder to put into words.

Was I a good mother? I'm aware now, from the vantage point of elapsed decades, that the answer is yes and no. Some things were great. Some should have been a lot better. I see in my children a number of wonderful qualities I helped them acquire. I see some weaknesses I know to be mine, too. And I see much that came from elsewhere: injuries and blessings that formed them as they walked through their growing-up years.

What a remarkable thing it is to see it all begin again! I see my grandchildren with the eyes of experience. I see things I recognize: the flash of a dimple here, a certain open-hearted gaze there, the same one I used to meet from another little girl long ago. They carry us in them, their mother and me. And they go forth into the world that will form them differently from the way our two different worlds formed us. I now know, better than I knew it when I was a young mother, how glorious and how painful their journey into an unknown future will be. I ache for their futures at the same time as I rejoice for them. And, perhaps, I also ache and rejoice for my own past, and their mother's. Her motherhood, her girlhood, my motherhood and girlhood, mingle with told and retold stories of my own mother's girlhood, and a few from my grandmother's. They all rest in these little girls.

For the larger portion of their lives, I will be gone. They will have stories of our times together to tell, I hope, but I will be only a memory. I want them to pay attention to the ache and to the joy of life, more attention than I paid—more, probably, than young people can. But I can do so now; I am the link between them and the past, as they are my link to a future I will not see. Blessings on it, little girls, and on you, forever and forever.

*"Greatly have they oppressed me since my youth, but they have
not prevailed against me."*
PSALM 129:2

>‹

A friend remembers, when he was in junior high school—a schol-
arly, skinny kid with a crew cut and thick glasses—that a group of
boys used to lie in wait for him every day on the way home from
school. One boy in particular—large, redheaded, and as brash as my
friend was shy—took great delight in tormenting him: he would
knock him to the ground and sit on him, banging his face against the
pavement repeatedly, while the other boys laughed encouragement.
Sometimes my friend would try to elude them, take another route
home for school. He longed for his mother to pick him up in the car,
but hated the thought of telling her why.

How long the torture continued I do not know. I do know that
today my friend is a respected engineer, supervising the work of many
other engineers in the largest and most successful communications
organization in the world. I do know that he won scholarships to college and was invited into the honors program there, that he graduated
with honors, that he was something of a legend among his fellow students because of his brilliance. I know that he makes a tremendous
amount of money. I don't know what the redheaded bully is doing
now. I think it unlikely that he has surpassed his former victim.

I also don't know why the boys, especially the redheaded one, felt
that it was all right to torture another student. I doubt that they grew
up to be criminals; I imagine they grew up and got married and had
jobs and kids and did all those things pretty well. It just doesn't fit, this
little piece of cruelty. Or does it? Is it there still a sadistic little pocket

of hidden self within them, biding its time until the opportunity for inflicting pain comes again?

There is evil in the world. I don't know where it comes from, and neither does anybody else. But it need not prevail against you, although it sure can ruin your day. For evil to win, you must become evil yourself. If you do not, whatever else it has done to you, it has not defeated you.

Evil wants recruits even more than it wants victims. We cannot always choose not to be victimized, but we can always choose not to allow the evil we have suffered to fill us with vengeance and make us as cruel as the ones who hurt us in the past.

MAY 2

If you, Lord, were to note what is done amiss, O Lord, who could stand?
PSALM 130:2

✦✦

*T*here are those who take considerable pleasure in pointing out other people's flaws, either behind their backs or in person. Why this is I am not sure: is such faultfinding perhaps something in the nature of a preemptive strike, getting in there with a criticism first in order not to be singled out for attack oneself? After a few encounters with one of these grown-up Hall Monitors, all I have to do is catch sight of her from a distance and I find myself hoping she won't see me.

I am the opposite: I find it very difficult to correct people, even people whose relationship with me has correction built into it, like employees and children. I frame a stiff reproof in my mind, but I find that it fades into thin air before it reaches my lips. I am excessively concerned with their feelings, afraid I might hurt them terribly, as if they were much more fragile than most people really are. I believe this is because criticism stings me, and I think that others are like me. This isn't true: lots of people can just brush it off. We are all very different in how we respond to it.

I do know that it is not being without fault that commends us to God, or to one another. People don't love you because you're perfect. They love you because you are loving—and even sometimes when you're not very loving at all. They love you, just because they love you.

Dick was dying of AIDS. It took a long time and it was very hard. He was weak and tired. He was often incontinent—a clean person all his life, he found this especially humiliating. Often he could not eat, and so he was impossibly thin: about ninety pounds, at the end, on a six-foot-two frame. He had been a handsome young Irish fellow with an engaging grin; now his cheekbones seemed about to break through the skin stretched tightly over them. The lesions of Kaposi's sarcoma on his feet made it difficult to walk. He had trouble breathing. Sometimes he saw things that weren't there.

His companion of thirty-five years cared for him. This, too, was hard. When an attack of diarrhea struck, fouling the sheets and blankets and Dick's body, it was Bill who cleaned him up. When Dick couldn't breathe in the middle of the night, it was Bill who drove to the hospital as fast as he could.

Usually Dick was patient, but sometimes he was peevish and fretful, frightened and angry if Bill left the room even for a moment. Once in a while, though, out of the blue, Dick would remind Bill that he loved him. Just that simple declaration: part apology, part thanks, and part sorrow in anticipation of their parting, which could not be far away. *And I love you, too,* Bill would say, his face grey with lack of sleep, his eyes red. Dick's death, when it finally came, was a relief for both of them, sorrowful though it was. Bill read a poem at the funeral, stopping more than once to accommodate his tears.

The scriptures, both the Hebrew and the Christian ones, are full of images of God loving human beings in full knowledge of the ways in which we fall short of perfection. There's not a one of us who's perfect, this verse points out. Love can take that in its stride. That's one of the ways you can tell it's love you're looking at.

MAY 3

I do not occupy myself with great matters, or with things that are too hard for me.
PSALM 131:2

➳✦

Like me, Corinna did not begin college until motherhood had already struck. Right now she is at the tail end of a required math course, a summer school course that crams a semester's worth of work into seven fun-filled weeks. I sneak a look at her textbook. The stuff looks familiar; I used to know how to do it, I know, but now I don't even know where to begin. I realize with mild shock that I don't remember a *thing* from the one college math course I took. Not a thing. Wait, I take that back: I do remember that the lecture was on television, and that once the professor used a supermarket display of soup cans stacked on other soup cans to illustrate something or other. His point is long gone, though, as is every jot and tittle of the course's content. It is as if it never happened.

I do still have dreams, though, about being enrolled in a math course that I haven't attended in weeks. The final examination is fast approaching, and I am clueless about anything we have covered. *Why haven't you done something about this sooner?* I scold myself, and try to find the professor, whom I have never met, to see if I can cut some kind of deal. He isn't around, and so I end up just going to class. I always awaken before I actually have to solve an equation.

My mother—may she rest in peace—had those dreams, too. To the end of her life she had them—she died in 1980, but she graduated Class of '34. That's almost fifty years. I remember how pleased I was to hear this, how we both laughed about it. I wasn't the only paranoid on the block. We're all scared stiff by the prospect of failure. The effects persist for decades.

Corinna is getting through this math course, as I got through mine and my mom got through hers. Wicked little Anna transferred into a division of NYU that doesn't require it, and she did so for that very reason. We're all victims of math anxiety, the fear of confronting our own incompetence in the world of numbers. My husband's university has a math anxiety program targeted specifically at women, it's such a common problem. How strange. *Didn't you ever have those dreams?* I ask him, and he says no. But everybody needs a sense of competence, and nobody likes its opposite. It's so necessary to have the satisfaction of doing something well that my dreaming self awakens me in terror at the thing I don't do well. Strong stuff.

MAY 4

I will not allow my eyes to sleep, nor let my eyelids slumber.
PSALM 132:4

✢

Ed Towt always came to the eight o'clock service. This was because we used Rite One then, the rite that used the Elizabethan language Ed loved, rather than the contemporary-language Rite Two, which he detested. He pointedly used an older version of the Nicene

Creed, one that began with the words "I believe" rather than "we believe," as the rest of the congregation was saying—*How the hell do I know what* you *believe?* he would demand. *Speak for yourself!*—and in doing so always finished up by himself, a syllable or two later than everybody else. When it came time for the sermon, Ed would lean back in his pew and close his eyes until it was over. For a couple of years I thought he was asleep. But then one Monday he stopped in to disagree with a point in my sermon of the day before. *I hear every word you say,* he said indignantly, when I expressed surprise at his powers of retention, *I'm just resting my eyes.*

Carol hosted the Daughters of the American Revolution at their house once a year. Once I was the speaker for a meeting she hosted. I arrived just as Ed, with a wicked grin, was hoisting the Union Jack up the flagpole in front of their house. It wasn't that he was unpatriotic; he just enjoyed a little humor. Actually Ed was *very* patriotic: he had a big iron bell out in their back garden and every Fourth of July he would proclaim liberty throughout the land—at seven in the morning or thereabouts, waking all the neighbors.

Don't forget that I want to be buried in my tartan beret, he would say, *and I want the old prayer book and I want bagpipes.* Toward the end of his life, Ed took up the pipes himself, hired a young Scotsman to come to the house and tutor him. The pipes require a lot of effort. Often Ed didn't have the strength himself to play. On those days, he would just sit in his chair and listen as the music skirled through the house. *Don't forget, I want them to carry me high,* he said, and when he died, his coffin left the church high on the shoulders of his sons and stepson and sons-in-law, the pipes leading it out with their strangely bracing wail.

I sure hope they use Rite One in heaven, Carol said to me after the funeral.

They'll hear about it from Ed if they don't, I said. *Do you suppose he sleeps through the sermons?*

This is Carol's second go-round as a widow. Her first husband died at thirty, and she raised three children on her own. Same thing happened to Ed, and he raised his two boys alone. *I'm going to the seashore with Mr. Towt,* she told her children when he asked her for their first date. *You mean the guy who sits in front of us and can't carry a tune?* her son asked. Ed loved to relate this story. They were full of drolleries about each other when he was alive; now, when I visit, his chair is empty. The anecdotes are still funny, but we miss that presence. Life on earth is good that way: it puts such interesting characters in our path. Nobody *has* to be funny and interesting, but many people are: a little bonus for all of us.

MAY 5

Oh, how good and pleasant it is. . . . It is like fine oil upon the head that runs down upon the beard . . . and . . . upon the collar . . .
PSALM 133:1–3

✹

Well, to each his own, I suppose. Oil running all over my face and hair and clothing certainly isn't *my* idea of a good time. It's interesting to consider how standards of pleasure and of beauty have changed over time. Many men wore heavy makeup in the eighteenth century. In seventeenth-century France, only men were permitted to wear diamonds: today, Tiffany's refuses to *sell* diamond rings for men. The Roman emperors are alleged to have enjoyed eating until they vomited, and then filling up again and repeating the whole messy business. Women's ideal figure, of course, changes from era to era; I should have been born in the seventeenth century, when what we now consider *avoirdupois* in women was greatly admired. And nobody in days gone by would have understood the current exercise craze very well, or thought it was much fun to run and sweat for hours. To accommodate the new realities about the ozone layer, our aesthetic where skin is concerned needs to revert to that of earlier centuries, when fashionable people were pale. Back then, people used to take arsenic to achieve the proper pallor, and would sometimes overdose and die from it.

And yet, there are constants that survive the vicissitudes of time and fashion. This psalm is about how lovely a thing it is to dwell in peace and friendship with one's fellows—in every time and every place, friendship has been one of life's greatest joys. Human beings need loving human companionship. Babies who don't get enough cuddling sometimes die from a condition known as "marasmus," a profound failure to thrive. The souls of adults, often depicted in medieval paintings as tiny children, also wither without love. Life may not be quite as simple as the Beatles suggest—that *all you would need is love*—but without it, nothing else we have satisfies.

MAY 6

Lift up your hands in the holy place.
PSALM 134:2

❧

The posture for prayer in ancient Israel was standing with the arms upraised. Most American Christians bow their heads automatically when somebody says *Let us pray*. Lately, though, there has been less unanimity about this: you'll go into a church and half the people will be kneeling, a handful sitting, and the rest standing up, or in some combination of these postures. Most people fold their hands, although sometimes you also see people lifting their arms, as if holding a hula hoop aloft, or resting their hands quietly in their laps, the palms upward as if to catch something from the sky. I've known congregations in which these differences became quite divisive; for some reason, people just couldn't seem to leave each other alone about standing versus kneeling and all the rest of it. It is amazing what people can come up with when they really want to argue.

My own choice? I behave myself in church, of course, since what an Episcopal priest does in the liturgy is usually spelled out for us fairly completely. But my normal prayer posture at home is lying down in a bathtub full of warm, scented water. The pages of my prayer book are wrinkled from having been turned repeatedly by wet hands; they look as if I had cried on them. My back always hurts at the beginning of the day because I haven't moved enough yet and then again at the end of the day because I have moved too much. My self-pity is at a fairly high level as I fill the tub, but then I sink into the water and understand all over again what gratitude is.

I'm not convinced it's necessary to choose one body language for your spiritual self-expression, any more than you would want to confine yourself to the same set of words over and over again. I feel comforted and nurtured praying in my lovely bath, but I also like to stand and pray—it reminds me that God's image lives in me, and I am strong and joyous. And I also like to kneel, to enact with my body the humility a human being feels when she is confronted with the awesomeness of the divine mystery and power. And the hands? Wide open to embrace God? Folded in quiet contemplation? Lightly cupped, to catch a blessing from heaven? Or, as mine so often are, wet with sweet-smelling water from my healing bath? They all sound good to me. I'll have one of each.

Let the nations be glad and sing for joy.
PSALM 67:4

✦

*A*aron Copland had no way of knowing when he wrote *Appalachian Spring* that the war in Europe would end on the day he won the Pulitzer Prize for this haunting setting of a simple Shaker hymn tune. They're playing it on the radio today, in between clips from old newscasts of people all over America, people in England and France, singing and cheering as the long years of fear came to an end. For the first time in years, wives could look forward to their husbands' return without the pang of dread to which they'd become so accustomed. Little children would at last get to know their fathers. Families would sit down to dinner again, couples would sleep safely in their beds again, under the same roof again, the way it's supposed to be.

Appalachian Spring is like that: a hymn to the beauty of daily life and love. It's only a ballet score about nothing very special, really: a girl and her lover get married. They are not royalty. They are not glamorous. They are just country people. Her friends and his friends come to the wedding. The parson is there. At the end, the two are left quietly alone in their new home, in their new life, beginning their decades of partnership in love. That's all. Nothing special.

But somehow this strangely dignified, achingly beautiful music helps us understand something that we need to understand: this is what is really important in life. Not money. Not power. Not glamour. Just love. Just being able to see and love trees, to smell the grass when it is newly cut. Just being able to touch the hand of your love. This is all you really need. For God's sake, don't run around after other things so hard that you forget these things. These things were what the soldiers had missed so much. These things were what those who did not return died for: the right of ordinary people to live ordinary lives. Back into the ordinary they came, up the garden walks, the apartment stairs, into the waiting arms. Ordinary life. There is nothing lovelier.

MAY 8

The idols of the heathen are silver and gold, the work of human hands. They have mouths, but they cannot speak; eyes have they, but they cannot see. . . . Those who make them are like them.

PSALM 135:15–18

✦

*T*he biblical writers took a very dim view of idol worship. People were always being tempted by the various cults of their ancient Near Eastern neighbors—a visit to that part of the world, even now, when the ancient temples and statues are crumbled memories of their former glory, makes it easy to understand why: the statues of ancient gods and goddesses were glorious, made of bright colors and precious metals, sometimes precious stones, the temples huge and filled with treasures. Pretty impressive, even in ruins. Of course the Israelites were tempted to be part of all that glamour when it was new.

But their god didn't have an image. The worship of this god was something beyond the admiration of precious stones and gold leaf. Also beyond the healthy respect for nature's power that convinced the ancient mind that gods lived in the wind, the sea, the clouds. Beyond anything that could be pictured—because something that can be pictured is no longer a mystery, and we who have looked into our own small souls know that even *they* are mysterious and unknowable. How much more unknowable is that in which is all that is and has ever been and will ever be?

I look around our church. There is the hanging pyx, a little round box suspended from the ceiling, in which we keep the consecrated wafers—*the Body of Christ,* we say, as we hand them to one another. There is the cross—we bow when it passes us in procession. There is the icon: Christ enthroned on a rainbow in a stylized heaven. On Sunday I sprinkle it with holy water, and swing a censer billowing sweet smoke three times in its direction. If we have no idols, what's going on with all this bowing and smoke?

The difference is that, to the idolator, the idol *is* the god. The icon and the holy water and the bread, on the other hand, are some of the many things that can help human beings express the idea and the feeling of holiness, but they are not God. I bow to the cross and to the icon: not because those two crossed pieces of wood, this painting on wood, are divine, but because God is.

Both the practitioners and the detractors of religious faith and practice often cross that line. Both often mistake the aid to worship for the object of worship. It is easy to do: the physical beauty and sensual appeal of ecclesiastical hardware are potent for many people. Hardline Protestants try to guard against this: no statues, no incense, sometimes even no music. I love beauty too much ever to be happy refusing it, so I keep on singing and swinging the incense, crossing myself, bowing—closer to the creator, if I desire to be closer, through these small pieces of the created world.

. . . for his mercy endures for ever . . .
PSALM 136:1

✦

Justice is what everybody wants, of course. Fairness. We want the good rewarded and the evil punished. We want there to be enough to go around. We want innocence protected.

But I'm not sure that justice—if we really got it—would be exactly what we had in mind. Pure justice, after all, leaves little room for forgiveness. Its impartial equations don't factor in the human capacity to learn from error. And justice is minimal, content merely to restrain evil, and more than a bit solitary, making sure that each of us is treated fairly, but not concerning itself with us beyond that. Justice doesn't acknowledge love; it must factor it out, in fact, lest it create a bias. Justice, you remember, is portrayed allegorically as a blindfolded woman.

Isn't righteousness, rather than justice, what we really need? The stories we all grew up with, stories of people risking or even sacrificing their lives for others, people like Dietrich Bonhoeffer or Raoul Wallenberg: justice does not prompt such nobility. Justice is simple: an eye for an eye, a tooth for a tooth, and no obligation beyond that. Make it all balance out somehow. Righteousness might prompt me to do much, much more in the name of love.

Mercy and forgiveness spring from righteousness, not from justice. The bare minimum of justice is the starting point, not the zenith, of the human potential for the good. And there is another reason to value righteousness above justice: besides the pleasing possibility of being noble toward someone else, there is the far likelier eventuality that I will one day be in a position to hope for mercy to be offered me, rather than the stern justice I may well deserve.

I will give thanks to you, O Lord, with my whole heart.
PSALM 138:1

>‹

Brunch after church with a friend who is preparing for the ordained ministry. *I still hear a voice in my head sometimes that tells me the whole thing is a lot of nonsense,* she says. *That I'm giving my life to something that doesn't care about me at all—like a scientific process or an evolutionary force or whatever. That my idea of God is a big joke. Can you believe that I'm preparing for this life and I still have these thoughts?*

She shakes her head with a smile, but it is a rueful one. I can easily believe it, I tell her. It's hard for a lot of us to do *anything* with our whole hearts. I've known a lot of religious people in my day, and many, many of them have had frequent moments of terribly painful cynicism. I have had such moments often. My idea of God may be a complete fantasy on my part, from start to finish: my own fantasy, or someone else's. I don't know that it's *not*, and there's no way on earth I'm *going* to know. Faith isn't about knowing. It's about following. It says, *This is how I want to live my life, and I've bet the farm on it.*

And why not? If I am wrong in my vision of God's bringing meaning to life and to the life of the world, it will soon be clear. I'm certain to be wrong, in fact, at least about some things. But am I any worse off than someone who did not try to push the envelope of knowing beyond its limit, who confined herself to the things that can be demonstrated? I don't think so. If she's right, we'll both return to our constituent electrons someday and that'll be it; she won't be better off than I will because she was correct. And if I'm right, that there is much, much more to life than meets the eye, then I will have had the chance to explore it, an exploration that will go on and on. Sounds like a good deal to me.

Where can I go then from your Spirit? Where can I flee from your presence?
PSALM 139:6
➤❖

I remember being told, when I was small, that God was everywhere. That concept was—and remains—an elusive one for me. I used to turn around very quickly, sometimes, when I was all alone, to see if I could catch a glimpse of God. Sometimes I would look under the bed. The idea was to give me an ongoing sense of the divine providence, I suppose: that God was looking out for me wherever I might go and whatever I might do. I didn't take it quite that way, though, not at first. The idea of God lurking, unseen, around the perimeter of my world seemed a touch sinister. Why was God hiding? If he's everywhere, why doesn't he just show himself if he really wants to reassure me? My brothers were always leaping out at me from behind large pieces of furniture and scaring me half to death. It wasn't my idea of a good time, and I didn't appreciate it.

Rather than encouraging my too-literal imagination to believe that I was being stalked, perhaps it would have been better to tell me that God is *available* everywhere. There is no situation to which the spiritual life is irrelevant. The element of possibility, the chance for good to be found in the midst of trouble, that unbidden, peculiar sense of heightened awareness that sometimes transfixes a person for a moment or two—no matter where you go, you don't get away from that.

I often have those moments in the early evening, out in the yard, when the light is a certain way: golden and gentle, preparing for the coming darkness. The leaves dapple the light, leaving their shadows on the ground before them. The smell of green things is in the air, and the sound of cicadas. At those times, my love for the earth almost hurts, and I am very aware of its passing. And of my passing, for that matter. At those times—unlike some other, anxious ones—I don't mind the thought of dying. Everything dies. My body will return to the earth, part of all this beauty. And that part of me that wonders at all this—I don't know much about where *that* will go. But it will not leave the comforting presence of the love that made it.

MAY 12

Protect me from the violent.
PSALM 140:1

→←

We didn't have a metal detector in the elementary school I attended. I'm sure you didn't have one in your school either. Didn't need one. The term "drive-by shooting" had not yet been invented, and a Saturday Night Special was something you might look for at a soda fountain. It was not considered foolish to pick up a hitchhiker or to leave your house or your car unlocked. It was a more innocent world.

On the other hand, we did have regular air raid drills at school, in which we all crouched under our desks with our hands clasped behind our necks and our eyes closed. All that I had heard about the atomic bomb made me more than a little skeptical about the efficacy of these precautionary measures: didn't the bomb turn you into a sort of X ray and then into a little pile of dust? What protection would my desk be to me, my small hands behind my skinny neck? We also had a modest emergency shelter at home, in the basement, where my brother had his model train. Cans of food, army cots, bottles of water. People who were richer than we were had elaborate underground bunkers. The ethical problem most often discussed: do you let your neighbor in when he begs to come into your bomb shelter after The Big One, reducing the amount of food and water and air available to your own family, or do you shoot him?

So that gentler age was a violent time, too: you might be sitting in your house, quietly watching TV, and then the next minute you might be an X ray, courtesy of someone in a control room eight or nine thousand miles from where you were. The despoiling of innocence was the same, and the absurd anonymity of modern violence, whether that of the 1990s or the 1960s: someone you don't know might just kill you one day, and there's not much you can do about it. The fallout shelters were card houses, like the air raid drills. And the metal detectors. And the car alarms that shriek through all our nights.

Protect us from violence—not just the possibility of injury at the hands of an unknown evil person, but from the hobbling of our spirits caused by our fear of that future injury. Don't let violence injure us twice: once when we live in fear of it and then again when it happens. Don't let it rob us of the sweetness of a reasonable trust in our fellow men and women, and in our own ability to take care of ourselves.

Be careful. Don't be stupid. But don't let the presence of evil in the world make you live in fear.

Let the righteous smite me in friendly rebuke; let not the oil of the
unrighteous anoint my head.

PSALM 141:5

>+<

*I*nteresting: the psalmist would rather have the righteous haul off and slug him than have the unrighteous do something nice for him, like anointing his head with oil. (I know, I know: I don't want oil poured on my head, either, but the people in the Bible seem to have liked it.) This psalm is about the seductiveness of bad folks' good parties: don't hang out with the wrong people, or you will become like them.

Last year I stopped for gas at a station in town. I've known the proprietor for years. He's always been friendly to me, and respectful, and I've always enjoyed a brief chat with him. More than once, he's given me some special treatment when my car needed repair: a ride back to the church or something. This time the talk turned to my forthcoming trip to the city. *I never go in there anymore if I can help it,* he said in a relaxed way, as he squeegeed the windshield. *There's just too many niggers there now.* He was not angry or combative as he said this, nor did he have any sense of having just said anything especially provocative. His tone was matter-of-fact, the tone of a person who is confident that he's speaking to someone whose agreement he can count on. He assumed that I felt the same way.

I was speechless. I handed him his money and drove off. What a coward—it's been more than a year, and I haven't been back. I am ashamed at whatever it was in my demeanor that made him think I was like him in this regard, and have wondered more than once what it was. I genuinely liked him. He was polite and funny and helpful. He liked me, too, and people like to share a worldview with the people they like. I guess he just wanted to celebrate the bond he assumed we had, one of the many things upon which we pleasantly agreed.

No more friendly chats. No more rides back to the office. I feel a little guilty every time I ride past and see him there.

MAY 14

No one cares for me.
PSALM 142:4

➣➣

$\mathcal{S}$ooner or later, somebody's probably going to have to.

We're living longer and longer. If this new fat pill I just read about works out, the number one risk factor (obesity) for America's deadliest killer (heart disease) will be history. I, for one, am ready—if you're reading this and happen to work for one of the drug companies that will be doing the trials, I want to talk to you. But there sure will be a lot of old people around—and none of us can count on popping off suddenly at a time convenient for all concerned. We may be thin, but we'll still be old. And most of us will need some help.

Both my grandmothers lived with us and died at home. It was difficult for my parents, but they managed with the help of friends and relatives. Both my parents died in hospitals—much more the norm now. My father-in-law dropped dead, the way a lot of people say they'd like to die, and my mother-in-law died in a nursing home of Alzheimer's disease, unsure for years of where and who she was, eventually forgetting everything: how to swallow, breathe, live.

People usually say they don't want to be a burden to anyone, but then they delay taking the steps that would help them avoid it. They can't see the signs of decline in themselves that are so visible to others, so they don't make new arrangements for retirement living until a crisis forces something upon them that nobody wants. It would be good if we could stop thinking of old people as family heirlooms that need to be maintained, unchanged, in the family jewel box—usually a home they've loved and lived in for years—and thought of them instead as people who are entering a new stage of life that is likely to go on for a long time. Your life is your own—just because you're old doesn't mean you have no responsibility for planning it sensibly anymore. In old age, as at any other time in life, others will govern you unless you govern yourself.

MAY 15

I remember the time past.
PSALM 143:5

✧

*L*ate at night, I am alone in the living room, writing. The window is open—a summer breeze carries the smell of freshly cut grass into the room. A vase of flowers from the garden sits on a table piled high with my husband's books. Except for the light of my lamp, the room is dark to cut down on the heat. Somewhere in the house a radio is playing.

I turn out the paragraphs best when I am undisturbed. I *can* write at the swimming pool while the kids jump and splash, and I *can* write on the train to New York, but I do my best work in a quiet and beautiful room. I have loved the quiet of late summer nights since childhood, a serene quiet full of flower smells, the smell of books and paper, of newly cut grass.

A piano begins to play "The Last Rose of Summer," and my father is suddenly in the room. The vase in which my husband has arranged our flowers belonged to my parents; my father was the flower arranger in our family, too, and in late summer vases of them filled the house. Sometime in the fall he would come in from the yard with a rose. *The last rose of summer,* he would say, and find a little vase for it. One last brave bloom, a last breath of flower smell before the sharper scents of burning leaves and north winds replaced summer's lushness. Sometimes he would hum the tune, a sentimental one—older than he was, I think, a song more from his parents' youth than from his own. The piano continues to pour out the tune. The people for whom it was new have all been gone for years. The melody is sweet but melancholy. *Why am I still here,* it wonders, *when the ones who sang me first are gone?*

Put these in my darling's hands, my stepmother said, her strong voice quavering a bit, as she handed me a few red roses, *he loved flowers so,* and then she covered her face and wept. *I will,* I said, my own eyes filling, and went to the funeral home for one last look. His gnarled hands felt the same as they had when he was alive as I slipped the stems between his fingers. The last roses of his summer, I think now as I hear the old melody.

You should be a writer, he used to tell me, *you write well.* He would give me books he admired. When I had my first child, he gave me *The Wind in the Willows*; was it to read to my little girl, I wondered, or was it really for me, because he wished I were still little and time had not passed so quickly? The first story I sold for real money was about him. Some of my best writing still is. I wouldn't know how to notice the bittersweet beauty of small things if I hadn't seen him do it all my life. Who today bothers to notice the last rose of summer? Who today knows the song? The gift of quiet, the smell of books? The flowers?

Bow your heavens, O Lord, and come down; touch the mountains,
and they shall smoke.

PSALM 144:5

✙

Volcanoes: Corinna was fascinated with them when she was five. I still have a little volcano paperweight she made in kindergarten on my desk: a bright blue plaster cone with lurid streams of orange and yellow lava creeping down its sides. Like the psalmist, Corinna was a moralist: she saw God's hand in the power and placement of volcanoes. Bad people should be cast into one, she thought, never to bother the righteous again. She even made up a vindictive chant about it, a tuneless little commercial for punitive legalism; I would hear her singing it to herself over and over. *If anybody's bad to anyone, if anybody robs anyone, put him in LIQUID!* Charming. She was very conscious of good and evil, Corinna, and even then enjoyed watching police shows. What does she do today? Works for the county prosecutor. We'd all better behave ourselves.

A lot of people have been fascinated with volcanoes, though, not just my one-time five-year-old. A mountain that smokes and puts forth fire. Liquid rock snaking through a city's streets, catching the people as they hung out the wash and baked bread, as they slept, as they strolled in pairs. A lovely cloudless day, turned suddenly white-hot, deadly. The idea of sudden death is incomprehensible to most of us: we, like Corinna when she was five, want to believe that wickedness is somehow attached to it, so that we can behave in such a way as to avoid it. The volcano, showering fire upon the righteous and the unrighteous alike, troubles us deeply.

Moral ambiguity is a very adult concept. It doesn't come immediately to small children, who view moral decision-making primarily as avoiding behavior likely to lead to punishment. The nuances of other people's behavior occur to us only later on, after the even-more-shocking consciousness of our own mixed nature hits us. If only society could be cleansed of evil simply by sorting out the bad people and restraining their evil deeds, even if not as violently as Corinna at five thought it could. The good and evil in human beings is just not that simple to delineate, not every time.

MAY 17

Put not your trust in rulers.
PSALM 146:2

➤❖

We didn't always assume that political leaders are crooked, the way we do now. I distinctly remember being surprised when somebody in authority was caught with his hand in the till. Of course, we were all much younger then.

When the psalmist talks about not trusting rulers, though, he doesn't really mean things like Watergate. Trust in the Hebrew scriptures usually means reliance upon strength: I might test first to see if I can "trust" a tree limb to support my full weight. Trust is about help. Who will help you? Whom do you trust?

Then as now, there were many places in which a person might put her trust. The Israelites' neighbors in the ancient Near East were all polytheists, so there were lots of different gods among which to choose. Kings and military figures rose and fell. As cities developed, some people became wealthy; they could trust in their business savvy and their money. We are not much different three thousand years later. We trust money. We trust military might. We trust scientists and doctors. We trust our own youth and beauty. These are the things that will help us, we hope.

But they all come and they all go. There will be an end to the saving power of all of them. One thing alone does not end: the spirit whose power survives even death. Perhaps the psalmist was a little more magical in his thinking than we are; perhaps he meant that trust in God would stave off death and misfortune forever, something we know to be untrue. But still the choice of whom to trust is yours: do you travel through life's uncertainties relying utterly on things you know will one day fail, or do you turn instead to a powerful love to supply your courage and serenity through victory and defeat alike?

MAY 18

He counts the number of the stars.
PSALM 147:4

➤◄

I am told that some of the stars we see in the night sky are actually no longer there. They were so far away that the light which emanated from them ages ago is only just now reaching our eyes. That which radiated the light in our direction eons ago may no longer exist.

So the number of the stars, from an earthbound human point of view, is not only ridiculously large, it is also uncertain. It is dependent on time, from our point of view. The whole of the universe, then, encompasses both the future and the past: for part of it, the star exists, while part of it does not yet know that particular star, and another part has long ago forgotten that it ever was.

How confusing. But oddly comforting, to me at least: it means, after all, that the light emanating from me has not yet reached a far-away place. That somebody, somewhere, could now be receiving the image of my mother brushing my hair on my first day of school. My grandparents' wedding day is winging its way across the vastness of space even as we speak. Somewhere William Shakespeare puts the finishing touch on *A Winter's Tale* and lays down his pen. With enough distance between image and reception, time becomes less obvious a prison. Under the eye of God, there is no such thing. No past and no future: all is present.

People usually conjure up a fairly concrete image of eternal life when they try to think about it: streets paved with gold, meeting up with loved ones, clouds, angels, no midriff bulge. We see the biblical writers applying their imaginations to the concept. But it *is* imagination: we don't have a clue about what it is, and neither did they. It's probably *not* just like the way we live now, only perfect. The reality of God is probably not nearly so easy to understand. When I hear something like this business about seeing stars in the sky that aren't really there anymore, when I think about the beauty of my encounter with them, when I imagine their encounter with me years from now, after I have died, my head may spin, but I suspect my soul understands.

Young men and maidens, old and young together.
PSALM 148:12

❖

When we were little, my brothers sometimes had a club whose governing principle was "No Girls Allowed." My next-door neighbor and I would retaliate with something we called the "Tomboy Club," designed to exclude not only boys, but also females our own age whom we called "girls" with a derisive sneer, meaning girls who enjoyed feminine pursuits such as dolls and dresses (this made hardly any sense: on days when we weren't being Tomboys, *we* enjoyed playing with dolls and dressing up).

There's the self-destructive power of prejudice for you: it can make a person scorn her own tastes and seek to exchange them for the tastes of a more powerful someone else. In our aping of the exclusiveness of the boys' clubs, we had not yet hit upon this particular feminist insight. We would understand it better when we grew up. The Tomboys tried to be boys in girl bodies, a way of fighting back that stopped short of celebrating girlishness and instead affirmed boyishness as the really desirable state of affairs for a human child, as if a girl who did daring things must be some new kind of boy, rather than just a brave girl. And as if daring and dresses couldn't both be fun.

Madeline longs to be as old as Rosie. It is one of the unkindnesses of her young life that she never will be, that her sister's two-year head start is permanent. Right now, Rosie is in a theater class for which Madeline is too young. I take Madeline to Main Street for some compensatory fun while Rosie tends her muse. We browse through one of those frilly stores with lots of potpourri and little china figurines. What Madeline chooses as a prize, though, is none of these; it's a little metal car whose doors and hood really open, the kind you can propel by revving it up with friction from the wheels. Cool.

That's a boy's toy, Rosie says in disdain, annoyed because Madeline got a prize and she didn't. *It is not,* Madeline answers loftily, *it's a person's toy.* That's my girl.

MAY 20

Let the praises of God be in their throat and a two-edged sword in their hand.

PSALM 149:6

✦

"*P*raise the Lord and Pass the Ammunition"—that was the title and first line of a soldiers' song during the First World War. So many centuries of enthusiastic warmongering in the name of Christ have gone by that a lot of people don't realize that the earliest Christians were pacifists. They were, though, not only because of their radical appropriation of the prohibition against killing in the Ten Commandments but because serving in the Roman army meant acknowledging the divinity of the emperor. In their view, not even self-defense provided justification for taking a human life. It was only later, when the new faith had become a lot more mainstream and had begun to spread throughout the Roman Empire (by conversions among Roman soldiers, among other means) that the idea of a Christian soldier began to seem like something other than a contradiction in terms.

That's so often true: it's easy to be a moral absolutist about situations in which you yourself are not involved. Once the Church began to include people who made their living soldiering, *Thou shalt not kill* just didn't look as simple. Extended contact with the world usually produces compromise. That's one reason teenagers and young adults often find their elders hypocritical: they see our compromises and don't know yet that life will force them to develop their own.

This is not a moral defeat. To live in the world as it really is is simply acknowledging the truth. And there is more: the untried absolutism of the young is essentially self-absorbed. It is somewhat like the pacifism of the early Church: in my youthful absolutism, I was much more concerned with my own clean hands than with another whose need might force me to dirty them. But the moral question to the moral adult is not always a simple *Are you yourself clean in thought, word, and deed?* Quite often it is more like *What did you sacrifice for the good of another and what did it cost you in terms of your own purity?* The adult will acknowledge the cost, even as she acknowledges the necessity of paying it. If a soldier kills in battle, he may be awarded a medal. A person who kills while committing a felony may get a lethal injection. But both have killed. Both have lost forever the purity they had before they did so: ask any soldier who has taken a life and can bear to speak of it. We do not explain away our actions when we accept their necessity. We just join the human race.

MAY 21

Praise him with the blast of the ram's horn.
PSALM 150:3
➜❰

*T*he Seamen's Church is in Lower Manhattan, right at the foot of the Brooklyn Bridge, just below Chinatown. Out on the street, you can hear the Lunar New Year getting ready to happen for three or four days before it actually does: day and night, nonstop explosions. Most of them are just a series of small *pop-pop-pops*, but some of them are darned loud. The federal courthouse is also nearby. This year it was terrifying to walk by the courthouse: inside, they were trying the people who blew up the World Trade Center, and outside it sounded like World War III. Not to worry. It was just happy Chinese people having fun. Okay.

Psalm 150 is all about that kind of noise. Maybe some of the instruments it mentions sounded okay—I've never heard a timbrel—but I have heard a ram's horn, and it would wake the dead. It makes an awful racket, something like a wounded tenor elephant. I don't really know why it should be that human celebration demands loud noises, but there it is, spanning cultures and centuries.

It is true that noise signifies power. I go to watch Rosie and Madeline in their tae kwon do class. The instructor executes an airborne kick, equal in grace to its obvious strength. *HEYAH!!* he yells, and then his students attempt the same, chirping their own treble *heyah!* at the appropriate moment. *It makes you stronger to yell,* he explains, *it focuses your power.* And I guess it does: eight-year-old Rosie can break a wooden board with a well-placed (bare!) foot. Power and noise: the roar of a hurricane, the subterranean thunder of an earthquake, the deafening collision of invisible masses of air that wakens people out of a sound sleep during a summer storm.

So when happy people of any era make a racket, one thing they are doing is making themselves strong, borrowing the gift of noise from God's thunder and oceans, scaring themselves a little with the noise of a power quite able to destroy: *The world is loud and dangerous. With timbrel and dance, with firecrackers and with the ram's horn, we turn our fear into play.*

Why are the nations in an uproar? Why do the peoples mutter empty threats?

PSALM 2:1

✦

*E*very time I think I understand what's going on in Bosnia or Rwanda, I read something in the newspaper or hear something on the radio that tells me I've got it all wrong. War is complex, all right; almost a century and a half after our own civil war, the factors that brought it about are not always agreed upon. Slaveholders said it was about states' rights. Abolitionists thought it was about freeing the slaves. Both turn out to have been pretty simple descriptions of a very complex series of events.

Yesterday the Japanese finally got around to apologizing for their aggression during the Second World War. Twenty million souls perished as a direct result of their brutal sweep through Asia. After the war, a constitutional prohibition against deploying Japanese armies abroad found its way, under duress, into Japanese law, and it has been observed for fifty years, as the vanquished transformed themselves into an economic superpower. All in all, we can say that the past fifty years have been more profitably spent by Japan than was the decade or so that preceded them. And, although the neighbors continue to grumble about the apology and its lateness, and to look upon the rising sun with substantial leftover trepidation, nobody really thinks that Japan will turn aggressor again anytime soon. There is too much money to be made doing other things.

Things rise and fall as the world wags on. Enemies become allies and vice versa. What brings this about is usually not changed hearts, but changed economic possibilities: it is amazing how readily the human mind can come up with a moral reason for doing almost anything likely to turn a profit.

Knowing how disposed to war the human family has always been, how facile our excuses for our own violent propensities have always been, can a person realistically pray for peace? Or, as many people believe, is earnest talk of peace just an irrelevant, flower-child decision to ignore the complexities of real life?

Here are some things we know:

1. I have almost no control over what anyone else will or will not do.
2. I do have some control over what I will do.
3. The power of hatred and violence in the world is immense.

Given these three indisputables, recourse to a power greater than ourselves makes a lot more sense than reliance upon a human peacemaking that has never been known to work. To pray commends the whole mess of whatever it is we're praying about to God. To pray is *not* to decide against working for it—most of the people I know who pray regularly for peace are also very actively involved in some effort to promote it. To pray is to admit that many things are beyond us. That's not being naive: it's just facing the truth. *Not* to pray in the face of human hopelessness is what's naive.

MAY 23

You will break the teeth of the wicked.

PSALM 3:7

✦✦

I've got to get my teeth fixed, says the woman who has come to see me, *and then I can look for a job.* She is hanging on by her fingernails to a tenuous and very recent recovery from cocaine addiction. It is not her first. I nod encouragement, torn between wanting to affirm her realism and not wanting to be insulting about her teeth, which are really quite badly stained and also seem somewhat jagged. She covers her mouth with her hand when she smiles, which is not all that often these days. My understanding of an addict's decision not to use cocaine is that it is like deciding not to sneeze. Not much to smile about.

Almost all the addicts I know—and not all of them are homeless ones, although many are—mention their teeth early on in conversations about their hope of getting back into responsible life. Even middle-class teeth, pampered veterans of thousands of dollars' worth of adolescent orthodontia and years of fluoridated suburban water, deteriorate badly when a person spends almost all her time getting high. I guess you just have other things on your mind besides flossing. Diet plays a role in this misfortune, too; an addict may not eat for days at a time, and is apt to fill up on junk when he does.

I can't go on interviews looking like this, she continues, and she's right. Her teeth are a problem, of course, but her face is also grotesquely thin and her skin is dull, rutted with lines too deep for a face that age. Her hair hangs limply; she is constantly brushing it out of her face. She fiddles with her hands as we sit, and appears to tremble a bit. She projects no particular emotion, and speaks in a flat voice. The marketplace is full of dressed-for-success young things who don't have ADDICT tattooed across their foreheads. She is no match for them. As out of touch as she has been with the world around her, she knows that much.

She will try again to drag her wrecked life out of the mud. She will go to several meetings of Narcotics Anonymous a day. I give her the name of a dentist who sometimes helps me out in situations like this. And we pray together before she leaves. You know what she says as she prays? She thanks God for getting her through a day without coke. Nothing about the mountain of difficulties the demon of addiction has set squarely in her path. Her words are words of gratitude.

Will she make it? More than half do not. I wish I could bolt the door to my office so she wouldn't have to go back out there, where a half-dozen "friends" want to help her get high tonight. But it's not my job to shield people from their lives. And she does have what she needs to stay straight: the conviction that being clean has come to her through a power beyond herself.

She does need to get her teeth fixed. She needs to do something about that hair. But before she does any of those things, she needs to lean into the power that has brought her this little distance and allow it to carry her a little further.

MAY 24

You spread a table before me.
PSALM 23:5

✛

*A*cres of food—that's what you see in a Turkish restaurant. You're supposed to point at what you want, and the waiter will get it for you. There is more than anyone could ever eat—and this is just the appetizer. And in a Greek home—all day in the kitchen, both the husband and the wife: four different kinds of olives, the fish salad *taramasalata*, fresh calamari cooked with tomatoes and garlic, stuffed grape leaves, flaky squares of spinach pie. Just the appetizer.

I am often struck by the importance of hospitality in poor countries. People who barely have enough themselves seem to be the ones most eager to be lavish in offering food and drink to their guests. I doubt if there is a Greek or Turkish expression for "Why don't we just split this?" The vision of plenty, of more than enough, of delight in the presence of the stranger is not a vision common here in the richest country in the world. Odd, our stinginess and their openhandedness. I don't understand it.

Once a Turkish imam was traveling and stopped at a poor family's house for a rest. Of course, food was served. He took one taste of the eggplant dish set before him, and it was so good that he swooned right at the table. Here is the recipe for that potent dish, called in Turkish "Imam Bialdi," which means

THEN THE IMAM FAINTED

3 medium eggplants,
   cut in 1-inch cubes
4 medium onions, chopped
12–15 cloves fresh garlic,
   minced

5 medium ripe tomatoes,
   quartered (or a 1-pound can)
1/2 cup good olive oil
3/4 cup fresh parsley,
   chopped

Combine all ingredients in a large Dutch oven—spray it with nonstick coating first for easier cleanup. Bake at 300°F. for about 3 hours, stirring occasionally. Wonderful hot or cold on pita, as a cross-cultural accompaniment to polenta, on a baked potato, on pasta, or alone. *Serves eight.*

I will celebrate your love in the morning.
PSALM 59:18

➤<

I used to be up very early in the morning—four or five o'clock. I would use that time to write, savoring the silence of the sleeping house. For as long as I can remember, I have loved morning. When I was little, my father and I were the early risers. We would go outside first, in the spring and summer, to look at the garden: he poking this or that emerging plant with his hoe, I following along behind, the early morning dew squishing delightfully in my sneakers. *Beans are coming,* he might say, or *Onions are coming,* and I would say a word or two in response. We didn't feel the need for much talk in the early morning, and to this day I am quickly exhausted by incessant chatter. Then we would go in and have breakfast, sharing a pot of tea and some toast with fried tomatoes or, sometimes, fried kippers. He would read until his ride came to take him to the office. I would read, too, sometimes, or I would just eat in silence and watch him.

My mother was still asleep. Not a morning person, my mom. Just before his ride came, my dad would pour a cup of coffee and take it up to her to help her creep into her day. When he left I would transfer to their room to begin my second morning shift, accompanying my mother's coffee in bed. This was more conversational, dealing with plans for the day and reminders from her about what I needed for school, and unanswerable non sequiturs from me, like *What makes Jell-O get thick?* and *How did people figure out the way to make bread?*

I felt love in the morning in those days from the two people I loved most, love and security that have contributed, I think, to the fact that morning is still my most creative and peaceful time of the day. A good time to pray. A good time to work. A good time to walk and talk quietly. A good time to savor being alive.

MAY 26

You will shelter them.
PSALM 5:14

→←

I never carry an umbrella. People are always coming at me with them when it rains, wanting to shelter me from the storm. No thanks, I always say, I hate umbrellas. And I do; I am taller than all people who carry them, which means that either I walk politely along with my neck uncomfortably crooked if we try to walk together or my companion umbrellas me while I walk upright in the knowledge that I am causing the drenching of another human being, one who apparently dislikes drenching enough to carry protection against it, as I did not.

It's only water. Well, I suppose there's a little acid and whatnot mixed in with it as well these days, but basically it's just good old H_2O. If my hair gets wet, it will dry. So will my clothes. So will my skin. It's only uncomfortable if you dwell on it.

And there is something very freeing about being under the sky when the heavens open. We are so sealed away from the natural world. In many cities, you can go from building to building and street to street, go block after block without ever being out-of-doors. *What's the weather like?* people say when you come back to the office after lunch. They have no earthly way of knowing in their airtight little cells, but then, neither do you: you've been scurrying from place to place through glass-covered tubes, like a gerbil. It's easy to begin *feeling* like a gerbil in so managed an environment. But under the sky, even if the sky is dumping bucket after bucket of water on your head, you get a sense of really living on the earth. I don't need to be sheltered from the sky: the sky *is* my shelter, appointed in creation so that I and the rest of creation won't burn up or suffocate or get flattened by a meteor. So I slog through the puddles and come inside, soaking wet and looking like hell. So? I wasn't that great-looking before I went out there.

MAY 27

Lord, do not rebuke me in your anger.
PSALM 6:1

✦

Can't stand criticism. Never could. I always think it means people don't like me, and I have more than the usual need to be liked—a more serious personality flaw than you might think. So if you love me, you're not allowed to complain about any of the things I do. Needless to say, nobody's ever been able to refrain for very long, because I do some pretty annoying things.

Why so sensitive, I wonder? I think it is because I have a certain amount of difficulty telling the difference between who I am and what I do. My earliest memory is of making a very large and elaborate painting and being praised to the heavens for it: a nice earliest memory, in comparison with some I've heard, but one that definitely left me wanting more. I gloated over compliments my parents paid me, and did everything I could think of to garner lots and lots of praise. All I wanted to be was the best, and I wanted it with great passion. To my self-absorbed ears, just hearing another person praised sounded like an indictment of myself. Not a very generous spirit, for someone who would grow up to be a priest, but there it is. To this day, few things bring me close to tears faster than not being able to do something someone else can do.

To forestall the sting of other people's criticism, I sometimes write my own bad reviews, getting in there first so that, if I must acknowledge a flaw, I can at least pick up a little bonus bouquet for being humble. I have to admit, though, that the whole calculus of praise and criticism has been pretty unsatisfying just about every time I've engaged in it, regardless of what I may have hoped would happen. The truth is this: whether one is feverishly collecting compliments or carrying out a preemptive strike against criticism by running oneself down, conducting an inventory on yourself all the time is boring.

MAY 28

For you test the mind and heart, O righteous God.

PSALM 7:10

➥

I thought we were going to see Troilus and Cressida *tonight,* my husband says mildly. *Oh, no,* I think, *I've done it again.* This is the third time we haven't gone to see *Troilus and Cressida* because I've scheduled a play rehearsal. I think I hear a slightly resigned tone in his voice, and I feel guilty. So I do what guilty people always do: I try to focus on ways in which this state of affairs is unfair to me, instead of the other way around. *I'm a busy woman. I've got a show to produce. Can't you see I've got to get these rehearsals in? Maybe other people can take time off for an evening in the park, but I've got a busy, important life. People are depending on me to be there.*

Obnoxious. And also a lie, or at least a half-truth—this crazy life of mine is a life I chose. People do depend on me, but it is I who have invited them to do so. Nobody put a gun to my head and made me produce and direct a play while being a pastor and writing a book and watching my grandchildren and doing six or seven other full-time things. One person alone is responsible for my lack of private time, and that person is me.

When the things you overschedule into your life happen to be good and useful things, even educational things—godly things, even—it's easy to feel a fair amount of moral superiority about your frantic state. *How dare you criticize me—look at all these fine things I do! It's not as if I were curled up on the couch watching TV all day!* But whether the things I've stuffed into my life are good or not isn't really the point; the point is that my life just shouldn't be stuffed as full of *anything* as it currently is.

We have a tremendous capacity to fool ourselves about our own motives. Most of them are very mixed, unless we get very clear about what we're doing and why we're doing it. Watch out especially for the good things you do—those are the ones whose leafy branches are most effective at concealing other, less attractive goals. Maybe I can get so busy at my important work that nobody will notice that I'm not paying attention to my spouse. Maybe my self-sacrificing commitment to my volunteer work will make people forget about my poor performance in my profession. If I'm a terrific confidante to my friends, maybe it won't matter so much that I never talk to my children.

But there's just no substitute for seeing things as they really are. Every situation has its truth, and in the end that truth is always revealed. It's a waste of time to hide.

*When I consider the heavens. . . . What is man that you should
be mindful of him?*
PSALM 8:4–5

❧

Since the theory of natural selection became part of the wood-
work in the ongoing conversation carried on by the human race
about itself, the idea of the mindfulness of God has suffered. Once we
begin thinking in terms of a process other than the six-days-on-one-
day-off creation described in Genesis, is there any role left for God in
creation at all? The psalmist wrote down this question a long time
before whatever process it was that culminated in Charles Darwin had
finished its work; this writer assumes an intelligent creator who has
fashioned the universe on the basis of a rational decision to do so. If it
all just sort of *happened*, instead, what does that do to the place of God
in our lives?

This question is precisely why people still burn textbooks in the
Bible Belt. It seems to them that removing the creating initiative from
God also removes God's agency in day-to-day life: if he didn't make
it, he probably doesn't run it, either. But this seems to me much too
simple an approach. We didn't know, before Darwin came along,
how God made the world. And we still don't know. Those poetic
lines in Genesis didn't tell us much of anything about just how all that
we see came about after the first "Let there be light." Genesis just
doesn't say. It's not a book about science.

You miss a lot if you don't allow yourself to "consider the
heavens." Belief in a book is one thing; faith in the God whose history in the human family is recorded over a period of several thousand years is another. In scripture, we have a chance to see how
the people of other times thought God acted in their lives. Were they

right or were they wrong? I imagine they were about as right and about as wrong as we are when we puzzle over the things of God.

The Lord is known by his acts of justice.
PSALM 9:16

➤✦

*I*f we know God by acts of justice, who is it that we know by all the other stuff?

People of faith don't have a problem with God's sovereignty when it comes to the good and the beautiful. Most of us can look at the Rocky Mountains and have the feeling of somehow having been in church. It's when some lunatic parks his explosive-packed car in front of a day care center and saunters away that our confidence sags.

People often ask me if the devil is real. How would I know? I do know that there's such a thing as evil, though, and I respect my own intelligence and that of whoever I'm talking to enough not to try and explain evil away, as you sometimes hear people doing: that this or that terrible occurrence is really *not* terrible because it's all part of God's plan, that it's a little corner of a beautiful picture we're too shortsighted to see, and so forth and so on, until you just want to smack them. Evil isn't good, damn it: it's *evil*. God's self-image is not so delicate a thing that we need to make up lame excuses for what happens in order to make him look good.

Christians believe that Jesus was truly God as well as truly human. (How was this so? We don't know—so don't let anybody tell you we do.) We believe that he died a miserable and humiliating death by one of the many barbaric methods people have devised over the centuries to kill other people. But we do not believe that he did this so he could hop nimbly down from the cross after the three hours were up and say *See? Nothing to it!* He didn't suffer at the hands of evil to show us that there was no such thing. *Au contraire.*

I don't think knowing God means having everything figured out. If I can see the divine possibility in the things that point toward justice and the good, I don't need to pretend that I understand injustice and evil. I don't. I don't imagine I ever will. But I won't let that stop me from longing for the goodness that I do understand.

MAY 31

So he lifted his hand against them.

PSALM 106:26

Can't you just spank me before daddy gets home and get it over with? I was crying when I asked my mother that. My father would be home soon, but there was still time to take care of the spanking I knew I would get now, so he would never have to know that I had played with matches. *No,* my mother said, *you wait until your father gets home.* She was really angry.

My dad didn't spank me much. Maybe hardly at all—I don't remember. My brothers got it more often: our father was from England, where corporal punishment was an integral part of child-rearing. Definitely gender-related, too: I know I escaped most of it by being a girl. On this day, though, the jig was up. I had done something serious enough to merit equal treatment. I had never been so frightened; I don't know that I have since. Absolutely filled with dread.

I remember the spanking. His heart wasn't in it: a few formal whacks on my corduroy-covered bottom. I still have the marble-topped dresser in front of which we stood: me across his knee, he standing with one leg braced against it, the two of us arranged in an uncomfortable Pietà.

Already, on television, scenes such as that one had taken their place in the past. Fathers on television called their penitent children into book-lined studies, and sweet reconciliation followed forthwith. Most kids I knew didn't have fathers with book-lined studies, though, so we got whacked instead.

Today it is considered child abuse to spank a child. Was it? I'm not so sure. It was a convention of parenting in which my folks reluctantly participated—at least, that's the way it looked from where I sat. It was one we are all better off without: there really are better ways to instill moral behavior and good manners than that one.

JUNE 1

"When the foundations are being destroyed, what can the righteous do?"
PSALM 11:3

➤◄

I must do something about these old photographs. They were taken at various stages in my father's life, beginning with one of him in a lacy dress and a headful of golden curls, sitting on his mother's lap while his father and his older brother leaned against her chair, and ending with the pictures I took of him lying in his coffin eighty-five years later.

When he was born, there were no automobiles. There were no air-planes. There was no brain surgery. No one had used chemical warfare, not yet, although that oversight would be remedied in just a few years. Almost everybody in England was Christian.

By the time he died, none of those things was true anymore. Almost nothing was the same. People's understanding of their moral selves, of work, of war and peace, even of what constitutes life itself—everything was new.

People who have given serious lifelong attention to spiritual things have always known that the foundations of human history are prone to distressing shifts. Life in the material world is fundamentally a matter of decay: nothing you count on in this world is permanent. It is all passing away. The spiritually thoughtful have always known this.

But was it always so obvious to everyone else? Change has been a part of life since the beginning, but not always as fast as it has happened in this busy century. Previous generations could assume some similarity between their own experience and that of their children. They knew they had many things to teach them. That is by no means certain now. Our children enter a world about which we know nothing. A different planet from the one we know.

No wonder religious and political conservatism is in style these days. People don't want to live on another planet. They like this one. But it's slipping through their fingers, and they can't stop it. Perhaps, if they are adamant enough about their preference that it not change, they can arrest it. But I doubt it.

Help me, O Lord, for there is no godly one left.
PSALM 12:1

➤⬅

$\mathcal{E}$xcepting, of course, the psalmist himself. A self-congratulatory bunch at times, the psalmists, just as we are now. It's somehow reassuring to see that it has always been so. Bear in mind that most Bible scholars agree that the psalms formed the hymnal of ancient Israel: people *sang* these things together during their worship services. Think of it: song after song about how perfectly dreadful other people are and the terrible things we'd like to befall them.

Almost everyone wants to be considered good. One way people sometimes try to bring this about it is to point out the faults of another. It doesn't work, of course. Whose attention are we trying to divert from our failures when we talk about those of others? Other people's, certainly. God's, absurdly. But probably the one I am most hoping to impress is myself. Looking at my sins is painful. I'd much rather look at yours.

All of the above is not to say that it's never okay to mention the ungodliness of the age, or that another's actions can never legitimately be discussed. Merely that a courageous self-inventory should precede my judgment of anyone else. If I've told the truth about myself—to myself and to others—I don't have to be Hall Monitor to the world.

Right now, there are many voices that sound like this particular psalmist. Sometimes I think ninety-five percent of our political problems would be solved if people would just mind their own business a bit more. You think homosexual relationships are sinful? Then don't enter into one. Look to the nourishing of your own virtue and let others look to theirs. But not every moral issue can be worked out so simply—some things involve injury to others and are thus matters of civil responsibility. Still, some of the biggest headline-gatherers fall into the live-and-let-live category: we each have the right and responsibility to decide for ourselves.

JUNE 3

See how they tremble with fear.
PSALM 14:5

➤◄

Where is my date book?

I had it Thursday night. I missed it at home on Friday, but figured I must have left it in my office by mistake. So yesterday I looked there and didn't see it. A slight foreboding settled upon me like a runny nose. Now it's early Sunday morning. I'm about to go to church, where people will want to ask me about meetings and make appointments to talk. I try to reconstruct the next few days in my mind's eye; I know I'm leaving a lot out. I think of people tapping their feet impatiently, waiting for me to show up for appointments about which I've completely forgotten. I think about the eighty or so telephone numbers I've got in the back of my date book, and about how many of them are written *only* there. I suddenly feel very tired.

That little book, like its predecessors, has been both friend and foe. *I'm going to needlepoint you a cover for it,* says friend Robin whenever she catches a glimpse of my datebook's obscenely inky pages. *It'll read "Just say NO!"* Good idea. Somebody makes a request and I open the book and look in the appropriate square. If there's a blank space, I feel obligated to fill it with this new task. But the fact that I can squeeze something in doesn't necessarily mean that I should. That has been the most difficult lesson of my professional life, and I cannot yet claim to have mastered it.

I know people who schedule regular time for rest and play, who use their date books to protect their time, as well as to make it available to others. That's so sensible it takes my breath away. But it is what they're *for*, after all. When I find my book—or when I give up and start another one, a more likely scenario—I want to turn over a new leaf. I want to take control of my days. I've never done this in my life, but I want to do it now. So help me God—it will require no less.

JUNE 4

Lord, who may dwell in your tabernacle?
PSALM 15:1

❧

Human beings love to exclude other human beings. Who qualifies for membership and who doesn't is a central part of any human institution's self-definition. Like it or not, we understand who we are in large measure by understanding who we aren't.

With that human characteristic in mind, it is not surprising that our vision of eternity is arranged according to the principles of exclusion. Different sets of people in different places have understood heaven's entrance requirements very differently. Sometimes the content of belief has seemed key, and people thought their prospects at the pearly gates were very dependent on their theological opinions. Often, behavior has been more central, with certain actions guaranteed to exclude the soul from eternal bliss. Heaven's prerequisites have always been community-relative: the ethical dilemmas of the day set the standard against which people's applications stood or fell. Dante thought simony a serious enough sin to consign people guilty of it to his *Inferno*; ninety-nine out of a hundred people today don't even know what simony *is*.★

The human love of shutting the door in other people's faces is such a powerful force that it's hard to tell, sometimes, whether an ethical opinion is really ethical or just a veil for this unacknowledged bigotry. What's the real story, if the criteria for inclusion and exclusion have changed so often over the centuries? Is *anything* we esteem timeless? My sense is that we'd best go slowly in assuming that we know what God loves or hates. God is not just a larger version of ourselves and our obsessions. Spiritual realities are much more mysterious.

JUNE 5

My heart therefore, is glad, and my spirit rejoices; my body also shall rest in hope.

PSALM 16:9

➤✦

She lives in a little museum in Malta: a tiny pottery woman, sleeping on her right side, her head resting in the crook of one arm. Her body is very curvy, with round hips and breasts, plump arms. She looks supremely comfortable, for a woman her age: she is believed to be twenty-five thousand years old.

Lying on one's side is supposed to be the best position for someone with back trouble. That also happens to be the way I've always loved to sleep. Among the many things that are different since I broke my

★Simony was the practice of buying or selling spiritual benefits.

back a few years ago, though, is this one. I can't lie on my side for more than a few minutes without experiencing pain. If I don't change position, it just gets worse. If I revert to my favorite sleeping posture in my sleep, as I often do, the pain will awaken me. You would be surprised—or maybe you wouldn't at all—at how blue this change in my life can make me feel at times.

I love the little pottery woman, curled up for a nap on her pottery couch. I wish I could be like her. Ancient people may have believed that a work of art had special powers over its subject—that you could improve your chances of landing a deer in the hunt, say, by painting a picture of one on your wall. People do this even now—sometimes you'll see, speeding along the highway, a recreational vehicle decorated with pictures of ducks and other game. I wonder if the little sleeping woman is that kind of a figure. Illness and pain were experienced for a longer portion of one's time on earth in those days than they are for most of us. To be plump and comfortable, to sleep serenely: there must have been many people for whom that was only a memory. Did someone hope for a lovely night's sleep just from having the pottery woman in the house? I understand perfectly.

But the truth is that painting a buffalo on the wall of your cave doesn't really help you bag one. The main problem with idolatry—which is really what cave paintings and animal decals on the side of your panel truck and my beloved little clay woman represent—is that it focuses attention on something material at the expense of the truly real. I can daydream about the little pottery lady's comfortable nap all I want, but the fact remains that I can't do what she does without hurting myself. She embodies my longing but cannot reward it. And if my focus remains that narrow—my longing for that one thing I no longer have—I may not be alert to the new possibilities that are certain to unfold in my life. A literal representation of my hope can tell me only what I already know. But my hope for the future lies in the things I don't yet know.

O Savior of those who take refuge at your right hand.

PSALM 17:7

❧❧

$\mathcal{M}$adeline is a lefty. Like all left-handed people in this right-handed world, she is pretty ambidextrous, but hand her something and she reaches for it with her left hand. At five years old, then, she is heir to a modest subculture of oppression based on this seemingly neutral trait. Almost all scissors, almost all desks, almost all tools, almost everything: right-handed. There is even an ancient moral preference in our language for right-handedness: the Latin word for "left" is "*sinister.*" When the Bible talks about the right hand of God, it means God's mighty power. Scripture never mentions God's left hand.

Parents and teachers used to try to change a lefty's handedness. Imagine being asked to do something poorly with one hand that you could accomplish easily with the other. I try to teach Madeline to tie her shoes, remembering to reverse the procedure. It's not easy. I think, in fact, that I haven't fully reversed it. No matter. Madeline's good for it. She's accustomed to transposing the righthanded world's operating instructions.

The hand you are built to use is your strong hand, whichever hand it is. The way you are intended to be, the path you are best fitted to walk: that's where you will find your greatest strength. I have known people who made serious changes in their lives, changes that mystified all their friends, because they knew themselves to have been "using the wrong hand" in their lives, trying to live from a place in which their strength did not reside, and they knew this had to change. You have your strength and talent in the way you have them for a reason.

*In the deep he has set a pavilion for the sun; it comes forth like
a bridegroom out of his chamber.*

PSALM 19:5

✦

*T*he rising of the sun is beautiful anywhere. This psalm chooses the
sunrise over water as an image with which to start a description of
the day. First the lightening of the eastern sky, then the greying and
pinking of the horizon, then the streaks of gold on the water and the
gilding of clouds, then the orb of the sun, showing more and more of
itself among the clouds piled high on either side of it like a throne,
until it's so bright you can no longer behold it.

We see the sunrise in colors because of what it is in the air: tiny
droplets of water vapor, each one a prism through which the sunlight
is refracted. We're not really seeing the colors of the light directly—
we're seeing them through the experience of these little drops. If there
were no little drops of water, we would see no color. They testify to
its existence in a way our eyes are equipped to see.

So many people have trouble with the existence of God, and long
for some direct showing of the divine presence. Such things are rare.
Much more common, and available to everyone every day, is the tes-
timony of things we do see, things through which the divine presence
shines. You can't look directly at the sun. Its light is mediated to your
eyes by drops of water. The presence of God is like that. We most
often know it indirectly.

Unsatisfying? I remember often thinking that it was unbearably so:
*If God's so smart and powerful and wants me to know something, why doesn't
he just come right out and tell me?* But now I don't feel that way. Now it
seems to me that there is no end to the things in my life that testify to
God's presence in it. What caused the change? I'm not sure. It cer-

tainly hasn't been a life in which every lottery was won and every door opened. It's been happier than many, sadder than some—a normal life. More sinful than it should have been, but less than it might have been. I *have* been looking for signs of God in it for many years. I have been learning to pray for many years. I've been reading about other people's experience of God for many years. You might say that I have been hoping and expecting to find God—and, since this is my life and not a science experiment, I have been far from neutral. So I see increasing signs of that for which I hope. I have prepared myself to see them.

JUNE 8

They collapse and fall down.
PSALM 20:8

➤➤

*T*hat is exactly what I'm planning to do a week from today. The play I've had in rehearsal for six weeks will have opened, and there will be little or nothing I can do to make it better than it is; at that point it's all up to the actors.

Directing a play is intense. Producing and directing one is more so. Besides the eighty or ninety hours of rehearsal, there are the decisions about set and costume, light and sound. The ticket and publicity deadlines, budget worries—none of these are someone else's problem. Every night for the past two weeks I've dragged myself through the door at around midnight. I'm so keyed up by all I have to do that I'm up at five the next morning.

At several points in this play, one character or another must fall down. One character takes a swing at another and misses, falling against a pillar. Two women fall to the floor and weep. The clown of the piece falls down all the time, tripping over a rock or a ladder or just his own feet. But it's not easy to fall down on purpose. Actors have to learn how to do it. We're built and programmed to keep our balance. Learning to contradict the body's natural equilibrium is hard.

I watch them fall, over and over again. At first, the falls are unsatisfactory—clearly staged. We go over them many times. As the actor's craft asserts itself, the unnaturalness disappears. The characters become real. Events actually happen. And the falls are real. The actors no longer pretend to collapse: they actually do.

I know myself. When this is over, I will not be able just to fall down. Too much adrenaline for too long. Like these gifted players, I'll have to learn how to collapse, to convince my body that it's safe to sink to the floor. It goes against the grain. But I can do it.

JUNE 9

The king rejoices in your strength, O Lord. . . . You have given him his heart's desire.
PSALM 21:1–2

✥

Some of the psalms are about the king of Israel. When these old songs were new, the king of Israel was a figure whose fortunes were closely watched: it was assumed that God's will for the nation was heavily dependent on his behavior, and that the country's favor in God's eyes matched that of the king.

Theocracies like ancient Israel are rarer these days, although they still exist. The expectation that the behavior of political leaders relates to God's will for nations, however, continues. Even secular societies like ours, complex aggregates of many converging social structures and political interests, whose processes are much larger than any one person's power, invest the personal virtue of the leader—or its deficiency—with great significance. We often call upon him to represent us in a ceremonial way, by laying a memorial wreath, say, or visiting the scene of a disaster, or eulogizing an important person who has died. The public is annoyed when a leader's personal morality is too openly other than it should be. Let him fall too far south of the good in the public eye, and he's gone.

What constitutes "the good" in public life changes. Different eras tolerate different things. Robert Packwood would not have had to resign from the Senate for his sexual peccadilloes had they come to light in the 1950s—they wouldn't *have come* to light in the 1950s. I don't mean to suggest that we are more righteous now than we were then. Hardly. Just less in awe of famous people's auras, I think, and considerably more interested in watching important people crash and burn.

There is a limit to the amount of public good an amoral person can accomplish. Eventually, the public and private must meet in the same person. We are right to hope for goodness in our leaders—as much goodness (and no more) as we are willing to demand of ourselves.

The poor shall eat and be satisfied.

PSALM 22:25

➤‹

*E*ntering Minka's living room, where our children had been playing, we beheld Carrie's child-size table, set with a cloth and dishes, ready for tea. No little girls in sight—they'd gone off to the bedroom or somewhere. Just the little banquet table, all set and ready. *The heavenly banquet,* Minka said when she saw the little table, and we laughed. But that was exactly what it was: a feast, set forth in the certainty that a wonderful time is in store for all. Carrie and Anna didn't know each other well. They were not neighbors who played together every day. But they knew all they needed to know: *This is another little girl like me. We will immediately be friends. We will have a special meal of invisible special food. It will be lovely.* And it was.

When people have imagined heaven, it has always included a feast. Plenty of food for everyone, eaten with pleasure in company with others. The communal nature of the heavenly banquet is constant; nobody envisions people stockpiling food in huge heavenly storehouses or stuffing themselves in private. It is a party, made by love.

Madeline will turn six on November 1st. She has been planning her birthday party for at least two months now, and it is months away. Should it be at the roller rink or at home? What games should they play? She arrives one morning clutching a paper crown, covered with round crayon-dot jewels and her name in crayon across the front. *It's for my birthday,* she explains. *Can you save it for me?* I look at the calendar. Still 120 days to go. What trust!

You know what happens to that feeling about birthdays as the years pass. And more than a few people learn to dread parties as well. Adults are so aware of the pain of time passing that we forget how to celebrate it.

JUNE 11

You spread a table before me in the presence of those who trouble me.
PSALM 23:5

✣

No fantasy beats the one in which you're publicly honored in front of people who have been rude to you: you're Cinderella, sweeping out of the house with your shiny new prince, leaving your mean stepsisters, open-mouthed, behind. Delicious.

Usually, though, the folks who have held you in contempt keep right on doing so. That wonderful *So there!* moment usually doesn't happen. Sometimes the fantasy includes an even-more-delicious bawling out of the one who has hurt your feelings: you perform the tongue-lashing you will administer over and over in your head, and your acting is so good your heart pounds.

Is it or is it not a good idea to administer that tongue-lashing in real life? In your fantasy, its recipient stands there like a sheep brought to slaughter; in real life, though, he's likely to get in a zinger or two of his own. If your relationship is an old and strong one, perhaps the blowup will clear the air. If it's not, though, it will doubtless end right then and there. In your fantasy, you stay on your script. Your rebukes shoot brilliantly through the air straight into the heart of their stricken object, who has no choice but to fold immediately. In real life, you're liable to mix things up a bit, to bring in things "while you're at it" that have nothing to do with the offense, to become so carried away with your anger that you're not expressing yourself nearly as well as you did in rehearsal.

Call me a coward—and there's some evidence for that—but I don't think it's ever a good idea to burn your bridges in anger, however much you may long to do it. You don't know what the future holds. You don't know what your relationship with someone who has treated you with disrespect might become. And you don't always know what your own part in this difficulty has been—there are two sides to everything. You may or may not be the wounded innocent you feel like right now. So stay tuned.

But what do you do with your feelings of anger and hurt? I was raised by a woman who believed that these feelings should never be giving a hearing. *You catch more flies with honey than with vinegar,* my mom used to say, and I guess that's true if you're catching flies. But my mom died young of heart failure; I've sometimes wondered if the stress of all that pleasantness might not have taken its toll. Anger frightened her. But that didn't mean she didn't have any. Bottling it up may not have been a healthy thing.

So who do you yell at? You can always yell at God—he's probably gotten very used to it by now, and he can't be hurt by it. We are known by God, inside and out. We are not surprising to the one who knows us so well, so there is no point in putting on an act. And, while you're yelling—as loudly as you can, with every bit of fury you feel— be alert. You may get a gift. You may get a feeling of release. You may see your hurt in a way that did not occur to you until now. God may use your noisy call to speak a word you need to hear.

Lift up your heads, O gates . . . and the King of glory shall come in.
PSALM 24:7

➻

We're going to knock down the kitchen wall facing the garden and go out about eleven feet. There will be a new porch, a new pantry, a new and larger dining area in the kitchen, and a new bathroom upstairs. There will be a new island in the kitchen, so my husband and I won't have to rhumba around each other over by the sink when we're trying to cook together. Pretty exciting.

I thought we'd leave the cabinets as they are, I told the architect when he asked if we'd like new ones. I painted the doors and drawer fronts myself, six years ago: a deep wine red. I left the dumb-looking fifties frames around them in their natural pine color and added white ceramic knobs. I think it looks pretty good. *Well, they may look a little dated with the new island,* he said. *What about the countertops? Oh, they're fine,* my husband began—but I cut in, *if you like little green snowflakes. We need new ones.* I look at the cabinets again. Now they don't look the same.

I can see that this remodeling project could grow into a lot more than we anticipated. New things make the old things look tired. We want the house to be beautiful and fun to life in, and we want it to welcome guests in a less haphazard way than it now does. In the hundred years of its life, it has had several experiences like the one we're about to inflict on it: the current kitchen, for instance, seems to have been the porch once upon a time, and my study may have had a cupola on top. I wish it still did.

Imagine a building with feelings. Imagine my house, embarrassed about its fifties countertops, naked without its cupola. Mad at us because we won't spring for new kitchen cabinets, like the ones the kitchen next door got. Poor thing. Imagine if houses were like *we* are—excited about expected visitors, deliciously conscious of looking *really fabulous* one day, hoping nobody drops in the next. Willing to undergo surgery—the loss of an entire wall, the graft of another—in order to provide a suitable welcome for our guests.

I glance in the mirror when the doorbell rings, not wanting to look *too* frightening for whoever is coming to see me. Common courtesy. What if the caller were God? God would see through my hastily-applied lipstick, would see through my concealer to the dark places under my eyes and the darker ones in my heart. I would be just as I am. The house would be as it is: tired kitchen cabinets clashing with little-green-snowflake countertops, saying whatever it says about its occupants.

JUNE 13

He guides the humble in doing right and teaches his way to the lowly.
PSALM 25:8

✦✦

$\mathcal{F}$or the eighteenth time, I tell the young actor to slow down. He grimaces and says he will. But when we continue the scene, he races through his monologue like a bat out of hell. Hardly a word can be understood. The nearness of opening night combines with my frustration to make me very angry, and I scold him—much more mildly than I'd like to, but enough to make me ashamed of myself afterward.

Why did I lose my temper with him? I'm surrounded by people who make mistakes and I make plenty of them myself. Why did his send me around the bend? I suspect it's because he has a somewhat inflated view of his own acting ability. His large ego—not a rarity in the acting profession—makes him unteachable, and it gets in the way of his ability to be all he could be. You can't learn if you don't think there's anything you don't know.

Everyone wants to be esteemed, competent, and wise. But nobody knows everything. If I am more concerned with defending my competent image and demonstrating my correctness than with finding out the truth, the truth is going to drift out of my reach. I may even become its enemy. It is the humble, in this psalm, who are guided by God, not the people who know everything.

JUNE 14

If the Lord had not been on our side, when enemies rose up against us, then would they have swallowed us up alive.

PSALM 124:2–3

➤✦

The island of Malta is just south of the Sicilian coast, a little drop of land in the blue Mediterranean Sea. Its convenient location—close enough to Greece, Italy, and Turkey to serve as an excellent staging area for invasions of Europe and the Near East—and its fine harbors have insured that tiny Malta would be coveted by larger countries with conquest on their minds. Sure enough, just about everybody has ruled Malta at one time or another: the Greeks, the Romans, the Ottoman Turks, the various Europeans who made up the crusades, the multinational Knights of St. John, Napoléon Bonaparte, and, most recently, the British Empire, which granted Malta its first-ever independence only in 1964. As a British colony during the Second World War, Malta was bombed by the Italians and the Germans 965 times, suffering massive destruction, the loss of many lives, and terrible fear. But the Maltese stood firm under the relentless attack, continuing to provide an invaluable strategic location to the Allied effort. After the war, the king of England awarded the Distinguished Service Cross to all Maltese people.

Malta is a country of churches—365 of them, the natives say proudly, one for every day of the year. The churches are dedicated to saints, and the neighborhood within which a church stands understands itself to be under the protection of the saint for whom the church is named—the usual understanding in a European town. In Malta, though, besides the usual masses and processions carrying statues, the people celebrate their respective saints' days with fireworks. Since there are so many saints to be honored, it's a rare day that is not punctuated from morning to evening with explosions somewhere or other—muffled if they are shooting them off in a neighboring town or loud enough to shake the earth beneath your feet if it's happening in your neighborhood.

If I'd been bombed a thousand times, I'm not sure I would enjoy all this as much as the Maltese clearly do—I know veterans of wars who have all they can do not to dive under the nearest desk when they hear an automobile backfire. But the people of Malta never pass up a chance for a *festa*, and they always have fireworks.

From my window, the curtains drawn back as I lie in bed waiting for sleep to overtake me, I watch the fireworks in honor of St. Sebastian explode over the medieval walls of Valletta. The window is closed, to keep in the air-conditioning; even so, the bed shakes with each explosion. With a gentle *whoosh*, a rocket climbs erratically into the night sky, a small bright light, then disappears. I hold my breath for the explosion, and in a few seconds it comes. But it does not rain down death on Malta tonight; instead, it blossoms harmlessly into a lovely coral flower, filling the midnight and lighting the ground below. Perhaps it is not odd at all that they love fireworks here, I think as another giant starburst fills the window. A memory, perhaps, for some of the people, of other nights, many years ago, when each thunder might have meant death. And—at least for those who survived—did not.

JUNE 15

Give judgment for me, O Lord, for I have lived with integrity.
PSALM 26:1

❧

*I*n a number of psalms, the writer imagines heaven as a court of law, with God as the judge. Trial by jury was a long way off in those days: when a disagreement arose, or a person was accused of a crime, he presented his case directly to the judge—sometimes the king—who might be advised by counselors but was alone responsible for rendering a verdict. *Probably God is like the king,* the psalmist told himself, *rendering decisions and dispensing justice. I'll take my problem to court.*

What a shame, my mother-in-law said to my husband when he told her I had been hit by a car, *she never hurt anybody in the whole wide world.* I guess she didn't know me all that well; I can think of a few people I *had* hurt in the course of the forty-two years leading up to the accident. Enough to merit five broken bones? I'm probably not the best judge.

Give judgment for me. Make the world make sense. Make it so that my goodness is rewarded, because that is sure not what's happening. This is the psalmist's cry to God: make the world something other than it is. It's our cry today, too. We long for sense, and so much of what happens in life makes none at all.

In real courts, the verdict is not rendered by a judge acting alone. The case is argued by lawyers, and it is often decided by a jury. This is because things aren't readily reducible to simple, black-and-white solutions, because things so often don't make sense, or make several different kinds of sense, all at the same time. Just so with all of life: there is never just one reason for anything that happens.

JUNE 16

One thing have I asked of the Lord; one thing I seek; that I may dwell in the house of the Lord all the days of my life.
PSALM 27:5

➤◄

Churches have a special smell. A blend of many smells, actually: the smell of old hymnals. Forgotten vases of flowers. Remembered incense, in some churches. The smell of furniture polish and candle wax. The smell of vestments worn for decades. Each church has its special smell, but they all somehow smell alike. I walk into one in Florida or Minnesota or the British Virgin Islands and take a deep breath: with my eyes closed, I would know I was in a church.

I love that smell. It connects me with the early years of my ministry. It connects me with the people in the congregations I have served who have died. I remember their lives and some of their deaths. It connects me with my own childhood, with my father who did the same work I do, with my mother: the smooth, clean altar linens, the gleam of silver, the black and white organ keys.

There is one more smell in city churches, one I don't remember from my childhood. It is the smell of unwashed bodies. The poor wait outside the churches for the doors to open in the morning; they know which ones will allow them refuge to sit and which ones will tell them to move along. Some of them sit all day. Many sleep, the blood pooling dangerously in their feet because they can't lie down. That is the reason so many homeless people have swollen feet. The swollen feet of the people who have no beds—feet covered with running sores that refuse to heal—create another smell I don't remember from the church of my childhood: the smell of rotting flesh.

The order and the cleanliness of the house of God. And in the midst of it, the stench of despair. The life of the soul in the world is not just beauty.

JUNE 17

Therefore my heart dances for joy, and in my song will I praise him.
PSALM 28:9

I saw you drive by here a week or two ago, the man at the gas station tells me as he cleans my windshield. *You were singing.* How embarrassing. I feel very private in my car, but of course I am not. Cars have windows. People can see me. They probably can hear me, too.

I come upon Rosie and Madeline dancing in the living room. The dance is an exaggerated bottom-wiggling thing, and they accompany it with their own deafening voices. Nonsense syllables: *KOOCHIE MOOCHIE, YEAH YEAH!* over and over. Then they fall down on the floor, laughing insanely. *Show me your dance,* I ask, and they are suddenly quiet. They giggle and blush and shake their heads. I don't insist; I see that the dance was intended just for themselves. It was not a performance meant to be seen by others.

Caught in the act of singing or dancing. Or both. All by oneself. Unproductive activities—I was embarrassed that the gas station man had seen me singing all alone in my car. How undignified can you get? But there have been times when I have sung myself from despair into acceptance. I have known the needed release of tears in the singing of a hymn. I have danced, all by myself, when my back hurt, and I have felt better. Perhaps something opens up in us when we sing or dance—an extra channel through which the soul can hear the creator's song.

JUNE 18

The voice of the Lord makes the oak trees writhe and strips the forests bare.
PSALM 29:8

✦

This is really dangerous, I shout to my husband as we walk to the car in the blinding rain. I am terrified. Thunder cracks the night in two as we make our way along the avenue. It is impossible to avoid being under a tree, as everybody knows you're supposed to during an electrical storm: the avenue is lined on both sides with trees, and their branches meet over the middle of it. A flash of lightning reveals other scurrying people, freezing them in midstride for an instant in an eerie black-and-white snapshot.

What lightning can do is weird. It can strip the leaves off one side of a tree and leave the other side unruffled. It can kill one person and do nothing at all to the one sitting next to her. It can make the hair on your head stand straight up. It can erase short-term memory, or it can pick and choose which memories to take—a three-month period in 1968 might be missing, never to be recalled again, for instance, after a lightning strike in 1997. It can drill a perfect smooth hole in a great tree trunk in a half second—a hole that looks like a master woodcarver worked on it for a month.

So lightning doesn't just look *strong*, which it certainly is. It looks *deliberate*, which it is not. The things it does look like *choices*. No wonder people like the psalmist thought of it as an efficient and very deadly weapon in the hand of God. We don't think of lightning as a weapon today. But we remain rightly in awe of it as one of the more dramatic showings of the mightiness of creation. Does God hurl it from the sky? In a manner of speaking. Do we really know how or why? Nope. But we know it is great, far greater than we are. Its power helps us to know our smallness. There are many things in the universe we do not control.

JUNE 19

Weeping may spend the night, but joy comes in the morning.

PSALM 30:6

➤◄

I am tired. My back hurts. Spitefully, it has also decided to send fiery little darts down the back of one leg, too, a painful unalleviated by lying down flat. Not to be outdone, the phlebitis in the other leg is causing it to throb in a scary way.

I am extravagantly sorry for myself because of this state of affairs. The fact that there are many people going to bed in much worse shape than I am matters not a bit to me on this evening. I am utterly self-absorbed. I rummage in Richard's drawer for a handkerchief and take it to bed. I cry myself to sleep.

In the morning, the pain is better. No throbbing. Fewer darts. Great mood—ready for anything. Ready to do it to myself all over again. Blessedly amnesiac about my tears of the night before—I do *remember* that I cried, but I don't feel sad now, so who cares?

In the darkness, unobserved: sometimes it feels good to feel bad. No need to explain my tears to a concerned husband or anxious daughters. People who love you always want to stop your tears. But there are times when just letting them come helps immeasurably. Keeping a stiff upper lip takes energy. Sometimes it's a good idea to let yourself go a bit. The sorrow coursing through my body is a cleansing river, sweeping all my tension along in its current. I am limp and tired when my crying stops. I sleep an exhausted sleep, and I awaken a clean slate.

Tears are a gift. They come for a reason. Sometimes they are a warning of trouble that needs special attention and healing—if you're crying every day, think about talking to someone about it. But don't try to stifle the occasional weepy bedtime. It may itself be healing for your spirit.

JUNE 20

Into your hands I commend my spirit.

PSALM 31:5

✣

I have known many people who did not have a religious life because, they said, it "did no good"—meaning, I suppose, that things still went wrong in their lives. That's a pretty narrow definition of what it means for a belief to "do some good," if you ask me: I cling to belief, and it's not because I think doing so will be my talisman against misfortune and nothing bad will ever happen to me. Every believer who ever lived has eventually died, and most of them, I think, would maintain that their faith did them much good.

These words from Psalm 31 may have a familiar ring to you, especially if you grew up Protestant in an American small town. The line is among the "Seven Last Words from the Cross," through which many an entire town sat—and still does, in many places—for three hours every Good Friday, listening to the local ministers outpreach one another on Jesus' final recorded utterances. He was quoting from a psalm—something he did a lot. *My God, my God—why have you forsaken me?* is another one you remember—it's from Psalm 22.

This one, like many psalms, is a song of hope, which is why Jesus chose it. About to die, he entrusted his spirit to God. Not to stave off death, but in order to embrace its inevitability in peace. Your death and your life and everything on the way between the two—you live it more serenely if you don't try to go it all alone. A power greater than your own supports you.

JUNE 21

My moisture was dried up as in the heat of summer.
PSALM 32:4

❧

If your young skin acts dry . . . That's what it says on the little green bottle of moisturizer Anna hands me. *If your young skin acts dry:* that is really very kindly put. It assumes that our skin is, by definition, young. That some of our complexions are just having momentary lapses and "acting" in a manner unlike their dewy norm. That the bottle's contents will help my skin snap out of it and come back to its young self.

I'm afraid, though, that it's not really an *act* in my case. I have a face like one of those dried-apple dolls if I'm not after it constantly with hydrators or liposomes or whatever. The heat of summer is bad; the forced-air heat of winter is worse. Without the aid of all my potions, I would look like a puppet all winter.

"Drenching Solution,"™ they call this stuff. The very name makes me feel better. Drenched. Soft young skin. Moisture to spare. *In the winter you might want to use this,* Anna says, handing me another little bottle. "Steady Drencher,"™ this one's called. There's that abundant D-word again, with its promise to lavish soft moisture on my thirsty hide, its generous assumption that my dryness isn't really *me,* that it's an "act".

I know it's not true. Or is it? The assumption that well-being is one's normal state is a good attitude to carry through life. It is even a biblical one: we are created good and lovely, in the image of the god who fashioned all lovely things. We are naturally beautiful.

I open the Drenching Solution and pat some on. *Just a little bit,* Anna tells me, *it goes a long way.* It feels and smells wonderful. My skin looks pretty. I follow with some Steady Drencher. Another lovely smell and beautiful feel. *Here,* Anna says, and hands me a bottle of shampoo. *Try this.*

When your hair acts bored, it says on the bottle.

JUNE 22

For the word of the Lord is right, and all his works are sure.
PSALM 33:4

➤✦

$\mathcal{M}$y husband likes to make pies. He only makes one kind: rhubarb. *Rhubarb's the only kind you need,* he says when someone asks him about branching out a little.

Richard accomplishes two purposes with his pie-making: besides being good to eat, the pies carry political messages. He makes a lattice top, and then he spells out a message in strips of dough on top of the lattice. Recent pie headlines have included:

1. LABOR AND LOVE	The one that appeared this past Labor Day.
2. UNITE OR	Do you give up? I thought so. It was for the Fourth of July—an obscure pictorial reference to Benjamin Franklin's remark after signing the Declaration of Independence: *Gentlemen, we must all hang together, or assuredly we shall all hang separately.*
3. ERIN GO BRAGH	He made this one for the widowed Irish mother of a friend. She is still talking about what a nice young man he is. Richard is sixty-eight years old.

What an interesting character my husband is. Sometimes he comes to get me at the train station and there on the seat beside him is one of the cats. *She wanted to go for a ride,* he explains. I find that hard to believe. Once, when he was out of town, I went to change their water dish and saw that he'd taped a picture of a tiger up over the bowl at cat eye-level: a feline pin-up.

Most of his humor is like that: verbal, but silently so. Comically putting things where they don't belong. Anthropomorphizing animals and inanimate objects. So a pie spouts political slogans. A house cat admires a tiger as a teenager does a movie star, and goes out for a spin in the family car. Reinventing the world, absurdly out of kilter. A person must really know what's going on to be this off-the-wall.

Happy is the nation whose God is the Lord!

PSALM 33:12

➤✦

*W*e're still a Christian country, the man said with an injured air. We were in England, not here. We were talking about religious pluralism. He wasn't enjoying the discussion.

I suppose he is right about his own country—technically, at least. The Queen is still the titular head of the Church of England. But there are a lot of people from other places with other faiths living there these days—not as many as in the United States, but more all the time. Making allowances for the experience of others seemed to this man to be somehow at his expense. It often seems that way to members of a dominant class that feels itself to be losing dominance—as if they will be in exile if they are not in charge.

Right now, there is a sense among some people of faith that it is time to make America a Christian nation, with some very explicit criteria for just what that Christian America will look like. Homogenized, I'm afraid, like milk that comes in a paper carton. Do you remember the way milk used to come—those glass bottles with the bell-shaped thing at the neck, where the cream collected? They stopped making those; it was easier on the consumer not to have to separate the cream.

Well, yeah, life *is* easier when everybody is the same. It *is* easier not to have to allow for people's differences. But it's not better. The homogenization of milk conceals what milk really is; it makes it impossible to see the cream in it. Milk left to its own devices shows itself honestly.

Lately, I've seen a few of those old-time milk bottles in stores. Some dairy has decided to bottle its product that way again. Imagine.

Look upon him and be radiant, and let not your faces be ashamed.

PSALM 34:5

➤←

*I*n ancient times, people thought that a human being would die from looking directly upon God—the contrast between God's goodness and our sinfulness would surely kill us. So this invitation, to look upon God and be radiant, is not so much about seeing God in a physical way as it is about the healing of human shame.

There may be a deed in your past you regret. You may have done a great deal of atoning for it, and you may have gone on to build a good life that visibly upholds values the world rightfully respects and admires. But still—there is this thing in your past. *Except for this one thing,* your soul keeps saying, piteously, over and over again, lugging the thing around with her everywhere she goes. *I am good, except for this one thing.*

The soul is dumb that way. She doesn't have to tote your sins around, day in and day out, but she does. She doesn't have to keep bringing them up whenever you think you're doing pretty well. She can confess them, and then she won't have to carry them anymore. But for some reason she is afraid to do that, so she holds on to them, sometimes for decades.

When you finally get around to confessing your soul's burden to someone else in the presence of God—who, of course, already knows about it—it is amazing how easy and freeing a thing it is. Finally you can put it down. Finally your soul has her hands free. And the person whom you chose to hear your confession, whom you were afraid would have no respect for you after hearing what you had to say—you were wrong about that. The confessor is never more aware of her own moral failures than when experiencing the courage of another person getting honest about his. All of us live in glass houses.

Strangers whom I did not know tore me to pieces and would not stop.
PSALM 35:15

✦✦

Part of the chaplaincy training program my friend has begun consists of visiting patients in the hospitals every day. It can be daunting: the patients are ill and frightened, often angry. Some of them are mentally ill. Many of them are dying. That's not the hard part of the program, though.

The hard part is what happens every afternoon, when the small group of student chaplains gathers to critique one another's working style. Nothing is off-limits in these discussions—the way one speaks, sits, stands, avoids, embraces. There is really no way to describe the effect of hearing person after person pinpoint the same negative thing in your style of interacting with others until you've been through it. This training is required of all Episcopal priests, and of many other denominations as well. We get very good in a very short time at hearing people criticize us.

Linda was on the hot seat last week. She called me—long distance—after it was over. *I'm not sure I can take this,* she said, her voice tight. *Was it like bearbaiting, with you as the bear?* I asked. I remember it well.

Exactly. I wanted to tell them Okay, I heard you. Can we go on? I don't know how often I needed to hear these things, but I think I've got it by now.

How painful, to hear certain truths about ourselves. And how rare. Mostly, people don't tell you about the things that are wrong with you—they tell others, behind your back. But there is a gift in this painful experience: if five or six people see something, it might really be there. Maybe I need to ask myself if it's true. Maybe I could be better in my calling if I worked on changing it. If some habit or unconscious attitude is having a negative effect on others, it's probably not doing me any good either.

For with you is the well of life, and in your light we see light.

PSALM 36:9

✢

The medical test that I thought would take a half hour turns out to be a five-hour job—they have to do before-and-after shots, it seems. I've now read the two *Modern Maturity* magazines and the 1979 *National Geographic* in the waiting room. I've made all the phone calls I can think of and I've done some office business over the phone. There are still three hours to go.

If only I'd brought some work. Then I remember that the reverse sides of the agreements I signed so that I can't sue the hospital if they accidentally kill me are blank. So I can write a couple of essays while I'm waiting. In fact, I can write essays about waiting.

What a gold mine of unused time we have in train stations, doctors' offices, supermarket checkout lines. I'm not sure I want to know how much it all amounts to—it's got to be a couple of years, at least, out of the average lifetime. I know women who carry knitting or needlepoint around with them to work on when they're in waiting situations. They also do it at meetings, some of them—it makes the men think they're not paying close attention, which can be a good thing for people to think sometimes. Or, if you've left the 12′ × 24′ hooked rug you're working on at home, or the only thing in the waiting room is *A Brief History of Time*, here's a thought:

You could pray. This is the perfect time for it. You won't be tempted away by some niggling little job you haven't done. Nobody is going to call you on the phone—turn off the ringer on that annoying little cellular thing in your purse, why don't you? Look upon this delay in your life as a pure gift from God, plunked right down in your lap.

It's not necessary to fold your hands or close your eyes. That could empty out the room in a hurry, and will open you to the sin of pride, since people will think you're holy. Just sit in your chair and look at the ground, or at a point on the wall, or at a picture. Not at the television. Listen to your own breathing for a while—it will help you not listen to the noise around you. Think of the breath, and of your life sustained by it since you first drew one. If you are at the doctor's office, this would be a good time to consider the miraculousness of this lifelong sequence of breaths. If you're waiting for a bus or train, pray your tiredness. Your busyness. Pray your worry about being late—what *else* are you going to do about it?

After a time, your mind will empty a bit, of its own accord. Don't worry about it or try to empty it yourself. And then there will be quiet in your soul, which God will fill with whatever you need at the moment.

Works anywhere.

JUNE 27

The little that the righteous has is better than great riches of the wicked.
PSALM 37:17

➤◄

*I*t's not right, though, Paul says to the lady walking next to him down the back stairs of Sagamore Hill, home of President Theodore Roosevelt. She looks startled. *It's just too much. Too much for one person to have.*

The house is a Victorian sprawl of stone and dark wood. Animal heads are everywhere inside, mostly animals shot by TR himself, although some of them—the Kodiak bear snarling perpetually before a fireplace, for instance—were gifts. There are one or two rhinoceros-foot inkwells, and an elephant's-foot wastebasket. There is a silver cup from the emperor of China, a carved wood and silk screen from the emperor of Japan. There are thirteen bedrooms. As the homes of the rich and famous of the Gilded Age go, though, it is fairly modest.

Paul lives in a one-room apartment in the Bronx. He was a seafarer for thirty years. His union pension and his social security don't go very far: his clothes are shiny with age, and display his competent darns and mends on the buttonholes, on the underarm seams. He cooks his own meals in his tiny kitchen. He comes to the seamen's dinners and puts three dollars in the plate: Paul's night out.

His mood was different when I took the old guys to Franklin Roosevelt's home. FDR's place in Hyde Park is elegant, too, in much the same way as his granduncle's—minus the animal heads. Eleanor and Franklin didn't get to keep their state gifts, as TR did, so there aren't as many silver punch bowls around, but the Roosevelt home in Hyde Park is one nice place. Paul wasn't as hard on FDR as he had been on his uncle. He and his friends were busy remembering their president, their war. *I never knew he was so tall,* Paul said softly, looking at the president's pinstripe suit and wool cape, *but then, you never saw him standing up.*

Truly, I am on the verge of falling, and my pain is always with me.
PSALM 38:17

I look at the ground when I walk. That was not the case before my accident, but these days I am conscious of a fear of falling, something I never used to think about at all. My balance and reflexes are not what they were. If I fall, I will not catch myself as adeptly as I would have a while back. Pain is always in the background and frequently in the foreground of my mind. I think of falling, of bones hitting bones, of nerves flattened against joints, of my crooked spine trying to absorb a new shock, and I feel a momentary panic. I must avoid falling at all costs.

I set out on a walk with a group; soon, I am at the end of the party. I am slow. I stand aside to let another precede me up the stairs. *You go ahead; I take forever.* I listen to the sound of somebody running down the stairs. It sounds scary.

Such fearfulness robs me of more than speed. Everybody falls now and then. Try as I may, I will not avoid it, even if I creep along for the rest of my life at my current snail's pace. Life cannot be lived well if the awareness that something bad might happen is so primary a factor in one's decisions. Never to run, because I might fall. Never to marry, because it might not work out. Not to take that new job because I might not do it well. The sweetest of life's fruits come to all of us through the acceptance of some risk.

So I held my tongue and said nothing.
PSALM 39:3

➤❤

My friend has a problem at work. She's been asked by her boss to participate in something unethical. She has written a memo stating that she can't do it and why. On Thursday he called her in and told her she was fired. Then he called her at home over the weekend. Could they meet on Monday? She is nervous. Should she maybe talk to a lawyer before this meeting? *I don't know what he wants,* she says. *I think he's afraid I'll go to the media. And I just might do that.*

She loves her job. It's work that has bettered the lives of thousands of people, and she's been proud of it. She wonders if her boss is going to offer her money to keep the incident quiet. That would be so crazy. *If it were money I wanted, I wouldn't have said anything in the first place.*

On Monday morning she goes in. He says hello, as if nothing had happened. Somebody asks her a question about another project. She takes a routine call at her desk. Is it still her desk? *I guess he wants to pretend none of this ever happened.* Not a word is said about the project in which she refused to participate. *I guess he'll get someone else to do that,* she says. *I guess I'm not fired after all.*

This strange victory leaves a bitter taste in her mouth. The misdeed will still be done. It just won't have her fingerprints all over it. Will that be good enough? *I don't think I can stay now,* she says with tears in her eyes. *I don't think I can go on as if nothing happened. Guess it's time to look for something else.*

This is her life. Her financial life, her professional life. Also her moral life. Many of us say we have the courage of our convictions. When the time comes to act on that courage, will we be able to pay what it costs?

Princely state has been yours from the day of your birth.
PSALM 110:3

>⟨<

When we turn into the driveway, there is grandson Conor, sitting in a dishpan in a few inches of water, with his father sitting on the ground beside him. A perfect pool for all six months of him on this hot June day. He catches sight of my husband and me and breaks into his big jack-o'-lantern smile, as if our coming were the most wonderful thing that had ever happened to him. Gratifying, even though we know that he blesses everyone who comes within his field of vision with such a smile.

Right on schedule for his age, this expansive love of company. It won't last, though—I forget when babies begin to be suspicious of people they don't know well, but it's coming right up. Eight months, maybe. That's how old he'll be when next we see him. Oh, dear—I suppose he'll regard us sternly and then bury his face in the shoulder of whichever parent is holding him. Only gradually will he allow us into his heart, and he will make his overwhelming preference for his own two favorite people very clear to us.

A year is forever in the development of a child. We're missing the little milestones that make up daily life with a baby. Two of our grandchildren live in our town. We see them every day. But Conor lives halfway across a continent; we think we're extremely lucky to be seeing him four times this year. And we are—I know grandparents who don't see their grandchildren even once a year, and I know a couple who have never laid eyes on theirs.

I wish I could explain how amazing a thing a grandchild is, but I can't—you know about it if you have one. I remember very well how wondrous a thing my grandmother was to me, how magical she seemed to make the most humdrum things, what a haven of peace and delight she was. To be that for a child is worth just about anything it costs, however often it is given you.

JULY 1

He put a new song in my mouth.
PSALM 40:3

>+<

$\mathcal{M}$r. Smith stops by with another photograph of his wife for me to see: she is on a beach with their granddaughter. He took the picture. I tell him how lovely she is in it, and he nods. He brings something in to show me every week or two: pictures of her, a copy of a tribute her club prepared in her memory, the order of service for her funeral. We talk about how brave she was, right up until the end of her life, how she visited other sick people to cheer them. She was physically beautiful, even as her chemotherapy stole away her black hair and her appetite, leaving her stick-thin and pale and bald: she wrapped her head in a turban and continued as best she could.

A familiar story: decades together, two lives joined in so many places you couldn't have separated them if you'd wanted to. Very, very few are granted the favor of a simultaneous exit from life; usually, one or the other must carry on alone.

I have a story to tell you, he says when he stops by one morning. *Would you believe that three different women in one day wanted me to meet lady friends of theirs?* He smiles and shakes his head. His face turns just the smallest bit pink as he relates the story of each encounter. *Just four months since my wife died. I told them I'm not ready to think about that yet.*

Four months isn't very long. I was pleased to see the embarrassed smile, though, and the faint blush. Although part of him was shocked at the idea, another part was pleased. He would never have chosen to be alone. It may be that love will come again some day. Maybe it will not. But there is a tingle of excitement, to think of himself in that role again, after all these years: maybe a new song.

JULY 2

The Lord sustains them on their sickbed.
PSALM 41:3
➤⊱

*B*ecause I'm often around people who are dying, able-bodied people sometimes get into conversations with me about what they want to happen should they ever fall ill, almost as if they could order up the kind of disability they'd be willing to endure, with a second or third choice in case the one they want is unavailable. *I don't want you to have to take care of me,* my husband tells me. *That's stupid,* I tell him sweetly. *Since when do we get a choice in the matter? Besides, how do you know it'll be you needing care? What if it's me?* I think he wants to drop dead suddenly: less fuss and fear.

Just because you're sick and weak doesn't mean you're useless. It won't mean that the people who love you will suddenly become bored with you. *I don't want you to have to take care of me*—who does want that? It's just part of life, the leaving of it, and sometimes it goes on for a long and difficult time. Nobody ever said life was going to be an unending series of rewarding experiences. Illness and pain are terrible. But your life isn't over when you have them. It isn't over until it's over.

It's hard to live with pain and weakness. The isolating idea that these conditions are unnatural and wrong just adds to the hardship. It discourages the sick person from trying to make the most of the energy she does have. It deprives both of you if you think you have to apologize every three minutes for being a bother. The people who handle debilitating illness best are the ones who find a way to live their lives realistically in the midst of it.

JULY 3

As the deer longs for the waterbrooks, so longs my soul for you, O God.
PSALM 42:1

✣

I look around my living room. Could stand to be a little neater, but I like what I see. Beautiful pictures. Furniture we picked out together, or brought with us. Photographs of the kids. His parents' beautiful carpet. Beautiful things. They do make me feel happy when I see them.

They are no substitute for my soul's peace, though, nor can they manufacture it for me. The soul's longing usually isn't in words. *There's something I want, and I don't know what it is.* The usual American assumption about this undefined longing is that it can be slaked by buying something; advertisers have become very good at playing to it. It's beautifully simple: first, we sell them something to satisfy their need. It won't satisfy them for long, so then we can sell them something else. As long as everybody agrees that satisfaction can be purchased, we can string them along forever.

When I was seven, my best friend and I ordered inflatable dinosaurs out of a comic book. The picture showed them to be taller than a child. We thought we would be able to ride on them, to bounce up in the air and arc back down. We couldn't wait.

When the dinosaurs finally came, they were nothing more than colored balloons with pictures of dinosaurs on them. They weren't taller than we were, and you couldn't ride them. *Every time I buy something, there's something wrong with it*, I remember my best friend telling me when we were kids. *Maybe just a tiny little thing, but something.*

You know, you're right, I said to her. I thought I was the only person that happened to. The one I buy is the one that will turn out to be just a little crooked, or to have a tiny hole in the seam, some minute imperfection.

It was the image we were buying: the dinosaur's ferocious strength and mystery, our own magical ability to tame the beast, the power to leap high in the air. Buying a self we could not supply on our own. Buying something that cannot really be bought: a satisfied soul.

JULY 4

I go about in mourning all the day long.
PSALM 38:6

＞＜

Do you have Wally's address? says the message on my e-mail. *I want to send him a note.* It's a colleague of mine from seminary days. *We've lost touch. I had heard he was ill.*

There's Wally, who has been HIV-positive since 1981. That's a long time in this epidemic; we didn't even have the acronym AIDS in 1981. *I was always a precocious child*, he told me in the hospital once. And Dan and Bob, who have both died: Bob first, down in Tennessee where they ministered, and Dan up here in New York, just last year. And Richard, who died just six months after his ordination. And Bernie who died last week. And many others.

When a priest dies, his or her body is dressed in liturgical vestments one. As long as my body can keep up with me, it's going to be a three-ring circus most of the time. It's going to be the familiar all-eight-cylinders/total-collapse cycle. I should be more moderate, but somehow I am not.

Maybe there's nothing wrong with that. Maybe we're not all supposed to be Henry David Thoreau. Maybe a week in the woods—or just a walk in the woods—is all some of us really want.

JULY 18

They hound me all the day long.
PSALM 56:2

✦

*U*sually the creditors call at dinnertime. If Susan answers, she says she's Nancy. If Nancy answers, she identifies herself as Susan and asks if she can take a message. It is humiliating. Nancy owes forty thousand in college loans. Susan went on to law school—sixty thousand. *Even at three percent interest, I can't make the payments and live in New York,* she says.

If only they'd gone to state schools. If only Susan had gone into corporate law, where the money was, instead of into public interest. If only Nancy were a computer whiz instead of an actress. They max out their credit cards. Nancy has five part-time jobs so she can get to her auditions. They have no couch.

Deferring the bulk of their college expense was the only way these young women could do what they wanted to do. Their choices had a cost, and they are paying it—not always on time, and not with anything that could accurately be called ease—but they're doing it. These years are lean, compared with those of some of their friends who chose other things. It's not always easy to keep the satisfaction of following their own dreams uppermost in their minds.

Most of us don't mind paying our way. Many of us, though, know that sinking feeling: *I'm in over my head. I'm not going to be able to do this.* We pedal harder. We rob Peter to pay Paul. Time passes, time and hard work. And finally, out of the woods at last. The last payment. The last exam. The last day of work. You made it.

JULY 19

Like a stillborn child that never sees the sun.
PSALM 58:8

✢✢

I notice that some losses are accorded more respect than others. Everybody's got a casserole for the widow, but nobody wants to stand too near someone going through a divorce. There is an outpouring of shocked sympathy for parents who lose an older child, but not much is said one way or another about a miscarriage or a stillbirth. Just not meant to be, people murmur, and go about their business. But the mother remembers that a small heart once beat under hers and now is still. Who are we to say what is and what is not meant to be?

It is easy to sweep a loss like that under the rug of your life, to be strong and brave, and keep courageously on. The world around you admires you for it, and is relieved not to have to deal with your unseemly grief. But you pay a price in your soul for doing that. You can't square your shoulders and smile your loss away forever. It is just there, and it must be acknowledged.

To whom do you speak it? To those who love you: they love the excuses our own selfishness. Or does it? *All the other kids are doing it,* **I** used to say sometimes when I begged my mother to let me do something of which she disapproved. *Well, you're not all the other kids,* she would say, and that was that. Even if it were true—which it isn't—that no one does anything good, what would that have to do with me? I'm still free to be generous if I choose to be so. We're not everyone. We are only ourselves.

JULY 16

My eye has seen the ruin of my foes.
PSALM 54:7

>⊁⊰

𝖸ou hear this a lot in the psalms: it's not going to be enough just to have my trouble go away. I also want to see the ones who did this to me get what's coming to them.

T. S. Eliot wrote a play in verse form about the martyrdom of Thomas Becket—*Murder in the Cathedral.* Becket was the most famous martyr of medieval times, not just in England, where he died, but throughout Europe. He knew, before it happened, that he would be killed. He returned to England from exile in France knowing that he was returning to die. In Eliot's play, four tempters visit Becket. Of course, they are from the Evil One, but they are also from Becket's own personality: after all, we are only tempted by that which touches something already within us. One tells him to forget his principles and just enjoy life. Another tells him to cooperate with the king who opposes him and wield tremendous secular power. A third tells him to join forces with the king's enemies and defeat him.

The Fourth Tempter is different. He counsels Thomas to embrace martyrdom for the sake of his conscience and to win heavenly glory. Moreover, he adds, Thomas will have the satisfaction of seeing his enemies in "another place."

Thomas sees this as the greatest evil: "to do the right thing for the wrong reason." Vengeance has no place in heaven. The truly good are not delighted by the suffering of the bad.

JULY 17

I would flee to a far-off place and make my lodging in the wilderness.

PSALM 55:8

✦

I have made once-and-for-all changes in my life at least seven or eight times. The forest of obligations and activities grows so dense that I can't move, and I resolve to chuck it all, say no to everything, pare my schedule to the bare bones and begin to have a life. And I do that—sort of. I announce the great change to all my friends. I resign noisily from a few things. I string together a few days of writing at home, doing what I've been telling people for years I want to do. My husband reads silently in the other room. The cat sits at my feet. I enjoy it immensely. *This is the way it should be,* I say to myself. Then somebody calls with an interesting idea about something we might work on together. I say I'll think about it, but I am already imagining how cool it'll be. Before I know it, I'm off and running on some worthy endeavor that sends me back into frantic mode.

This has happened so many times that it would be silly to hope for change at this late date. I often say I want a simpler life, but I must not really want one at all. If I did, I'd be doing more about getting whole package of you, not just the nice bits. These loved ones may be accustomed to the strong, calm you, and you may need the help of a counselor to learn to show them a weaker side of yourself. It doesn't come easily to some of us. But your loved ones can handle your sorrow, or they can learn how to handle it, and you should respect them enough to offer it honestly and trustfully. After all, how much do you love someone to whom you are afraid to show your true self?

And, always, you can speak your sorrow to God, who has always known about it anyway. Who never dismisses it, who never abandons. The loss the world ignores rests in the tender lap of God; in my imagination, I rest there, too.

JULY 20

His lightnings light up the world; the earth sees it and is afraid.
PSALM 97:4

✦

We stood on the porch, my father and I. There was a storm: mighty thunder rumbled and rolled to terrifying climaxes, and lightning bleached the front yard a momentary, unnatural white. I was four and crying at the top of my lungs in terror. He was forty-five and perfectly calm. *Look,* he said, kneeling beside me and holding me tight with one arm, *look at the marching men.* He pointed out across the yard at the road: row upon row of raindrops really *did* appear to march with military precision along the road in front of our house. *You have to have cannons when you have a big army like that marching,* he said, as the thunder made me scream again, and I gripped his arm as hard as I could.

I wanted to be as brave as he was. I stopped crying, and we stood together on the porch for a long time, watching the marching men. I felt safe in the crook of his arm. My body tensed every time the cannons roared, but I understood the necessity for them; after all, you have to have cannons when you have a big army like that.

I was too little to sense any incongruity in this: that a metaphor of war made me feel safe. That I was afraid of thunder and lightning, which would not hurt me, and that my fear was eased by a vision of war, which could. My father had returned from the war invincible. To me, the idea of soldiers marching was a vision of safety. What did I know then of the other children in the world that night, for whom that vision meant anything but safety, children who knew things about fear I didn't know, things no child should ever know?

JULY 21

They forage for food, and if they are not filled, they howl.
PSALM 59:17

➤✦

I peer into the refrigerator. There's nothing to eat.

Of course, I know this is not true. There are carrot sticks and a nice chicken breast I poached yesterday. There is whole wheat bread and there is peanut butter and there is raspberry jam. There are apples. There is plenty of water in the tap.

But I envision other things: macaroni and cheese out of a dark blue box. Chinese steamed dumplings. Vanilla ice cream with thick, rich chocolate sauce. Tortellini with tomato cream sauce. Kentucky Fried Chicken. None of the things I crave are good for me, like the apples or the poached chicken breast. The heck with those things: I dream of things that are bad for me.

When my husband daydreams about food, it's always about a salad. Imagine that: longing for something healthful. The heart and the mind in one accord: very unusual, I'll bet. I wish I were like that.

Looking back on my addiction to cigarettes, I remember the voraciousness with which I consumed them. Sometimes I would light one up, only to find that I already had one going in the ashtray; if that's not compulsive, I don't know what is. And then I would glance around, appalled, to see if anyone else had noticed. I remember times when I was angry about something or other: I would fling myself into a chair and light up defiantly, as if to strike back at—whom? No one but me. I was the only one there.

I am like that now about food, medicating away my disappointments and piques with whatever I can put in my mouth. I do feel better when I do that, for a while at least—that is, if you don't count the disgust with which I regard my weak will. One thing I learned in many a doomed battle against cigarettes is that guilt is of little avail in turning this sorry situation around. The fierceness of my need is stronger than my guilt, stronger than my will to resist. If there is to be deliverance, it will not come from me. It will have to come from God, if it's going to come at all.

I realize that this is a hard thing to read if you're not sure there even *is* a God, as many people are not. I'm sorry. I'm afraid I don't have anything convincing to say on that score. All I know is that I was unable to quit smoking on my own no matter what I did, and that a power beyond my own power delivered me. I saw it happen, and I trust what I saw, even though I can't explain it. So I trust that the same thing can happen with this food thing. And with anything else I can't do entirely on my own.

*Add length of days to the king's life; let his years extend
over many generations.*

PSALM 61:6

➤✦

The royals have been having a tough go of it lately. Sexual high jinks are nothing new in their history, of course, but they didn't used to elicit calls for the elimination of the monarchy altogether, as they do now. The one period in which England experimented with doing without a king was so dreary nobody's suggested repeating it for three hundred fifty years. But now a fair number of Britons, it seems, would just as soon do without them—not enough to make that occurrence at all likely, but more than I would have expected.

What was the king for in earlier times? He had a lot more power in ancient Israel than Prince Charles can anticipate wielding in the unlikely event that his mother ever gives up her throne to him. He was the central political and religious figure, larger than life. He was Israel. In some ways, the royals still *are* the country: important not because of their goodness, or lack of it, but because the community they symbolize matters to everyone. It's not true that former monarchs and their families were virtuous and this lot is tacky. But it may be that the community itself feels less important to many people, that they feel no particular loyalty to it.

God save the king! they say, automatically. *God save us!* is what they mean: God save our identity, our common cause. God save our ability to pull together when we must. This is an individualistic age. I'm not sure pulling together is a very highly valued skill today; it's every one for himself. But inside ourselves, we still know we need each other.

On the scales they are lighter than a breath.

PSALM 62:11

✦

No one has ever looked at me anxiously and asked if I didn't think I was just a little too thin. Not once in forty-four years. My blessed mother used to talk sometimes about how hard it was to gain weight; I would try to be sympathetic, but it was uphill work. *It's not hard to gain weight,* I would mutter, *all you have to do is look at a piece of cake,* and we would laugh.

I visit my friend Richard, who has AIDS: he is over six feet tall and now weighs less than a hundred pounds. The stubborn life and ongoing good humor in that skeletal body amaze me. He talks about the anguish of struggling to gain an ounce. This time my sympathy is immediate, and so is my appreciation of the irony in all this: why do I have so much more weight than I need while he wastes away? I tell him I'll gladly donate thirty or forty pounds I'm not using right now. We both laugh.

People with weight problems sure do laugh a lot. Might as well— making a joke of something that makes us sad is an old trick, an easier way to tell the truth about things that are not as we wish they were. To laugh at something—or at someone—is to refuse to adopt a subordinate posture with regard to it. That's why the employees of a tyrannical boss love to laugh at him behind his back, vying with one another for Best Imitation of the Dumb Way He Walks, or Best Mimicry of His Stupid Way of Saying Hello on the Phone. He may abuse his power over us, but we can form a community of laughter that puts that power into a perspective that can only be called divine, and we can draw strength from the laughter. If we can still laugh at him, he has not defeated us. Laughter gives power to the weak: get enough of us laughing at our oppressor, and one day we may even defeat him.

JULY 24

That they may shoot down the blameless from ambush.
PSALM 64:4
✢

*I*t never gets too familiar not to shock: a little boy lying face down in the street, his lifeblood trickling into a gutter that dates back to medieval times. Or an old lady, shopping bag still in hand, her sensible shoes neatly pointing downward in the dark pool of her own blood that widens all around her.

I just don't get it, somebody says. *I was over there in 1986 and everything seemed fine. Nobody cared who was Muslim and who was Croat.* What happened in Bosnia? Did they really just pick up where they left off before World War I, after seventy years of being best buddies? Was there really no trace of enmity and then, suddenly, utter blood-hatred? Of course not. Sure, you could find Muslims married to Croats. There were Yugoslavs who had no particular ethnic consciousness. But there were also ghettoes. There were neighborhoods defined by ethnicity. The combination of ancient and new tensions wasn't absent all those years. It was just underground. If one knew to look, it was there to be found.

None of that has a thing to do with the old lady or the little boy. They were trying to cross the street at what turned out to be a very wrong time. The casual prejudice of their society, fanned into sudden, malignant life, felt no need to determine their views before killing them. As it does not in other parts of the world, including our own. As prejudice—that which "pre-judges" before ascertaining fact—never does.

JULY 25

Our sins are stronger than we are, but you will blot them out.
PSALM 65:3

➤❖

We are talking about healing: a group of people between the ages of thirty and seventy-five. Some are divorced. Some are in recovery from alcoholism. Several are widows. Several are HIV positive. Two have disabled children.

Everyone nods when somebody brings up the *Why me?* problem. *What did I do to deserve this? This can't have just happened. It must have come from somewhere.* Almost everyone there knows it's irrational, but almost everyone there has entertained the notion that her suffering has come to her as punishment for some sin in her past. It's a lonely feeling: *I deserve my suffering.* We bat it around a little, and then people feel better. It always helps to talk.

But still: just because you don't think your cancer is punishment for your divorce doesn't mean that there aren't good reasons for taking a moral inventory of your life. Guilt *does* damage us. It has weight; we carry a burden when we carry it. If your life is threatened by disease, now is the time to get serious about mending fences. Before it's too late. If something else just turned your world upside down, now is the time to lighten your load wherever you can. That could mean squarely acknowledging something that you know wasn't as it ought to have been and fully feeling your regret without rationalization. Then you can spend the energy you were using carrying your guilt around on facing what you're facing.

JULY 26

"Because of your great strength your enemies cringe before you."
PSALM 66:2

➤◄

I have dreams, sometimes, of facing down a threatening force, of frightening him away with a show of physical strength. They are vivid: sometimes I awaken and my heart is pounding, I am so angry at whomever it was I was vanquishing while I was asleep.

Often a show of strength is all that's needed to make a bully back down. A stiff letter on a lawyer's letterhead works all manner of wonders that just don't seem to happen when you yell and scream all by yourself. The first thing that happens in an international crisis is the dispatching of a few impressive navy ships to visible points on the horizon near the trouble spot; don't mess with us, they say to a potential aggressor. It often works. I, for one, was astonished when Desert Shield actually turned into Desert Storm; I never really believed that the troops and guns and body bags we piled up on the Kuwaiti-Saudi border were for actual use. I thought we were just trying to scare them.

I'm not nearly as powerful in real life as I am in my dreams. I wouldn't really be able to vanquish much of anyone. The appearance of strength is borrowed plumage for me. In order for your show of strength to be permanently successful, you really have to have power, not just appear to have it. In my dream, the bad guys cower and run away. In real life, I *need* strength more often than I have it to spare. In my dream, I stand alone, self-sufficient and full of power. In real life, I am not self-sufficient. I can't prevail all alone, relying on my own power. In real life, I need strength from another source.

JULY 27

Father of orphans, defender of widows!
PSALM 68:5

❧

The orphan and the widow: two symbols of loss and vulnerability. They were very powerful symbols in the patriarchal society of biblical writers and are no less so to us, though we are slower to acknowledge need than they were. Women and children needed defending in those days, we think. Not like now.

The Million Man March made lots of people nervous. Some white people just don't like to see too many black males in any one place. Minister Louis Farrakhan is an unguided missile on a lot of important issues: gay people and Jews and women don't take his ridiculous and dangerous remarks about them lightly. But many thoughtful people listen to him when he talks about the importance of men in the black community, about reclaiming their responsibilities in their families. Thoughtful people of both races know that whoever is to blame for the desperate straits in which too many black men find themselves, only black men themselves can overcome them. Nobody—not even black women, and certainly not white people—can do it for them. The most others can do is get out of their way.

That's why many black women I know supported the march. They know their own strength, a strength that has been tested and tested hard for generations, but they also know they need their men to be strong, too. That the widow and the orphan may not be helpless any-more, but they are still bereaved. That the human race is composed of two sexes, and that they need each other.

JULY 28

But as for me, I am poor and needy.
PSALM 70:5

❧

I'm feeling that way now—some unforeseen expenses loom, and I'm not completely certain just where I'll get what I need to meet them. It makes me feel anxious and unattractively sorry for myself, as I begin to devise plans about what to do without for the next month or so.

Sorry for myself until I really stop and think. I think about the people who have so much less than I have—which amounts to almost everybody else in the world. My house would seem like a palace to easily ninety percent of the earth's population. I have enough to eat every day. I have more than one pair of shoes. I have a lot of other things. To many people, I am rich.

And then I stop and think about deprivation in my own past. I'm rich, also, in comparison to my younger self. I remember longing for things I couldn't have, and I remember that some of them were pretty basic things. And now I'm blue because maybe we should think about eating out less for a while? Big hairy deal.

This does cheer me up. It's really not that annoying you-think-you've-got-troubles routine that makes a person feel worse instead of better. It's just an honest counting of blessings. It puts my current incon-venience in accurate perspective. And it reminds me that everything comes to an end. I've been in tough places before. All will be well.

From my mother's womb you have been my strength.
PSALM 71:6
>←

These days women know they're pregnant long before we used to know. I remember when you could be two months along and still not sure; now, you pick up a kit at the drugstore on your way home from work and you know in a minute. You can also learn whether your baby is a boy or a girl. You can find out if your baby is dangerously ill in time to do something about it; these days, major surgery is performed on babies still in the womb—complicated surgery on organs no bigger than the mother's fingernail. You can hear your baby's heart beating. Amazing.

Even with all this knowledge, gestation and birth are still dangerous times in human life. So much can go wrong. A little boy was recently born to the daughter of a woman I've met only on the Internet—she and I participate in many of the same discussions online. The baby had a syndrome characterized by multiple disabilities: malformation of the hands, of the arterial structures around the heart, possible blindness and mental retardation. At three days old, he underwent heart surgery. A month later, he had another operation. Many more will be needed. A hard, hard time for a little guy.

On the computers scattered throughout the world, there was an outpouring of love and prayer. There were people online who knew children with the same disability; they referred the grandmother to the families of those children for support. People did research and sent her what they learned. Everyone typed messages of concern and assurances of their prayers. One person told another. People who had never heard of the woman, who would never meet her little grandson, prayed for them by name. Now and then the overwhelmed grandmother found time to send out a bulletin: that Jordan went home, that he was taken for a walk in his stroller, that he had to go back into surgery and it took an excruciating hour-and-a-half to find a tiny vein for his IV line. With every bit of news, the messages of prayer and support flashed through cyberspace again and again. *You will never know how much it all meant to us,* the grandmother wrote.

A little one in trouble, lifted in prayer by a host of strangers. Jordan faces many challenges in the years to come. But he does not face them alone. Besides those who know him and love him, there are those who will never know him but love him anyway. And there is another Love, from the source of all life, that keeps fighting against such formidable obstacles.

I know talk of *that* love enrages some people in situations like this: *If God's so all-out loving, why is this baby subjected to agony?* I guess if I thought God had sent this trouble, I'd feel the same way. But I don't. There is life. And there is evil. And in the midst of evil, we can find life, and that is God. Evil does not overcome it. Even at the end, when death comes upon us and snatches us from all that we know, that Love is there.

JULY 30

That the mountains may bring prosperity to the people.
PSALM 72:3

❖❖

*T*he longest period without rain in many years. No watering of lawns or noncommercial washing of cars allowed. The lawns are a crisp brown. Trees seem to be changing color prematurely. The summer has been hot, and has seemed abnormally long. I am eager to put it behind me. I want rain and snow, deep cold, no sun.

It's not really what comes out of the sky *here*, though, that will determine the water level. That happens up in the mountains, far from here. That's where it has to rain and snow. The mountains drink deeply and send the water down to us. Invisibly, underground, it flows downhill. We might get ten inches of rain in a day here—I wish we would; the trees and lawns would green up a bit. But our water supply will remain poor until the mountains get rain there.

Our prosperity comes from somewhere else. No one is an island. No *island*, even, is an island. Our life *is* shared, whether or not we have decided to share it. So when I behave as if you don't matter, I won't get away with it for long. My selfishness will backfire, and I will injure myself. And when society decides it's every one for himself, watch out. That's not the way things work. *Do to others as you would have them do to you,* says the Golden Rule. In a sense, an accurate description of reality can be derived from a paraphrase of it: *What you do to others will in some way affect you.* Better be careful what it is.

JULY 31

I had almost tripped and fallen, because I envied the proud.
PSALM 73:2–3

>←

I fall all over myself trying to explain to my therapist just what it is that's making me so mad at this person. *She whines about her problems,* I say.

So what? she says. *What does her whining have to do with you?*

Well, she doesn't appreciate what she has, I say.

Granted. Why should you *be mad because* she *doesn't appreciate what she has?*

The righteous reasons I produce for my anger just don't hang together, not until I add the one admission that makes it all make sense: I am jealous of this person. I don't just think she ought to appreciate what she has: I wish *I* had it. There's nothing righteous about my anger at all. It's completely self-absorbed.

I am impressed with the power of this particular deadly sin. Envy is very efficient. I spend a fair amount of effort trying to be loving and affirming of others. I work hard at it. I really want to be that way. And yet I am appalled at how easily envy slips into me, how ready I am to want what someone else has, to feel anger toward him because I want what is his. Appalled at how often this happens.

It's a crippler. Here's the truth: you can't be someone else. You can only be you. When I catch myself up in envy, it's as if I were ensnared in a sticky spider web: I can't move toward what I can be, what I can have. I can just gaze longingly at someone else's life and long for it. So Demon Envy wins big: I increase the sum of the world's anger, I increase the sum of the world's dishonesty by not admitting it, and I don't grow in my own joy.

There are no signs left for us to see; there is no prophet left; there is not one among us who knows how long.

PSALM 74:8

✦✦

Well, the prophets didn't always know *how long*, either.

Prophecy really wasn't as much about foretelling the future as it was about discerning the meaning of things that happen in human history. So Jeremiah wasn't soothsaying when he foretold the captivity of Israel. He was assessing the situation. *If you guys hold out here, they'll burn the city and take us prisoner. If you surrender, they'll spare the city and make us part of their empire over in Babylonia. You'd better surrender and preserve what you can. Someday we'll be able to return.*

It's not true that there are no signs left to see. There are signs aplenty. We've just lost the ability and the will to see them. That's because reading the signs usually requires people to change their behavior, and we usually don't want to do that. You don't have to be a fortune-teller to know that the United States in the near future will look like Bosnia does now if our racial relations do not improve. It's no magic to know that we can't continue as we are and expect everything to be fine.

Things don't happen for no reason. Everything has a cause, and a careful study of what's going on right now can yield some good predictions of what's likely to happen in the future. Human lack of direction usually isn't about lack of information. The prophet looks at the same history everyone else looks at. And he isn't magic. Just willing to tell the truth about what he sees.

I was glad when they said to me, "Let us go to the house of the Lord."
PSALM 122:1

➤✦

*T*here were times, when I was little, when I really *wasn't* very glad to go to the Lord's house. In the summer, especially, I would hear the early church bells and groan to myself as I lay in bed. Sometimes I would beg my parents to let me stay home—not very often, for I knew my chances of success were slim. Strange behavior, for me— I was the early riser in our family. Why didn't I want to go to church?

Well, it was hot, of course. The ladies fanned themselves with flat paper paddles printed with scenes from the Holy Land, supplied by the local funeral home. Those were the days when you had to wear a hat in church; mine had a loathsome elastic band that went under my chin to keep the thing on my head. So there was that. But my brothers were acolytes: sometimes one of them would fall over from the heat up there at the altar, so it wasn't as if I had a corner on suffering in church. You should have heard *them* on Sunday mornings.

I think there should be such a thing as casual church, John told my dad as he was tying his tie one sweltering August morning. *Jackets and ties are stupid. You should just wear a shirt when it's so hot.*

That's an impossibility, my father said. Many things which are now realities seemed impossible to him. Off we went: hats, wretched elastic bands, starched shirts, neckties, jackets.

Now there *is* such a thing as "casual church." Obligatory women's hats came off in the 1960s. People in my congregation wear jeans, tee shirts. Others wear business suits. In the hot summer, most don't wear jackets.

And me? And John, the one who rebelled against his necktie? We wear layer upon layer of heavy vestments, a stiff round white collar underneath it all—while everyone in the congregation is in polo shirts. Amazing what a person can grow into. But I am not completely conquered. Sometimes I sneak not wearing the collar: casual church.

AUGUST 3

"I will appoint a time," says God.
PSALM 75:2
✦✦

*W*hen your number's up, it's up. That's what George says. George is a gambler by avocation, and perhaps by demonic possession as well: it looks to me like he's well past the stage where he can take it or leave it. A wholesale signing over of one's own decision-making power to a roll of the dice: that's the game he plays, and that's his attitude toward his own life as well. He seeks out situations in which he knows he'll lose control: *Maria came over last night. We had a good time, but then she left. She didn't want to stay. So as soon as she left, I went right to the deli and binged. I mean, Friday night at ten o'clock and I'm alone, you know? I ate all day Saturday.*

Oh, yes, I do know. But he's been having this problem in his relationship with his girlfriend for almost a year. He knew the evening was likely to end in disappointment. He set himself up: gave himself a situation he knew he couldn't handle himself without turning to food, his drug of choice. *So then Sunday I went to Atlantic City and gambled. I've been okay since then.* One drug substitutes for another. It sounds dangerous to me. As I leave the meeting, George is talking to the therapist about using marijuana to make himself feel better. *I don't know about that one . . .* she begins, shaking her head.

There are many people in the world who rely on their own judgment. George and I are not among them, though: we are addicts. We look for ways to make it inevitable that we will "pick up," as they say in the addiction biz. He knows his girlfriend makes him sad and angry. He knows he eats when he's sad and angry. So he invites Maria over on Friday night. I do things like that: get myself in a situation in which all that stands between me and food is willpower. I don't have any willpower.

I will appoint a time, says God. That doesn't mean we have no responsibility for managing our days. Tell the truth about yourself. Don't set yourself up and then blame it on your girlfriend, like George. Don't skip a meal and then use it as an excuse to binge, like me. God appoints our times, but we are the ones who decide whether or not to help ourselves live well in them.

AUGUST 4

And I said, "My grief is this: the right hand of the Lord has lost its power."
PSALM 77:10

✢

The journey from the simple and straightforward assumption that God will always protect us from harm to an understanding that the truth is much more complicated than that is usually a hard one. Arrival is often surprisingly abrupt, and surprisingly long in coming: I've met hundreds of people whose first inkling of the truth was when something bad happened to them as adults. A divorce, the painful death of a loved one from cancer, and all of a sudden there's no God. As long as *other* people were the ones divorcing, *other* peoples' loved ones suffering and dying, God was in his heaven and all was right with the world. God turns out to have been a pretty narrow idea: God is me without any problems.

Well, all human beings since Adam and Eve start out thoroughly egocentric. We grow out of it. But we remember the grief of being cast out of that imaginary paradise. Thinking that the sorrows of the world could not harm me was very nice indeed. Learning otherwise was painful. And it opens up questions a lot harder to ponder than the old "faith=prompt deliverance" ever was.

Where is the power of God? Now that I know it's not that I'll live forever and never be sad, what exactly is it? Where do I see it? What happens because of it?

I've spent my life trying to answer these questions, and I still don't know. All I have are hints: that the power of God is unexpected. That it often brings good out of terrible evil. That it fashions all human fights for justice. That it lives outside our reality of life and death. That's about it: I'm new at this. As I will be if I live to be a hundred.

AUGUST 5

They shall still bear fruit in old age.

PSALM 92:13

➜←

*F*orty years old. Forty-four. Forty-seven. I think I read somewhere about a woman giving birth at fifty. Moms can be old these days. *I worry sometimes about her being alone as a young adult,* one woman tells me. *I'll be sixty-five when she's twenty.*

Well, maybe that's a problem. But people just *have* problems, no matter how old or young their parents are. You may not live to see your grandchildren if you get a late start. But you may not, anyway: you could go out for a quart of milk tonight and get hit by a truck and that would be that. Life is a risk for everyone. Young parents have more energy. Old ones have more wisdom and, usually, more money. There are gifts and curses no matter when you become a parent.

But children love their parents. They learn what love is primarily from them. However long a time we have with our children, we shape what they will be for as long as they live. They will give thanks for some of what we have given them and go into therapy to deal with things we might better have kept to ourselves. Almost always, they manage to transpose the life they learn into the world they enter, and almost always, they end up knowing what love is and valuing the good. If you die when they're in their twenties, as my mom did when I was, they'll be sad. If you die when they're in their forties, as my dad did when I was, they'll also be sad. That life together may end too soon is no reason at all not to let it begin.

AUGUST 6

One generation shall praise your works to another.
PSALM 145:4

➤✦

*I*t was the fiftieth anniversary of the dropping of the atomic bomb on Hiroshima. It seemed like a good day to spend some time talking about war, and so a group of us gathered after church—a circle of fifteen or so. One woman had been a three-year-old in London during the bombing. She talked about sleeping in her Anderson Shelter—a steel cage under the dining room table—every night. Another woman brought her mother's memoir to the meeting. Her mom was an army nurse in the Bataan prison colony; they could never discuss her experiences while she was alive. An older man had been in the German army; he sat next to a guy who'd fought in the Battle of the Bulge on the American side. The Englishwoman read a poem about Sadako, the little girl in Hiroshima who believed she could save herself from death by radiation poisoning if she made a thousand paper cranes. It didn't work. Bright paper cranes in memory of her were sprinkled around the parish hall, hanging in clusters from the ceiling, in a line along the windowsill.

None of us were in Hiroshima that hot August day in 1945, when the whole city shot suddenly up into the sky in a quick burst of white fire. Some of us weren't even born yet. The inconclusive sorrows of the human family since that day, the closeness of war to our lives, the deepening awareness of its tenacious grip on our hearts—the fiftieth anniversary of the bomb was a good day to think on these things.

August 6 is also the Christian Feast of the Transfiguration: Jesus goes up on the mountain to pray and his friends see that his face is glowing white. How ironic. Or, maybe, how appropriate: the power of God is the only power that transforms us and banishes war from our midst. We certainly don't seem able to do it on our own.

By your great might spare those who are condemned to die.
PSALM 79:11

➵➴

*I*n San Gimignano, a lovely medieval walled city in the Tuscan hills, there is a museum which contains all manner of devices human beings have employed to inflict pain and death on other human beings. Guillotines, stocks, wheels upon which bodies were broken, iron maidens—a real charmer, the iron maiden: a woman-shaped coffin, in which people were enclosed and then gored to death by long spikes inside the lid. There are devices on display too sexually perverse for me to write about in a book I hope will sell well among sensitive people. There is a modern electric chair.

It's odd to see the chair amid all the medieval stuff. The iron maiden, the wheel, the guillotine: these things are safely removed from our era. These are things people used in much more barbaric times. But the electric chair is still in use. Americans line up outside prisons and cheer when the switch is thrown and the lights dim. You don't leave the Torture Museum with a good feeling.

The catalog of the exhibits is a passionate protest against the use of torture and capital punishment in all modern countries. It was dedicated to a favorite son of Italy, Mario Cuomo. Cuomo lost the governorship of New York in 1994, in large measure because of his steadfast opposition to the death penalty. With many a flourish, his successor signed it into a law within days after his inauguration. People all but danced in the streets, as if the signing were an act of great virtue and courage. As predicted, the new governor's action made no difference at all in New York's crime rate, as capital punishment has never lowered crime in any of the states in which it was enacted. It merely added the state to the long list of potential killers, and honored one of the basest human motivations around: the desire for revenge.

AUGUST 8

Oh, that my people would listen to me!
PSALM 81:13

⇥⇤

I remember thinking, when my children were young, that motherhood would be really easy when they were grown. They'd be able to do for themselves all the things they needed me to do for them. It would be a snap.

Some things did lighten up: they do their own laundry and make their own money. I don't feed them anymore. But I didn't know, when they were little, how hard it would be to let them live their own lives when they were big. How hard it would be to watch them learn from their own mistakes. How hard it would be to let go, and then how hard it would be, also, to know when to help.

So much advice on the tip of my tongue. So many warnings. So many ways in which my experience could be of some use to them if they would just listen. So many times that they came to believe something of which I'd tried to no avail to convince them years before. So many, many *I told you so*'s blessedly left unsaid.

People just learn better from experience then they do from instruction. Almost always. We may wish with all our hearts to spare them the consequences of their actions by lending them our experience, but experience is something that can't be borrowed. We gather our own.

Thinking back, I remember warning upon warning that did nothing whatsoever to dissuade me from any number of actions which later proved every bit as disastrous as predicted. I didn't listen, and I lived to regret it. But I learned. As agonizing as it is to see someone you love flirting with disaster, there's always the chance for learning and growth. And, even if that learning never takes place—sometimes it doesn't— growing up means deciding for yourself. Go ahead and warn of danger—you'd be irresponsible not to—but then they're on their own.

AUGUST 9

Now I say to you, "You are gods, and all of you children of the Most High; nevertheless, you shall die like mortals, and fall like any prince."
PSALM 82:6–7

❧

Much is made, in the Judeo-Christian tradition, of our having been monotheists before anybody else was—well, almost anybody: the Egyptian pharaoh Amenhotep IV thought there was only one god, too, but the other Egyptians thought he was weird and the idea never caught on. And that singular belief did set the Hebrews apart from their neighbors. But snippets like this one show that they were not wholly innocent of polytheistic ideas: here, God is standing in the midst of his fellow gods, like a king in his court, and he is demoting them to the status of mere mortals. A very human scenario, if you ask me.

Just about the worst thing a person could do in the Hebrew scriptures was worship another god besides the God of Israel. And yet those ancient books are essentially the story of the people of Israel doing just that, in one way or another, over and over. They were forever wandering off somewhere and having to be brought back. They interpreted all their reverses of fortune as signs of the divine displeasure at this sort of behavior.

It's interesting: such a strong sense of having been chosen, and yet so consistent a tendency to just wander away and do other things. Interesting and familiar: people do take the most extraordinarily important things utterly for granted. He lavishes six times the care on his 1957 Chevy that he gives to his marriage. She allows her job to take over her entire life. They play with the dog more than they do with their children. Yet both say that family is the most important thing in the world to them.

Faithfulness requires concentration. The talk is one thing; what really counts is the walk.

AUGUST 10

Like fire that burns down a forest.
PSALM 83:14

>+<

All firemen are cute, says my young friend. *I mean it: there is no such thing as an ugly fireman. Have you ever seen one? No. I rest my case.*

My daughter agrees. I ask if they remember a television show they loved when they were little, a show about two handsome firemen who managed five or six daring rescues a week. I liked the show, too. It was exciting to see them come so close to the flames and then pull the victim out just in time. To risk one's life for one's fellows: what could show more nobility of spirit?

We feel this way about firemen, as if they were battling a foe that came out of nowhere, keeping the chaos of the whole universe at bay. They are most assuredly brave, but their foe is not quite so cosmic: most fires start because of some human error. Sometimes they are what the insurance companies call "acts of God," but usually they can be traced to carelessness. Yet we treat most house fires as if no one were responsible. We view fire prevention as an admirable extra, a wise and fine thing to do, but something rather less than one's civic duty.

In Europe, that's not how it is. The centuries have been crowded there; life is lived in closer proximity to one another than we live it here. And so it's not just a terrible misfortune to allow a fire to destroy property; it's against the law. People whose houses burn because of dangerous conditions they could have prevented are seen as both victims and perpetrators, the potential killers of their neighbors. They go to trial. They can go to jail.

You need a smoke detector to get a certificate of occupancy in most American towns. But no official will ever come to your door and demand to see that it's working once you move in, not if you live there for twenty years. Maybe today would be a good day to check that out. Not just as a practical matter, but as a spiritual one. The world will not take care of us if we fail to take care of ourselves. Life will furnish us with enough trouble; we don't need to court more.

For one day in your courts is better than a thousand in my own room.

PSALM 84:9

➤✦

*H*ere is something I have thought about the dead: they don't have time, wherever they are. I've also thought that they don't have space, either, that their continued existence is not in a *place*. That it's not so much "wherever they are" as "however they are" that hints most closely at their way of being. I can offer no evidence for these claims that would satisfy anyone disposed to doubt. But people who do a lot of funerals have occasion to think a lot about the larger life, and these two thoughts are what has occurred to me so far. Not much for almost twenty years of work, I'll admit, but these things take time.

If it is true that it is only we who are bothered with time and space, then some interesting and encouraging things are also true. The first is that the pain of loss, which we feel so keenly and fear so much, afflicts us here only. If there is no time, there is no past. No future. Only a permanent now. My mother, who is dead, lives in it. That first moment I remember with her when I was three is in it. My own death in our future is in it. All now. All at the same moment out of time. So nothing has been lost. It is all still there.

But, of course, it is not still *here*. Time can pass pretty slowly here, especially future time. Have a baby and think of her at twenty-one: sounds like a long time from the front end. It's when she really *is* twenty-one that you realize twenty years lasts about a minute. One reason among many why old people often handle sorrow better than we think they will: they know something of how quickly everything on earth passes, the joys and the sorrows alike.

You have withdrawn all your fury.
PSALM 85:3

✦

*B*eing from the Midwest, I find it difficult to express anger when I feel it. Our people have a powerful cultural interdiction against such things. It is often difficult for me even to feel it. I'll look down at my hands and see that they have become fists without my even being aware of it. Me, mad? Whatever can you mean?

I'm not sure exactly what it is that we're afraid of about getting angry. Perhaps we have a frightening fantasy of being unable to stop once we get going, that we'll just yell and scream and throw things for the rest of our lives if we ever do it once. Unlikely. Or perhaps we fear that our anger will be returned, that there will be a terrible fight that ends relationships and makes people homeless in minutes. Unlikely, also. Or maybe we cling covertly to a smug moral high ground, secretly enjoying the image of sweetly keeping our cool while everyone around us is losing theirs. Which, come to think of it, isn't all that nice.

Interesting, isn't it, that virtuous things—like being sweet-tempered—can become occasions for self-congratulatory behavior that really isn't very virtuous at all. It would be much better to be honestly angry than to make oneself sick pretending a sweetness that isn't the truth, for the sake of appearances.

Prior to any other goodness is being what you seem. In some way, at some time, false goodness is revealed as what it is. A smiling woman with clenched fists is a contradiction in terms and makes no sense. She needs to allow her outside to match her inside.

*Show me a sign of your favor, so that those who hate me
may see it and be ashamed.*

PSALM 86:17

⸻

*A*stute observers of human nature, the psalmists. *Do something nice
for me,* he asks, which makes sense—who doesn't want nice things?
But this guy is really thinking ahead: *Not only will I enjoy this nice
thing, but I will also have the pleasure of my enemy's shame.* Impressive
planning.

Enjoyment of what we have is so often mixed with other things.
We usually pretend to a purity of heart that isn't really there because
we've been taught that it isn't nice to be vengeful, but we daydream
about being vindicated when we're treated badly, and that daydream sometimes includes some groveling on the part of those who
have hurt us. *Just wait,* we console ourselves, *they'll be sorry.*

Usually, though, they're not that sorry, whoever they are. People
who hurt us usually aren't actively hostile toward us. They're just
indifferent. They usually don't seek out ways of hurting others; they're
just so self-absorbed that they don't notice when they do. And they
may never connect our vindication with any condemnation coming
their way; people who are casually cruel never know that they're
cruel, and aren't conscious of their sin.

Sometimes you meet a person who has become obsessed with
teaching a former persecutor a lesson. Who would rather see his
enemy suffer than enjoy his own new freedom from whatever he was
suffering before. Everything in life comes to revolve around this
vendetta. Nothing could be less free. If I'm being unfairly treated in a
situation I can't turn around, I don't need to get out and then get
even. I just need to get out and get on with life.

They are like trees planted by streams of water . . . everything they do shall prosper.

PSALM 1:3

➸➹

The hydrangeas we put in along the front walk last year fainted every afternoon in the August heat. They were young, still, and their stems were not yet the woody stalks they would be after a winter in the snow; they were soft plant tissue instead, well suited to the task at hand—rapid growth—but without the hard sheath of bark that would keep the water from evaporating right out of them. So over they went, every afternoon by two or three o'clock, their big puffballs bent almost to the ground, their leaves drooping like tongues. You could almost hear them gasp. We would go out front with the watering can and pour them something tall and cold. You could almost see them straighten up; in thirty minutes they were back on their feet and looking good. No staying power, though; by noon the next day, you'd walk by and there they would be again, toppled over, gasping on the ground. The hydrangeas would have been thrilled to be planted by streams of water.

Things have been much better for the hydrangeas this summer, even though it's been one of the hottest summers since people started keeping track of just how bad things get. The reason for the improvement is this: they survived a cold winter, growing tough skin on their tender outer stalks. The cold calloused them all up and down, so that this year their stems were strong pipes within which water could flow without being sucked right out of the plant by the parched air.

Well, there it is: we might all wish to live right by streams of water, so close to everything we need that survival requires no effort at all. But most of us don't live there. We grow and get tough another way: by living through hard times. Things are set up so that most of us learn more and get stronger from the hard times than we do from the easy ones.

AUGUST 15

My sight has failed me because of trouble.
PSALM 88:10

>‹

Well, it isn't really because of trouble in my case. It's just middle age. Things start to deteriorate. First bifocals, now trifocals. Where will it end? I know a woman who wears pentafocals. Incredible nuisance.

My friend John has been a loner all his life. Comes and goes, does John, disappears for months at a time and then shows up one day without a word of explanation. He owes no one an explanation for anything he does—at least, he didn't until recently. His age and his diabetes are catching up with him now, and the circulation to his legs is all but gone. He's lost a few toes on one foot; the other one is swollen and discolored. But he checked himself out of the hospital when they started talking about nursing homes. He's staying in my place right now—no home, either, our John: he just roosts in different places—and can't arise from the couch. This is no permanent solution to his problem, a couch in my apartment. He'll have to go to a nursing home, and I'll have to get tough with him if he refuses.

I was furious when I heard John had checked himself out of the hospital against medical advice. But then I remembered myself and my trouble with my glasses. I didn't tell you the whole truth up there at the top of the page: I *have* the trifocal lenses, but I don't wear them. Instead, I'm stumbling around with an out-of-date single-focus pair. The trifocals drove me nuts. I don't want to deal with the wavy lines. I don't want to accept the reality of what is, after all, a very small change. I don't want to bow to the fact of my age. I'm more like John than I'd like to think I am.

AUGUST 16

"I have set the crown upon a warrior."
PSALM 89:19
❖

*T*here are those who think that *only* warriors have what it takes to wear a crown. It's typical, after a war, for Americans to want to elect a popular general to public office—witness the many calls for General Colin Powell, a man who took the nonpartisan stance of the military so seriously that most people couldn't guess whether he was Democrat or Republican, to run for the presidency. The steely nerves, the high-stakes decision-making, the aura of strength the uniform bestows: they all look pretty presidential. The sense of common purpose facing a common enemy is symbolized by the figure of a general; people often refer to the whole fighting force by his name, as in "Patton pursued Rommel further into North Africa."

People much too young to remember the Second World War participated eagerly in its recent fiftieth anniversary observances. We envy the unity of purpose people had then; we feel our fragmentation and cynicism keenly by comparison. We wish we had a strong leader, someone like a general. Then maybe we would be more like an army: more uniform, more in agreement about our common purpose.

When we long for a general, we are really longing for something we ourselves have lost. Our political leaders will always resemble us: confused if we are confused, self-serving if that's what we are. Strong and honest if we value strength and honesty. A leader, a president, the rector of a church, a college president, even a husband or a wife: we get what we select, and we select according to what we value. If the outcome of our choice surprises us, we may need to understand ourselves a little better.

AUGUST 17

But they did not stop their craving, though the food was still in their mouths.
PSALM 78:30

➤✦

*H*ere's something I have learned: thin people eat only until they're satisfied. Fat people eat until they're full. We feel unsatisfied until we feel the pressure of our full stomachs. Not just unsatisfied: uneasy. An irrational fearfulness urges us on to eat until we are just short of physical pain. Or even until we have moved well into it. That full feeling makes us feel safe.

Now, I've been dimly aware of this for years. My support group is bringing it out into the open: compulsive eating, like any compulsive behavior, is something one does when one is fearful. *How silly,* I think to myself. *What on earth have I got to be afraid of?* I listen to my feelings before a meal and then after one: I hear loneliness. *Nonsense. You're not lonely. You have lots of people who love you.* Maybe so. Certainly so, in fact: I'm richly blessed that way. But somehow I fear loneliness anyhow, and somehow I've talked myself into believing that eating makes it better. And so, for years, it has. Temporarily.

Now that I understand that, I finally have some leverage. If I've been eating addictively to assuage loneliness, I can attack the loneliness head-on instead and drain away much of the emotional power food has over me. If I meditate on the many ways in which I am loved, if that becomes keenly real in my soul, I won't need to seek love through food. I'll seek love through love. I'll become more aware of love. I will probably become more loving, too.

So many destructive ways of behaving are really about something quite unrelated to their apparent goals. People who brag about their accomplishments are usually terribly insecure. People who are sexually promiscuous are usually wretchedly unhappy with the selves they share so lightly. People who wear themselves out doing good for others are sometimes deeply angry. We try in wrong-headed ways to get what we need when we're afraid to ask for it directly, and it never works. I may feel better momentarily when I stuff myself, but I lose much more in burdening myself with self-hatred than I've gained in security. Because food isn't love. It's just food. Booze isn't love. It's just alcohol. Even good deeds aren't love. Love lives in the spirit, and if it's not there, no substitute will do.

The waters have lifted up their voice.
PSALM 93:4

☙

You can buy a machine that will replicate the sound of waves breaking on the shore—scientifically proven, it says in the catalog, to induce relaxation and ease stress. It would work for me, that machine: that ceaseless foaming sound that ebbs and flows puts me immediately at ease. When you take little kids to the beach, they stand at the water's edge and shout at the top of their lungs. Even the most harried of mothers doesn't care how loudly her kids yell: the noise of the waves drowns them out. You sit and watch and listen to the waves breaking; they stand and shout uselessly into the surf. After a while you all get back in the car and go home, as relaxed as if you'd slept.

Why? Well, the sea is big and we are small, of course. Its hugeness puts me in mind of the smallness of my concerns: long after I and everyone else have been forgotten, the waves will crash onto the beach as they always have, bringing microscopic pieces of the world here from thousands of miles and thousands of years away, carrying pieces of my world today back out to sea.

And the sea is our former home: the cells from which our species of life emerged lived in water, and we ourselves floated in water for the first nine months of our lives. We remember its sound, our safe buoyancy—not in our conscious memories, but in a more primitive part of us. Our own past, our human past, our evolutionary past: they all sprang from the deep, the great mass of water that dwarfs the body and calms the mind.

The Lord knows our human thoughts; how like a puff of wind they are.
PSALM 94:11

➤⬝

*I*n the summer of 1967, I had a paper dress. Everyone was talking about them for a few months back then. Red, white, and blue stripes, mine was. If you wanted it shorter, you just cut off a length at the hem. And when it got dirty, you threw it away. Paper dresses were pictured in *Life* magazine. But by the fall of 1967, everybody had forgotten all about them.

In the early 1970s, AT&T spent a ton of money developing PicturePhone, a telephone combined with a video screen that would enable callers to see the people they were calling. You would have answered the phone in hair curlers and your old sweatshirt and there, on the screen, would have been your mother-in-law. It went nowhere so fast that the term "PicturePhone" became AT&T slang for "unworkable idea."

When my husband left for Turkey in 1950, toothpaste in America was white. When he came back in 1952, it was green—and so were a lot of other things, like soap and mouthwash. Chlorophyll. It disappeared almost as abruptly as it appeared. Plants need chlorophyll, but people really don't.

Some of our ideas just don't deserve to last. They are the red herrings of human progress. They answer a need nobody seems to feel but the people who invent them. Other ideas seem destined to appear, providing solutions to universal problems. Ideas whose times have truly come: vaccines for devastating diseases, for instance. They are developments so important in their times that it seems they will never be unneeded or revised. And yet even these pass away or change.

Everybody got a smallpox vaccination when I was little. My older daughter got one when she was little. By the time Anna was born in 1974, though, they weren't doing them anymore. No need.

The most important human achievements, the most long-lasting things we make and do: eventually they will be forgotten, quaint relics of a time only dimly understood by some future generation. We and our works are so far from forever—a puff of wind.

AUGUST 20

In his hand are the caverns of the earth.

PSALM 95:4

＞＜

Most of the earth's surface is under water, of course. Hidden from all but a few of us. Go beneath the surface, near the shore, and it's a different world, a world from a dream, another planet. Wondrous things, depending on where in the world you are: magnificent architectural corals, brilliant fish, undulating tall plants. The telltale little pile of rubble on the sea floor that indicates an octopus's nest: watch it and you may see a tentacle emerge in exploration. Then the animal herself wiggles out and jets off to find some food: a pale grey-brown, all head and legs. A flat disk outlined on the floor is really a flounder, coloring himself to match the pebbles upon which he drifts, looking up at you with both of his eyes on his top surface. Dive down toward him, and he picks up speed to escape, easily leaving you behind as his disk shape skitters along the bottom and out of sight. Enter into a school of three thousand golden fish; they will swirl all around you, but will not touch you. You will be unable even to graze one with your hand. Come upon a phalanx of squid, swimming in a wedge—the same formation in which geese fly. Trouble the water, and the whole wedge shoots away, staying in formation as it goes.

Sometimes, swimming along among the coral formations, you will come upon a cave. I don't think I have to tell you not to enter it. Probably you will already have thought of that. In the brilliant, sun-dappled blue water, the cave will yawn below you, dark, seeming to go down forever. Maybe it *does* go down forever. Maybe it goes miles down, down to the center of the earth. Its profound deepness is frightening. It may not have a bottom. You do not know who lives there, what pale, eyeless animals. You pass over the mystery quickly, as quickly as you can.

AUGUST 21

Ascribe to the Lord the honor due his Name; bring offerings and come into his courts.

PSALM 96:8

➤❖

This is one of the Offertory Sentences, the verbal signals from the priest to the congregation (and to the ushers, whose job it is to pass the offering plates) that the focus of the liturgy is about to shift, from reading and reflecting upon scripture to the offering of ourselves to God and God's self-offering in the bread and wine. For those of you from other traditions, to whom that last bit didn't make total sense, let me add that people know to go for their wallets when they hear it. This isn't the only Offertory Sentence you can use, of course; you can also say *Let us with gladness present the offering of our life and labor to the Lord,* or you can say, just a tad more threateningly, *But do not neglect to do good and to share what you have, for such sacrifices are pleasing to God,* just in case somebody out there was thinking of not sharing. I once heard a friend use *And Eve gave him the apple, and he ate.* Bold, that. I still don't know exactly what he meant by it.

I usually use the sentence that starts off this reflection. It's the one I got into the habit of using and the one that comes readily to my lips, after I've been ad-libbing announcements up there for two or three minutes and have run out of things to say. Every time I use it, though, I wish I'd used something else. Why? Because it reveals me as someone who uses the male pronoun when speaking of God, and I'm afraid I'll give offense. Nobody really thinks God is a guy, but we keep using these male words. I do it all the time, because I don't want to be clumsy and fall all over myself with "he or she," or be equally inaccurate and just use "she," or be *really* confusing and alternate between the two. I don't want to say things like "Godself" because it sounds silly. I can't bear to turn God into an "it," or into some kind of faceless force, like gravity or electromagnetism. My language about God is limited because of my limitations, not God's.

So sometimes you just need a pronoun. At least, I do. And we don't have a suitable one. I hope people who hear me and are offended will bear with me—I'm working on it. And I hope other people understand that it really is a problem and not just trendy political correctness.

Confounded be all who worship carved images and delight in false gods!
PSALM 97:7

✦

$\mathcal{M}$y colleague is a well-known liturgist, someone who excels at planning and performing the many symbolic actions that make up an Anglican worship service. People from far and wide consult Lloyd about large and small pieces of the liturgy; he carries in his head a tremendous volume of wisdom about where the things we do came from and what they mean. No bow, no change of posture, no placement of chalice or cruet is unplanned: each has a reason, a part to play in making the whole worship experience make sense. The result is simple, reverent, and beautiful.

In the sacristy, where our vestments and all the things used in the various services are kept, he has labeled everything. Everything has a place. If you can read, you can find it. ALTAR BREAD. PURIFICATORS. LAVABO TOWELS. Inside the key drawer are about a dozen little compartments, each one also labeled: FUNERAL KEY, OIL AUMBRY KEY, etc. Everything: TOOLS, SEWING SUPPLIES, ODD STOLES. Even the portraits of the three bishops to whom we relate are labeled, so we'll know who's who.

Naturally, the labels are the source of a fair amount of sacristy humor. *What happens if you get to heaven and find that it's messy?* the acolyte mistress wants to know. *I'll know why I'm there,* Lloyd says serenely.

The people who participate in the sanctuary must rehearse often, and must keep their wits about them during the service. It requires concentration. A new person is often nervous, and rightly so: there's a lot to remember. Many details. And it's expected that things will be done perfectly. Fortunately, we usually come pretty close.

Obviously this is not an experience in spontaneity. For some people, that's a problem: it might seem that the liturgy has become an idol, that God has been forgotten in an obsession with detail. That our practice in worshiping God has itself become a false god. I suppose that could happen. You could plod mechanically through all the bows and kneelings and unobtrusive signals, all the prayers you've known by heart for years and years, and not feel anything.

In my experience, though, it doesn't happen very often. The stateliness and dependability of the service has an oddly freeing effect. We don't have to decide what to do; we *know* what to do. Our spirits are thus encumbered, able to absorb the rich panoply of music, incense, color, and fabric at a level above the level of cognition. It takes planning, but in the end, it is so about God, so *not* about human compulsiveness. Not a label in sight, not during the service. None needed there.

AUGUST 23

Sing to the Lord a new song.
PSALM 98:1

➤❖

*B*ecause religious institutions have been the custodians of so many human traditions, it's hard to imagine what they were like when they were new. But they all were, once. The first Christians were Jews. The first Jews were believers in the nature religions of the ancient Near East who saw something beyond those religions. The first Methodists were Anglicans. The first Anglicans were Roman Catholics. Everything came from somewhere. Each new thing takes root in an old thing, but it does not stay. It becomes a new thing.

Neither does the old remain the same. The conditions that gave rise to the offshoot also change the community from which it emerges. This is true in every human institution, not just in religious ones. We are continually singing a new song. Each generation must find a way to understand its past in relation to its present, not instead of it.

Some of the things people did in the past are no longer done. Take a look at an old set of silverware—there are some strange-looking implements in it, utensils we no longer use. We pick them up with interest, but not with alarm; nobody's very frightened by the decreased use of berry spoons in the present age. Other differences with our ancestors' ways bother us a little more: I know hardly anyone who's not a little unsettled by our rapidly changing sexual mores. You can get into some pretty uncomfortable conversations pretty quickly.

All we can do in the face of change is talk and think together about it. Talk about what has led to it. Talk about where it may take us. Talk about what we fear and what it is for which we hope. Because out-of-hand rejection of change and uncritical acceptance of it are equally silly.

AUGUST 24

"You were a God who forgave them, yet punished them for their evil deeds."
PSALM 99:8

→←

*F*orgiveness is a hard concept. People hang on to grievous sins committed against them for years. People even hang on to trivial affronts for years. I know one woman who can't bring herself to forgive another woman for a cruel remark she once made to a third party, although the *recipient* of that remark himself has, in fact, long since forgiven her.

Why is forgiveness so hard? I think that it involves a serious misunderstanding of what forgiveness is and isn't. Perhaps I can be of help.

First, and most important: forgiveness is much more about the forgiver than the forgivee. It is not nearly as much about what you have done as it is about whether I can decide to be in relationship with you. Thus, the ranking of offenses—this, this, and this can be forgiven, while these six things over here are unforgivable—is not necessary to determine forgiveness.

Second, and following from the first: forgiveness does not wipe away history. It's not about *Oh, that's okay*. A person may be forgiven, but that doesn't mean what he did was "okay." In fact, the things appropriate to forgiveness are never okay. If what he did was okay, he is not forgiven: he is acquitted. The things we do have consequences. We may be punished for them, or they may carry with them very efficient punishments of their own, and to forgive one another doesn't change this fact of life and human society. It is a *person* who is forgiven, not an action. The forgiven are welcomed back into the community, not exonerated. Thus, we might forgive someone serving a life sentence for murder, but not recommend his release; in forgiving him, we acknowledge his membership in our society, the pain of his captivity as well as its justice.

Third, forgiveness does not wait upon feeling. People who forgive the killers of their loved ones—and you do read of such people now and then—are not angelic beings who don't feel rage and vengefulness and sorrow like other people do. They didn't forgive because warm fuzzy feelings about the murderer crept into their hearts. They forgave because of what their hatred was doing to *them*. Forgiving was part of learning to live again. It was a decision made out of their own need.

Finally, forgiveness is often out of our power. We often find it impossible. It is usually *supplied* to us by the God who desires our joy and mourns our sorrows. It's not something we come up with but a capacity we receive. A gift, not a job. So don't beat yourself up use-lessly because you can't forgive something in your past. Of course you can't. Just ask for the gift.

AUGUST 25

He himself has made us, and we are his.
PSALM 100:2

➤⟨

*A*mericans are so conditioned to individualism that it is difficult for us to understand any other way as something other than bondage. Our right to self-determination feels absolute to us, as if there were no value higher than that of personal autonomy. Some of our favorite stories are tales of people who set out alone, followed their own hearts, and triumphed.

In my years as a port chaplain, I had a chance to observe thousands of working people from many different cultures. I visited something in excess of four thousand merchant ships from all nations. Just about every visit began in the messroom, the place where seafarers are likely to have a few minutes of leisure time and welcome a friendly visit. The windows of opportunity are the same on every ship: coffee time at ten, lunch at noon, and coffee again at three in the afternoon.

Seafarers from different countries behaved differently during meals. South American crews laughed and chatted their way through lunch. Korean lunches were uproarious affairs, utterly unlike the silent inscrutability Americans attribute to all Asians. A buzz of chatter, interrupted by frequent laughter, in the Filipino messrooms. And you can just imagine the Greeks. The Germans, too, and the British, even the taciturn Swedes: anything but taciturn during a break in the day understood by all to be a social as well as a nutritional occasion.

I must report that American messrooms are often very different. Many times, more often than on the ships of other countries, I would see each man staring into his own plate, eating quickly and silently and then leaving. An opening gambit from me would often begin a worthwhile conversation, but the sense of isolation was sometimes profound.

It seemed to me that the other guys were better at making their fellow crew members into temporary family than our guys, and that this skill could be a real lifesaver when one was away from home. Our individualism has been a strength in some ways: in the fostering of the entrepreneur, for instance. But it can also make us very lonely people at times.

AUGUST 26

Your youth is renewed like an eagle's.
PSALM 103:5

>+<

The late afternoon and evening is hard. Times when I've been working hard and have accomplished a little something—like right now—I feel like I should have a reward. Just a few weeks ago, that would have meant wandering into the kitchen and fixing myself a snack. I would have made sure I was unobserved. I probably would have hidden the box or can, if there was one, deep in the trash can and cleaned up after myself, so that my husband wouldn't know that I had eaten. And I didn't think of myself as an addict. Denial, as they say, is not a river in Egypt.

Just writing these few lines that describe the way I lived my life then makes me feel better. That behavior was as dysfunctional as any secret drinker's ever was. To think that I am no longer living that way is an amazement and a great gift. I feel like the man who wrote "Amazing Grace": *I once was lost, but now am found, was blind, but now I see.*

Interesting: I lived like that for years. Its effects were obvious—all you had to do was look at me to know I had a problem. And yet I was a spiritual leader who enjoyed the respect of many people, and was able to be of help to many. My serious illness did not prevent my usefulness. Thank God.

And so I *have* my reward: the awareness that I have been delivered from the bondage to my appetites in which I lived for years. And that those years in which I lived in that bondage were not an utter loss.

AUGUST 27

How long, O Lord?
PSALM 13:1

✷

Rosie and Madeline don't want to go to the pool anymore. They don't want to go to the library. They're tired of all their board games. For my part, I notice myself being increasingly grouchy about the messes they make in the house. I am less eager to find exciting and educational things for them to do than I remember being in June. In the morning, they watch their *Grease* videotape for the five hundredth time; I don't even do a commercial for the National Geographic one about Tutankhamen's tomb instead. I look at the clock more often: when will their mother be home?

I think we're just tired of each other.

Madeline got her letter first: a welcome from her new teacher, on stationery with baby animal stickers in the corners. Her name tag for the first day of First Grade was enclosed. Rosie's came the next day, significantly less chatty but just as thrilling: a form letter containing the gratifying news that she has been selected for advanced reading. They read and reread the letters. They went to buy shoes and socks with their mother.

How nice when leisure ends just as one is getting sick and tired of it. This usually happens for children, in America at least. It is much less common for American adults; we return to the stepped-up post–Labor Day pace wishing it could have been postponed a bit longer. Did you know that the typical German annual leave is six weeks long? I'm really not trying to make you feel worse than you already do about going back to work after your two weeks off—I just want the record to show that there are productive industrialized countries in which the benefit of a holiday is better understood than it is here.

All Rosie and Madeline can talk about is school. The soles of their new shoes are brand-new and unscratched. They are rested and ready. It is time to begin. God bless their eagerness.

God bless those, too, who are discouraged already, before they have ever begun. God bless those who needed more time off from work than they got, and those who need work so badly they're dreaming about it at night. If only it could always be true: if only the world were always ready for us when we are ready for the world.

He turned their waters into blood and caused their fish to die. . . . Egypt was glad of their going, because they were afraid of them.

PSALM 105:29, 38

>‹

I don't know what previous generations had in the way of mental pictures when they thought of the ten plagues it took finally to convince Pharaoh to let the Hebrews go, but I can't help but see Cecil B. DeMille's *The Ten Commandments* in my mind's eye. Great flick. I remember the Egyptian women recoiling from the blood in which they suddenly found themselves bathing, the great sound of the waters rushing back to form a pair of enormous watery walls, the Hebrews walking neatly between them on dry land. Cool. That film has set the standard for miracles, as far as most people are concerned: big, impressive, in glorious living color and accompanied by a magnificent sweeping soundtrack.

But a miracle is really both more and less than that. It can be a lot quieter. And its purpose is not just to show off the divine command of special effects. It is much more important than that: a miracle is a sign of God's presence in human history.

Blood coming out of our faucets and the sea rolling back on its haunches would be highly unusual events if they happened today, but they probably would not convince most of us one way or another about God's presence in our lives. The miracles to which modern folk would respond would be about other things besides the inversion of natural processes. Our needs are different. The Hebrews needed to get out of Egypt, and the strange event that helped them accomplish that was their miracle. What is it that *we* need? In our longing we can find the shape of miracle for our time.

They grumbled in their tents.

PSALM 106:25

➤✦

I tried to get on the World Wide Web for the third time today. My parish has a "page" on the Web, don't you know, with my sermons on it and everything, and I've never even seen it because I don't know how to get on the thing. Everything was going along well for a while, but then a message came on my computer screen—something about my needing to upgrade. There followed a tense half hour in which I attempted to understand what I was being asked to do and failed repeatedly—too much gobbledygook. All over the world, people are downloading and upgrading and God knows what else, like it was a walk on the beach, and I'm sitting here not sure what those things mean and why someone would want to do them. I signed off in a sour mood, after firing off a whiny e-mail message to my two computer genius friends who had suggested I try to get on the Web in the first place.

Of course, there was a time when I felt this way about e-mail, and now I use it a great deal. And there was a time before that when I felt that way about computers, and now I spend as much time with my computer as I do with my husband. So we can get used to things. I just hate it because I can't figure these things out myself, like any self-respecting seventh-grader can. Some patient soul needs to walk me slowly through it.

Not knowing things other people know puts me in a bad mood. I feel ashamed of my ignorance. My focus narrows immediately to encompass only that thing I cannot do; never mind the many things I can. My patience is practically nonexistent in this circumstance. I am struck by the contrast between my lack of patience and the incredible patience so many mentally retarded people display. Many things are incomprehensible to them, but they keep right on trying, over and over again. They don't beat themselves up. They just try. That's impressive.

When my kids were little, we used to play softball every Sunday afternoon with a group of emotionally disturbed adolescent boys at a nearby group home. Their disabilities were various: some were autistic, some schizophrenic, some mentally retarded. One retarded teenager told me about his new job: he worked as a janitor. *That's good,* I said, and he answered *Yeah. I can do it!* What volumes of frustrated attempts at things he could *not* do lay behind those happy words. And yet that boy was wiser about his achievement than I am about mine: willing to take pride and pleasure in what he could do, rather than remain defined by what he could not.

AUGUST 30

He brought them to the harbor they were bound for.
PSALM 107:30

➤✦

Sometimes terrible things happen on ships. Dickensian things: sometimes the seafarers don't get paid. Sometimes they don't get fed. A year or two ago a captain murdered some stowaways.

But what's really remarkable about life at sea is not these terrible things, but the fact that they are as rare as they are. For the most part, the enterprise works with amazing ease and efficiency: a group of people who are strangers to each other, who come from many different cultures, who don't speak the same language, steer an enormous and expensive piece of machinery laden with valuable cargo across a dangerous ocean, and they usually get it where it's going on time and intact, without injury to ship or crew. They are very good at what they do.

I think of how hard it seems to be for different cultures to live in peace on shore. Why can't we be more like the seafarers? I think of the way they care for each other, of how conscious they are of their dependence upon one another. Death can come suddenly at sea, and everyone on board knows it. They form fast friendships with ship-mates; the friendships last for years. They are not angels: there is not racism on board sometimes. Sometimes it is virulent. Usually, though, it is not; usually, there is mutual respect, if not intimacy. These quarters are too close for enmity.

They are crowded and in danger, and so they behave themselves. But we are crowded, too, and we are also in danger. We also live too close together not to trust each other. We, too, cannot escape contact with people unlike us. We, too, depend on one another for safety. Our lives are more like theirs than it seems. Maybe our response to our lives can be more like theirs as well.

AUGUST 31

He loved cursing, let it come upon him; he took no delight in blessing,
let it depart from him.
PSALM 109:16

✦

What goes around, comes around, people say knowingly when someone who has hurt others is himself hurt. There's a symmetry to that idea that attracts us: we want things to come out right in the end, for an auditor with more authority than we have to step in and even the score. And, even more than we want the negatives in the lives of those who have hurt us addressed, we want our own goodness rewarded, to wear it like a talisman against the pain of life.

Anyone over the age of five will have noticed that things usually don't work out nearly so neatly. Some actions do carry their consequences very close behind them, but there is no guarantee of punishment commensurate with sin or prosperity commensurate with virtue in this life. No sure curses and no sure blessings. We must look deeper than that easy calculus for reasons to live a moral life.

What it comes down to is this: the only reason to live humanely is that you want to live that way. You could probably live selfishly and get away with it; millions do. The primary reason for living a life of service to others instead is simply that you like that life. You desire a spiritual dimension in your life. You do not wish to be alone. You want to love and be loved. You want to explore the mystery of the world's meaning, and you are willing not to make yourself and your prosperity the measure of all things. This life is not lived in the expectation of some external reward. It is its own reward.

SEPTEMBER 1

The Lord has sworn and he will not recant.
PSALM 110:4

➜➜

*T*he idea that God doesn't change is a powerful one for a lot of people. Change is such an enemy, giving daily evidence as it does for our own inexorable walk toward death. So God as the Unmoved Mover holds a certain attraction for some of us: here, at least, there is not diminution.

Yet there are many places in scripture in which the divine mind appears to change, in which God repents, or takes pity and changes plans. *Behold, I am doing a new thing,* God tells the prophet, and who are we to disagree?

New to *us,* these new things of God: our history itself is unknown to us when it is future, and only partially understood even when it is past. In the eternal present of the life that is larger than the one that constrains us, though, where everything is what has ever been and ever will be, all change is included. It is not a museum. God is not a mannequin. That life is, above all, a *life*: it moves, breathes, feels, loves. It contains all other living and breathing and feeling and loving. All that is in our now, all that was in our past, all that ever shall be.

Does God change? Yes. God *is* change. Visible from where we sit, it is diminution, alteration that paves the way for the great change we all fear because we cannot help but think it the end. But it is not the end. It is a whole new beginning.

SEPTEMBER 2

As the eyes of servants look to the hand of their masters, and the eyes of a maid to the hand of her mistress.

PSALM 123:2

✣

Most Americans are a paycheck away from real trouble. No cushion, no reserve: they don't work and it won't be long at all before they don't eat. Despite all the smiles on Wall Street, most people don't feel secure. They feel endangered. Retail was almost flat last Christmas: people were afraid to part with too much money. The downsizing fad among corporations shows no sign of abating, even though certain pundits have dared to wonder if it is entirely a good thing. People work at their desks in the knowledge that their employers are wishing there were a way to eliminate their jobs. Often, a way is found: with a month or two of outplacement help or with only carfare home, the worker is gone.

What is the economy for? Is my only economic duty really to myself? Obligation to others is decidedly unfashionable these days: those who wish to keep everything for themselves will tell you that helping others is really hurting them, that it fosters indolence and dependence, as if there were no middle ground between a hand up and the total welfare state.

The servants of biblical times lived in a system that no longer exists. Of course it was unjust: there was no opportunity to leave the class into which you had been born. But it did have a place for everyone. Ours is different: you're free to make your own place, but the sense of human interdependence that has been a part of life since civilization began is damaged. The world will be different without it. I predict that some among us will want it back enough to create it again, and that they will not come from the ranks of those who have designed the lonely self-sufficiency of the present age.

This is my comfort in my trouble.
PSALM 119:50

✦

*F*or the Labor Day picnic, everyone in the community who can brings something to share. The noncooks show up with potato chips and soda. Evadne has roasted a chicken with wonderful herbs. Sompit is from Thailand; she and her husband Walter have brought Thai-style chicken to cook on the grill. There are fabulous salads, including something amazing—involving salsa—from Delores, and my own contribution to the feast, my mother's potato salad: now served daily, stripped of all its fat calories, at the salad bar in heaven.

Work means different things to the different people here. The children are trying not to appear excited about their imminent return to school. The unemployed will return after Labor Day to more of the same: longing for a reason to feel as exhausted as they do. Others are uncertain of their future: downsizings rumored or announced. A college student is thinking of extending her undergraduate years: *No jobs out there anyway,* she says, *and besides, I really don't know what I want to do.* She sounds dispirited. Several elderly women sit together in the shade; they worked harder in their day than most of the younger ones can imagine. They hear the malaise in the talk of the others. It is hard for them to believe that there are situations in which a willingness to work hard is not enough.

We celebrate the importance of work today, and our love for each other, which we gather around ourselves like a soft garment. It protects us against the insults and disappointments of trying to make it in a hard world. We enjoy the day. Our problems will still be here tomorrow.

MY MOM'S POTATO SALAD

10 pounds potatoes	8–10 stalks celery
1 bay leaf	3 cups mayonnaise
8–10 eggs	$^1/_2$ cup milk
2 large red onions	salt and pepper

Boil potatoes in their jackets with bay leaf until tender—about 25 minutes, or until a fork inserted into center goes in easily. Cool in colander; skins come right off like magic. Hard-boil eggs (12 minutes), then plunge them into cold water so the shells will come off easily. Wash and chop onions and celery, cut potatoes into pieces, peel and chop eggs, and combine all in large bowl. Mix mayonnaise and milk and pour over salad by degrees, until it is the consistency you like. Salt and pepper to taste. Serves 20–25.

The mayonnaise and eggs used in heaven don't contain saturated fat. Ours do, though, so you might want to think about omitting or reducing the number of eggs and using soy mayonnaise instead of the kind made with eggs. Not the same as my mom's, but not bad, either.

SEPTEMBER 4

He makes the woman of a childless house to be a joyful mother of children.
PSALM 113:8

➤✦

Now that the baby boomers are finally having their very late children, marketing is all about babies, as it has been all about whatever the boomers were into ever since businesses realized that their numbers and buying power couldn't be matched anywhere else in the population. Sexy male models with no shirts on, who smoldered at us in the eighties from the midst of suggestively rumpled designer bedsheets, now tote naked babies instead. The gadgets for a well-supplied infancy have multiplied stupendously: six or seven different kinds of seats for various sitting venues, special ergonomic baby bottles, intricate odor-eliminating disposal units for paper diapers, elaborate sets of expensive nursery furniture in every style from country French to sleek industrial.

Childlessness has always been a special sadness for those who yearn to be parents. It underlines aloneness. Many more people live alone today than ever before in human history, so aloneness is not the anomaly it once was. Women don't have to explain their childlessness to strangers as much as they used to, but the questions of well-meaning friends and hopeful in-laws are still hard to take. Of course, life is full and rich for those who will make it so, no matter what their station. But part of what makes it so is the opportunity to nurture. Everyone needs to help something grow. This is a deep spiritual need; the soul is cramped if it can't happen.

So the baby boomers multiply and the cash registers ring. People who aren't parents aren't in the market for ergonomic baby bottles. But they can—and, for their souls' health, they must—find a way of nurturing something that will endure beyond their own lives.

*Who turned the hard rock into a pool of water and flint-stone
into a flowing spring.*
PSALM 114:8

✧

There are enormous pockets of pain in many people's souls that they
don't even know are there. Other people may know, of course. It may
be very obvious to anyone with eyes: life-threatening obesity, for
instance, or a destructive relationship. They may try to bring it up and
be rebuffed. *Everyone thinks I should leave him,* a woman tells me. *But
I'm okay. It's just not a big deal. He's not always like that.* But she has
physical symptoms related to stress. She has been hit hard enough to
leave a mark, more than once. She is *not* okay. Still, the fear of the
unknown is a powerful thing. She doesn't know how to live in a way
other than the way she's been living. So she does not allow herself to
feel her own pain.

I know you think I shall be unhappy about my weight, my friend says,
although I have not said so. *But honestly, I'm not. I just like to eat. It
really doesn't bother me.* But she eats alone in her apartment every night.
She has a hard time resisting food, and feels terribly deprived when she
does. She can't say no to it and retain her serenity. She is serene only
when she is full, and then only for a while. She really thinks that her
weight doesn't bother her. She has been heavy all her life. She does
not believe her situation can change, and so she cannot allow herself
to know how much it really hurts her.

This makes all the sense in the world: if you can't change things,
why make yourself miserable?

But what if you can? Then it is only coming to terms with how bad
it is that can get you started on whatever it is that needs to happen to

change it. The odd thing is, there is a tremendous feeling of well-being after the pain of that discovery. *I have really felt terrible about this all along, and hopeless, and I didn't even know it. And now that I see myself more clearly, I feel known and loved. This is really the person I have always been. The me that was always "okay" was really a shell in which I lived. Now it is breaking apart, and my soul is freer.* A hard rock is becoming a pool. A stone will be a spring.

SEPTEMBER 6

Both small and great together.
PSALM 115:13

➤✦

When actor Christopher Reeve was paralyzed from the neck down in a riding accident, people followed his progress on the news every day. Sometime after the accident he gave an interview. The contrast between his former athletic self and his current condition was shocking; even the interviewer was moved. But Reeve was graceful and brave. He was applying all of his wit and energy to the tremendous adjustment demanded of him.

Interestingly, some people sent him money. Christopher Reeve already had plenty of money. His spokesperson made sure the press understood that he wasn't using these donations to pay his medical bills, that they were being put into a special fund. I imagine they'll go to spinal cord research or to a hospital specializing in the care of these injuries.

Odd, isn't it, to send a rich person money? Spinal cord injury is devastatingly frequent among young people, especially young men:

guys like sports and they like to drive, and both can be dangerous. Most of these paralyzed young people aren't rich. Most of them will live with their terrible situation in much more humble circumstances. People don't send them money.

Certainly Reeve has more resources with which to cope with his condition than most other people similarly injured. But that will not remove him from their fellowship. He will still have much more in common with the poorest of them than he has now with rich people who are able-bodied. He has joined a fellowship radical and heartless in its equality.

We bring nothing into this world and we take nothing out. Our relative prosperity, or its lack, hides our ultimate pennilessness from us for a while, but we all understand it sooner or later.

SEPTEMBER 7

I believed, even when I said, "I have been brought very low."
PSALM 116:9

➤⃟

$\mathcal{P}$eople who are not religious believers often want to know what good it does to be one. This is after it's been established that faith in God doesn't cancel all your credit card debt, get rid of that cellulite, and make everything in this world go your way. *So if bad things are going to happen to you anyway, what's the point?* is a frequent and very sincere question. It comes of some bygone adult—one who didn't plan ahead—telling a child that God would always reward him if he behaved himself. Rather like Santa Claus. Things like that stick with a person.

So what *is* the point? Take away the affable genie who grants your every wish and what is left of God? Is belief a reasonable course?

Faith is just as much about me as it is about God. Since there is hardly anything in the way of hard data upon which to make a scientific judgment about what God is, it's really all in my court. It is actually a choice, a decision to orient myself in a certain way.

But because I can't weigh and measure God, does that mean that faith is *all* me? Me and my imagination? Oddly, no. Once you begin to walk that road, you begin to notice things you didn't see before. New rooms appear in a house you thought you knew pretty well. You begin to understand that the very decision you made to look for these things was, itself, a gift. There is, and has always been, another voice in your life that you now hear more clearly. These things can only be seen from the perspective of that walk; if you're not on it, it looks pretty silly.

Think of a couple you know whose attraction for each other makes no sense to you. *What the heck does she see in him?* you wonder. You may never know. But they do. They're on the walk, and their knowing is different from yours.

We do many things that don't "make sense." Most important loves don't make sense, and they certainly don't keep trouble at bay. They complete us, though, giving us other voices in our lives besides our own. This love is like those, except that it contains them all and abides when they fall silent. As all of them eventually will.

Hallelujah!
PSALM 117:2

✦

On Sunday nights when I was a girl, the Grange Hall in my little town rented out its second floor to a Pentecostal group that didn't have its own church building. My best friend and I sometimes wandered over there on a summer Sunday evening—not to attend the prayer meeting, but to eavesdrop on it from below the open window around the back. We would station ourselves on the ground beneath the window as the long rays of the evening sun slanted across the grass and wait for them to begin upstairs. Soon the singing would start: fast, rhythmic songs, nothing like the hymns we sang at the little Episcopal church. There was no organ; they accompanied themselves by clapping their hands, another thing we never did at Christ Church.

We would look at each other and grin when the clapping started. By the time people upstairs began to shout *Hallelujah!* we were red with suppressed laughter. The preacher would thunder along for an hour or so, his sermon peppered with the *Hallelujahs!* and *Amens!* of his flock. The two little girls on the grass below listened and laughed until it began to get dark and we remembered that our mothers would be wondering where we were.

Sitting on the grass, laughing at the worshippers, we were aware of a certain guiltiness in our pleasure. We would have died on the spot if anybody from the prayer group had seen or heard us. When we returned home on these Sunday evenings, we did not tell our families where we had been. Mine would not have approved. Neither would the rector of my church, had he known what we were about. And, in my heart of hearts, neither did I; I knew enough to know that I would have been ashamed of myself had I been apprehended.

I had the right to prefer our way of doing things over another way. But it was unnecessary to ridicule the experience of others. Not my finest hour.

SEPTEMBER 9

I shall not die, but live.

PSALM 118:17

✦✦

*L*ike so many other people's mothers, mine was an invalid for some years before she died. As her body weakened, her hospitalizations became more and more frequent. Many times she came near to the door of death; each time, her skillful doctor plucked her from it in the nick of time. She would rest and mend, get strong enough to come home. Each time was like a miracle: through the door of their little house she would come slowly, seeing again the curtains and the wallpaper and the furniture, entering her kitchen again, touching the stove. It was all still there.

Until the next frightening, middle-of-the-night run to the emergency room. The day she left for the hospital for the last time, she looked around her living room and began to cry. Knowing, in the way people often seem to know, that this would be her last look at her little world, she crept sadly out to the waiting car, leaning on my father's arm.

Years later, when my father grew frail, and endured similar frequent hospitalizations, he, too, had that miraculous feeling about his homecomings. After one grave crisis, one that kept him between this world and the next for weeks, he rode slowly and joyfully home with my stepmother at the wheel. Into their own street they turned, and there in their yard were all the neighbors, waiting for the first glimpse of the car. When he saw them all standing there in the bright morning sunshine, he wept. He had thought never to see those dear faces again. But eventually he, too, left his home for the last time, certain enough of what lay ahead to give instructions against the use of the ventilator that had saved his life before.

I'm going to go on home now, his wife told him with a kiss, *I'll be back later this afternoon.*

And I shall be going to my real home subsequently, he said. And it was not long before he did. To be granted life when it seems about to be snatched from us: a miracle. To face the day when that does not happen with acceptance, sorrowful though it may be: a miracle of a different sort.

SEPTEMBER 10

I myself will waken the dawn.
PSALM 108:2

➤❮

*M*y preferred awakening time is very, very early: anytime after five. I love the quiet house, the hushed street outside. I make a pot of tea and say Morning Prayer all by myself. *Lord, open my lips* is how it starts: those are intended to be the first words out of the mouths of the faithful after the night's long silence. In New York City, the sisters of the Community of the Holy Spirit, whose cross I wear around my neck, are saying the same words in their convent on 113th Street. In Australia, my dear Brother Justus is saying them, only it's already tomorrow there, instead of today. Rhoda in Rhode Island is saying them, and Liz in Boston. The Bishop of New York is saying them, and so is the retired Bishop of Kentucky. It goes on in its dependable, sweet way, through prayers and psalms and Bible readings, until at last it is over: *Let us bless the Lord,* the prayerbook invites us, each in our quiet home, and we each answer *Thanks be to God.* I turn on my computer and log on to my online scripture study group, a hundred or so people who are reading the same words I am reading every day. I jot down a note or two about what the reading said to me this morning and send it off. I read their notes about the readings of the day before. I love those people—some of them I know personally, but many of them I've never met and will never meet. It is like saying Morning Prayer together, the way we used to do in seminary.

By now, the trucks are roaring past on their way to the city. I turn to my word-processing program and settle down to work. I listen to the news. The phone rings; soon my granddaughters will be over and I will take them to school. I hope for a productive day, and a peaceful one. My days are always better when they begin this way.

SEPTEMBER 11

Those who have a haughty look and a proud heart.
PSALM 101:5

❖

This is Fashion Week in New York. Designers think up imaginative places in which to show their spring collections: warehouses, libraries, tents set up on closed-off cobblestone streets. An enormous tent goes up in Bryant Park. Important people attend important parties before and after all the shows, and the parties are reviewed as seriously as the collections.

This year, I understand, all the designers have decided not to use the supermodels. The supermodels are impossibly thin young women, so instantly recognizable that the press usually saves ink by referring to them by their first names alone: Kate, Claudia, Elle, Iman (actually, I think Iman only *has* a first name). Ordinarily the same six or seven girls do all the shows, dashing by limousine from one to the other and collecting hundreds of thousands of dollars each day. This year, though, everyone wants unknowns, or at least little-knowns.

I notice, too, that a few models in a few pictures are actually smiling. This, too, is new: ordinarily, the preferred expression is a bored pout or a grim, straight mouth, which must be difficult to summon to your face if you know somebody's going to hand you five hundred thousand dollars at the end of the show.

I bear Kate and Iman and the rest of the supermodels no ill will. They have enough money to do absolutely nothing for the rest of their lives and still live comfortably, so I don't feel sorry for them, either. I think it would be fun, though, for beautiful young women to smile as if they enjoyed their beautiful clothes and their beautiful selves for what they are and no more. Fashion is fun. It is sometimes beautiful. It is art that everyone enjoys. It needs a lot less reverence and intensity, though, to make sense.

SEPTEMBER 12

Sing praises with all your skill.
PSALM 47:7

✦

*T*ed expertly shuffled the cards. He bent the deck in a certain way, so that the cards fell down upon one another with the precision of a machine. He dealt them just as quickly and surely, and held his in a perfect fan. When my turn came, I tried to bend the deck and let the cards drop as Ted had done. Cards shot all over the room. It looked so easy when Ted did it, I thought, hating him as I scrambled around on the floor, picking up cards.

We were in the first grade. How Ted had gotten to be such a card-shark at such a young age, I can't say. I do remember the sting of my own jealousy, though, how hard it was for me to yield leadership in anything to someone else. *I should be the best at this,* I thought. It killed me that somebody else was.

I was so much older than six before I understood that I couldn't be the star every time that it's embarrassing to report it here. It certainly made it easy to get a handle on what original sin means, though, when I began to study theology. Original sin is the tendency in human beings to make ourselves into our own gods. To worship ourselves. I recognized myself immediately.

Of course, nothing is more annoying than false humility. You're good at the things you're good at, and you don't get brownie points by pretending you don't know what they are. Or that it doesn't feel good to have them acknowledged now and then. But to allow your skills to flower without letting your performance become a power-hungry tap dance of desperate attention-seeking: that praises the God who endowed you with them.

How shall a young man cleanse his way?

PSALM 119:9

✢

*I*t is well known that many adolescents lose their virginity at an early age these days. This phenomenon seems frighteningly new to many people, although it is not: many people in previous centuries were sexually active long before the age of fifteen, and many girls were married long before that age.

What is different now, though, is that modern childhood has been extended far beyond its former limits. A twenty-year-old was considered an adult a hundred years ago; most of us today would think of that person as still an adolescent. Dependence upon parents lasts much longer nowadays than it used to. The independence that sexual maturity confers upon a person doesn't go with the social situation in which young adults continue for a decade or more after its onset.

So lots of young people get started with sex long before it makes any sense to do so, long before they have become accustomed to weighing life's choices for themselves, as an adult must. Eventually, most of them grow into social and moral maturity at a level more consonant with their physical adulthood. By then, though, they may already have gone down some paths whose steps they cannot now retrace. Some of them look back on their earlier excesses with wonder—*Was that really me?*—and real regret.

But I have noticed that most young people transit fairly easily into a new chastity that fits their situations—and that this is true even if they have been markedly casual in their sexual lives. You can't get your virginity back just because you've figured out that you matter enough not to have to go to bed with someone you don't love. But you can act on that insight now—and my observation is that most of them do. It is not too late for them, as it is never too late for any of us to move toward wholeness.

SEPTEMBER 14

How hateful it is that I must lodge in Meshech!
PSALM 120:5

➜←

Meshech was in what is now Turkey. Probably, nobody the psalmist knew had ever gone there. Think of it as Siberia—or, if you are a New Yorker, think of it as New Jersey. But we are not really talking about geography. We are talking about isolation.

It is a cruel feeling to be out of the loop. Someone important to you doesn't consider you important enough to be included in the common life of the community you both share. You find out about things after they've happened. A sense of foreboding as well as injury fills you, especially if the person forgetting all about you is your boss and the communities from which you are being excluded are meetings you would have attended in former days. *I'm on my way to being canned,* you think, and you just may be onto something. Or if the person who seems to be living his life as if you weren't there is your spouse. *We're in trouble,* you think, and you're absolutely right.

What do you do when you find yourself in Meshech? The impulse when you're being isolated is to isolate yourself more: *Okay, fine—I know when I'm not wanted.* But this is dangerous. You will not be allowed simply to take up space while your community's life flows on all around you. If you do not fight for your place, you will be forced out. Or you will be physically left behind. And your aggrieved isolation will not feed your wounded soul: the remedy for aloneness is not more aloneness.

So you have to bring whatever it is that's making people leave you out into the clear light of day. Go to your boss and find out why it's happening. You may get an answer you don't like, but it is always better to know the truth, while you can still plan for it, than it is to be unpleasantly surprised. And if it's your spouse, or your friend, the same: you're not feeling this isolation because everything's hunky-dory, and the reality of your life together may be painful to hear. You may be able to save the relationship and you may not. There are very few guarantees in life, but here is something like one: if you don't move forward, you move backward.

SEPTEMBER 15

He who watches over you will not fall asleep.
PSALM 121:3
➤✦

When I was little, I used to make my mother lie down with me as I was going to sleep. *Make* her? Yes, using the power children instinctively understand, that of being so irritating their parents yield in self-defense. *Stay for a hundred minutes,* I would beg; a hundred minutes seemed safely infinite. Poor thing: my mom was frail when I was little, and tired after a long day. Often she would stretch out beside me and fall sound asleep herself.

If she was needed downstairs and couldn't stay for a hundred minutes, I was ungracious. I didn't want to be in my room in the dark; the furniture looked larger and vaguely threatening. Closed doors seemed ominous. The clink of plates being washed, the hum of voices from downstairs spoke a world of light and safety—upstairs in the dark, though, anything could happen. Something might be under the bed: I was careful not to allow a hand or foot to dangle temptingly over the edge of the mattress. *King Kong* had been shown on television for the first time, and I had seen it: the face of the great ape appearing outside the window as the people inside went about their business unawares. I dreamed of this, and avoided looking at my bedroom window.

It was during those nights, the nights when there were not a hundred minutes to spare and I was alone, that I first began to pray. I used "Now I lay me down to sleep" because that was the one I knew. I strung a long list of *God blesses* out after the little poem: my parents, my brothers, my grandmothers, my pets, the family car. I prayed that King Kong would not come to our house. And he did not.

SEPTEMBER 16

Pray for the peace of Jerusalem.
PSALM 122:6

✦

When Prime Minister Yitzhak Rabin was gunned down after a rally in support of the Israeli-Palestinian peace process, people were stunned to learn that his assassin was Jewish. Even his security men were unprepared for this, fatally so: they were so focused on keeping a sharp eye out for suspicious people who seemed to be Arabs that the young man in a yarmulke was allowed to come within a few easy feet of his target.

People wondered if that event would put an end to the long and painstaking journey toward peace in Israel. It was all the more sobering that this murder was the murder of a Jew by another Jew: how could peace ever come if Israelis themselves did not support it wholeheartedly?

I think the peace project will not derail. The fanatic's terrible projects do not have the outcome he desires: moderate people on both sides of any polarized issue recoil from radical violence, and they get very disgusted very quickly when the killing starts. The assassin's own mother called him a traitor.

But everyone who is party to the process will have to realize, as all human beings must realize, that there is no peace without compromise. Peace means that I will not get everything I am fighting for. If I did, that would not be peace; it would be my dictatorship, the conquering of my enemy. Nobody over the age of two thinks he's going to get his own way every time. Dress it up in fancy patriotic clothing if you like—but it's the uncompromising voice of the two-year-old that we hear in diplomatic failures around the world.

SEPTEMBER 17

We have escaped like a bird from the snare of the fowler;
the snare is broken, and we have escaped.
PSALM 124:7

➤❖

*M*y fast is going well. I have not eaten solid food for a month now, except for the bread of the Eucharist—more like fishfood than bread, really, so it's not what you'd call a taste treat. The man at the Italian restaurant around the corner, who is a Muslim, thinks

I'm doing this for religious reasons; every time I take someone there for dinner, he smiles broadly and tells me about his observance of Ramadan. I take people to dinner all the time; we sit down and they order and consume something delectable while I drink mineral water with a twist of lemon. I swear to you that this is not painful—and that's a miracle. I drink five little packets a day of a nutritional powder mixed with water; the mixture supplies me with every vitamin and mineral known to be necessary to human life and contains roughly the calories in two good-sized apples. I may look different already; I'm not sure.

But I certainly feel different. I feel as if I had been in prison and have been set free. I have lied to myself for years about how full of shame I was about my weight, and now I'm not doing that. I have felt hopeless and bitter, and I have lied, telling people that I don't mind the way my body is, that the reason I overeat is that I have this tremendous zest for life. Now I am different. I'll talk about it to anyone who will listen; I believe that my family and friends are beginning to be bored with me, and I don't care.

To come to the end of a lifelong lie makes an impression on a person. She is to be pardoned if she's making rather a big thing of it. Bear with me.

*Those who trust in the Lord are like Mount Zion, which cannot
be moved, but stands fast for ever.*

PSALM 125:1

➹❁

*M*ount Zion is one of the hills upon which Jerusalem stands. The
whole city came to be called Zion after a while—kind of a nickname.
Mountains figure prominently in religious story and symbol: Moses
received the tablets of the law on one and Jacob wrestled with the
angel on another. A collection of ethical sayings of Jesus were pulled
together by early Christian writers as if they were one speech, the
chapters in the gospel according to Matthew now called the Sermon
on the Mount. And it's not only good things that happen on mountains in the Bible: the crucifixion occurred on the hill ominously
called Golgotha, "the place of the skull."

The power of mountains inspires awe in all human beings: great
peaks of earth and rock, pulled up mightily from the face of the earth,
so high that snow caps them, even when the weather is warm down
below. Whatever made them comes to mind when we see them.
Nobody could see the Rockies and not believe in God, a friend who lived in
Denver told me once. Actually, many people *have* managed to do that,
but I do know what she meant. They certainly put a person who happens to be disposed that way in a prayerful frame of mind.

Enormous and unmoving, mountains. At least, they seem that way.
But the fact is that even the mountains are not impervious to the rav-
ages of time. Older mountains are rounder than newer ones, for
instance; a few million years of wind erosion takes its toll, even at sixty
thousand feet. Sometimes half a mountain just slides off down its own
slope, prompted by the tremors of the earth below the surface.

To derive one's spirituality from nature does not insure permanence. It embraces change. The vicissitudes of human life have their counterparts in the life of a tree, a river, even a mountain. Nothing here on the earth lasts forever. Enjoy it while you can.

·

SEPTEMBER 19

When the Lord restored the fortunes of Zion, then were we like those who dream.

PSALM 126:1

❧❦

*I*t may be that this psalm was written before the Lord actually *had* brought Israel back out of exile in Babylonia—"restored the fortunes of Zion"—rather than afterward. If that is true, the use of the past tense here, speaking of a longed-for event as if it had actually occurred, is a special statement of hope and faith, as if a college freshman were to say to herself in a daydream, *When I graduated summa cum laude. . . .*

Don't get your hopes up, people will tell you, *and then you'll never be disappointed.* Well, maybe so—but do you really want to live your life that way? In my work, I am often with people who are dying. I notice that even they cling to hope, and that their hope is crucial to their spiritual health as physical strength ebbs from them. Hope for a cure, at first—and then a different hope, for a blessed respite from a life grown too heavy to carry, hope for something beyond the existence they are leaving. Life is tough, too tough to survive without the hope that surfaces so deliciously in dreams: dreams in which the beloved dead are with us once more, dreams in which lost loves return, dreams in which lost physical health and wholeness are restored. Dreams speak hope as if it were a language.

Yeah, but then you wake up, objects the cynic, *and you feel worse.* I don't know about that—the facts of your sorrow are no more true than they were before you dreamed. Your sorrow is no greater than it was before. Hope doesn't make sorrow worse. So why not accept the comfort and courage it offers you?

SEPTEMBER 20

It is in vain that you rise so early and go to bed so late.
PSALM 127:3

➵✦

*I*t is nine-thirty at night, but the train is full of commuters. We sit in silence, most of us, staring into the middle distance while the conductor ticks off the station stops. Some are asleep: these he awakens with surprising gentleness as the train approaches their stops, so that they can gather their belongings and stumble off into the night.

There's got to be a better way, one of them says to his seatmate as he leaves, and the woman smiles ruefully and shakes her head. *See you tomorrow,* she says. *I don't know why we're bothering to go home,* he answers, and she shrugs and shakes her head again.

Six in the morning until ten at night. The children asleep when you leave and asleep again when you return. Exhausted Friday nights, when an innocent invitation to see a movie or go out to dinner feels like an act of aggression. A bitter feeling that you don't like very much as you count your shirts on Sunday night. You know that an already-short candle is being burned at both ends, and maybe in the middle as well. But you can't work less than you're working. This is what your job requires. Slack off, and pretty soon it won't be your job anymore.

Maybe that's so for you. Maybe it isn't—you are the only one who knows for sure. But this is the only life you will live in this world: it's a cinch they don't run themselves ragged this way in heaven. You read a story in the paper about a man who took his family to a tiny town in North Dakota and telecommutes. You doubt if your boss will feel as close to you in Fargo as he does here. But something has to happen to make your life livable, and you are the only person who can make it happen. For heaven's sake, take care of yourself. That's how you take care of the people you love. And aren't they why you're doing this?

SEPTEMBER 21

The plowmen plowed upon my back.
PSALM 129:3

➤❖

*T*he psalmist's lament is the ancients' equivalent of our *I feel as if I'd been run over by a truck.* Actually, I *was* run over by a truck a few years ago—well, not a truck really: it was a Toyota. But it more than sufficed.

I am fully recovered now, for the most part. But I am not myself—or, at least, I am not the same self that went for a walk on that bright spring day. She has never returned; I think she's gone for good. I am now a person who fears falling down: I descend the subway steps carefully, listening for footsteps behind me, hoping that nobody will bump me going down the stairs and knock me down. I am now someone who sometimes trembles absurdly crossing the street: what if someone doesn't see me and hits me? What if that horrid impact comes again? In a strange way, it seems likely that it will, even though I know that to be statistically quite unlikely. I now have dreams about being injured. I never used to dream about that.

I think of my new self while talking with a friend. She has spent the last two years battling a depression bad enough to put her out of work on disability. She is better, finally. *But I'm not myself,* she says, more wonderingly than sadly. *I just don't feel like the same person. I don't even like the same things. It's really weird.*

The things that happen to us in life change us permanently. We shouldn't be hard on ourselves because they do; what else can we expect? If somebody lost a leg, nobody would expect her life not to change. Our spirits change, too. It's not surprising.

But neither should our new selves be experienced purely as deficit. Some things are missing for sure, and I mourn their loss. But there are new things, good things: new respect for myself as a person who can endure a lot of pain, new sensitivity to the reality of the disabled. Those aren't deficits; they're real strengths, and I wouldn't have had them if this hadn't happened to me.

Today a plowman walking slowly up and down my back sounds like something that would feel pretty good. I must have slept crooked, or sat too long in one position yesterday: I hurt. I wouldn't mind a plow or two tiptoeing up and down my spine for an hour or so. A small plow.

For there is forgiveness with you; therefore you shall be feared.

PSALM 130:3

>‹

At first glance, this pairing of ideas makes no sense: if God is forgiving, then why should we fear him? Shouldn't we, rather, be afraid when God is *not* in a forgiving mood?

Until we stop and think a little bit about what the word "fear" might mean in this context. It means "to regard." To "fear" someone means to be in an accountable relationship; if I "fear" you in this way, I care what effect my actions have on you. I don't want to act in such a way that what I do comes between us. We are engaged with each other. We connect.

If I don't think you are forgiving by nature, I am unlikely to connect with you. I won't seek out relationship with one who I know in advance will punish me for failing. I will avoid you, so as not to find myself repeatedly in situations wherein I offend and you yell at me. We do not remain in relationship with those whose ultimate good will toward us is in question.

So people who have not understood God as forgiving sometimes look no further. They just clear out while the going's good. They don't relish tying their lives up in knots trying to please some cosmic Someone who can never be satisfied, and so they just ignore the whole God thing. Because much talk about God is not in rational terms, they can usually tell themselves that the reason they don't believe is that faith doesn't make sense, forgetting for the moment the many other things they do that don't make sense, either. I think it is often not "sense" people long for, even if they say it is. I think it is reconciling love.

But I still my soul and make it quiet, like a child upon its mother's breast.
PSALM 131:3

➤←

I can't help it, I just get upset, says my friend tightly, after she has blown up at a colleague in front of others. This happens all the time. She thinks, I guess, that people who don't publicly humiliate others can manage this because they *don't* get upset, which isn't really the case. The world is not divided into people who don't get upset and those who do. Everybody does. But why is it that some people seem able to make their souls quiet while others freak out? Can you learn to "still your soul"?

Yes, you can—but first you must really want a quiet one. Ranting and raving at people is habit-forming. It gets so it feels natural and good. It's also very intimidating to others, so ranters quite often get away with their bad behavior. They can handle the fact that nobody feels very much at ease around them because of the deference their associates learn to give their hot tempers. It may be that quiet just isn't very exciting once you've known the thrill of striking terror into people's hearts.

But if you have sometimes found yourself ranting and wish you hadn't, and you really would prefer a quiet soul, here are some concrete things you can do to get one:

1. Make allowances for your physical or mental tiredness. Things are harder to handle when we don't feel well. If you're tired or sick, be aware of it: your emotions will ambush you with ease if you don't realize that you are in a weakened state.
2. Ask yourself what is making you angry. Chances are, the quick answer will be that somebody else is doing something wrong. Okay. Now, set that aside for a moment and ask yourself what *you* are doing. You alone. And stay with that thought for a bit.

3. Now picture your soul as a miniature of you—a little person. The medieval painters imagined the soul this way, and you see a person's little soul being carried off to heaven by angels in lots of medieval paintings of death scenes. The image is not accurate—how on earth would any of us know what the soul looks like?—but it is useful. Think of this little version of your true self cuddled against your own breast. Think of its light weight over your heart. Think of it resting and being comforted there. Hold this thought for a bit— hold it for as long as you like.

And then go on about your business. You will not feel like reaming somebody out. You need never feel like doing that again if you don't want to.

SEPTEMBER 24

"This shall be my resting-place for ever."
PSALM 132:15

✢✣

I love this house. Its shingles are curling up at the edges, and the kitchen isn't laid out well, and it sure could use an exterior paint job, and my husband and I could both be a lot neater. But it is beautiful and gracious to me, comfortable. When I have been away, I walk through its rooms, seeing and smelling and feeling its wordless *welcome home.*

It is appalling, really, that I have such a snug place to live and there are other Americans who have nowhere at all. Such refreshment to come back to, warmth at the end of a day. To know that our things are just where we left them. Once, years ago, before the term "homeless" had entered our vocabulary in its current form, a woman and her two children showed up at the church without a place to live. They spent a couple of nights at our house. The little girl had fun with my younger daughter. They bounced on the bed and watched television. The boy said nothing. He was sixteen, a year older than my older daughter; I wondered what it was like for him to be a needy guest in the home of a pretty girl his own age. My heart ached for his humiliation.

The fire burns cheerfully beside me as I lie on the couch and write; the sunlight slants toward the few remaining leaves on the trees outside our window as the afternoon grows late. Years after the children and their mother stayed with us, I happened upon her at the hospital. She worked there now, and had for some years. Things had gotten better. The kids were fine, she said. It was thrilling to hear this. I think of them now. I don't remember what led to their homelessness, but I remember them. How the little girls bounced on the bed and laughed. How the boy was silent.

SEPTEMBER 25

Oh, how good and pleasant it is, when brethren live together in unity!
PSALM 133:1
✢

*A*nd how awful it is when they don't. I know so many people who don't speak to a brother or sister, who haven't for years. Something happened in 1978 and they're still mad in 1995.

Brothers and sisters are a shock to each other's systems from the moment they meet. The mother who was yours alone now has a new love. Children are greedy; sharing is something we learn, not something we're born knowing. Yes, the pleasant conspiracy of siblings in a house is part of family life, but there are often ancient rivalries that seem to take on a life of their own. When we try to explain to an outsider exactly what is behind the feud, the explanation sounds a trifle thin. It is really an alibi for old jealousies fanned to bitter new life.

At weddings and funerals the siblings stand, side by side, looking vaguely—or, sometimes, exactly—alike. The deaths of their parents leave them in charge: the power shifts to their generation, and also shifts within it. One of them sometimes becomes somehow like their mother; one sometimes becomes the patriarch. Our families are the mysterious crucible of who we are. They are never neutral to us. *I don't have much to do with my family,* someone says, and wishes it were true. Whether or not he ever sees any of them again, he has everything to do with them.

One thing that helps, I think, if family is more a source of pain than of support, is to remember that the perfectly happy family exists only in the imaginations of those whose families make them crazy. Every family has its ups and downs. Some are profoundly diseased, but there is none that is not a little so at times. And while the family is powerful, it is not the only thing that forms us. We are neither doomed nor charmed by where we originate. Besides all having a powerful past, we all have a future, too.

For the Lord has chosen Jacob for himself and Israel for his own possession.
PSALM 135:4

✣

A brief word about Jacob and Israel, for those who may not know: they are the same person. You remember Jacob, the wily son of blind Isaac, who hoodwinked his father into disinheriting his brother Esau. If you don't, look him up in the book of Genesis, chapter 27 to the end. Jacob went on to all kinds of other exploits, narrow escapes from various enemies which he accomplished by various tricks and deceptions. He is a character of very ancient folklore; the tales about him are whimsical hero myths, very like the exploits of Odysseus that the Greeks enjoyed. His name was changed to Israel after he wrestled with an angel one night, and thus he became the group noun under which the people of the land understood their emergence from a nomadic society. Jacob the wanderer becomes the patriarch of the twelve tribes.

Of greater importance than the question of whether or not Jacob was a real person, or whether all the things that happen to him in the book of Genesis really occurred, is what he reveals about the people who recorded all these stories: they understood themselves to be relatives. The descendants of one father, obligated to one another by ties of kinship. The figure of Adam is important for the same reason: whether or not we know where the Garden of Eden was, or ever find the discarded core of that fateful apple, we know from the story of Adam and Eve that the human family is one family. That we are relatives.

So there's a lot more to these old tall tales than just what happens in them. There are a number of forms of meaning, among which facticity is but one, and that not always the most important.

Who gives food to all creatures . . .
PSALM 136:25

→←

That great American irony—the fact that, while malnutrition is rampant in so many other places, it is obesity that constitutes a huge health problem here—is in my mind a lot these days. The world is not a fair place: I pay hundreds of dollars to starve my way out of a disease of abundance, sharing the same hemisphere with toddlers who pick through garbage in search of an edible scrap.

The bottom line is this: it is human avarice that perpetuates starvation. No, we don't cause the droughts in the Sudan, but we do pay people in America not to grow grain even while they're going on. We have chosen local prosperity over global survival, and it is very much a choice, not an inexorable economic necessity.

From our mother's first invocation of starving children in faraway lands, offered to shame us into eating our green beans, we have resisted the link between ourselves and the poor. We want our behavior to be our business alone. When challenged as adults about this attitude, we are apt to respond with something like *I'm not hurting anybody. There's nothing wrong with enjoying what I have.*

There certainly is no sin in enjoying ourselves. Maybe my mouthful of food doesn't hurt anybody else. But it doesn't help anybody else, either. Since when have we fulfilled our ethical destinies simply by doing nothing wrong? Are we only here to live for ourselves and not bother anybody until at last we return to the earth, a collection of dust and bone, no more uninvolved in our world in death than we were in life? There are animals more altruistic than that.

As for our harps, we hung them up.
PSALM 137:2

I often sing when I feel sad. It always lifts me up—it's probably not possible to sing and be hopeless at the same time. You may still be sad—that's what the blues are for—but expressing sorrow through song does something to it, makes it something that the soul can handle. Sorrow isn't beautiful, but the spirit's courage in owning up to it sure is.

St. Augustine said that the person who sings, prays twice. If prayer is hard for you to approach, as it is for many, you might think of song as a way into your own spiritual life instead. Who said prayer has to be little prose essays every time?

Even if I am too deep in the lassitude of despair even to open my mouth, I can always listen to someone else. I have fastened on certain symphonies at certain times, playing them over and over on the record player through lonely nights in my life, somehow feeling that something in me has been expressed in them that I could not have spoken.

I don't mean to imply that listening to a CD is praying. I only mean that sorrow blocks our emotions sometimes, numbs us so that it's hard to move sufficiently outside ourselves to do the kind of reflection on life that is the beginning of prayer. When words fail, as they sometimes fail all of us, there are other ways to pull the soul together and get in touch with what it's trying to say.

SEPTEMBER 29

Though the Lord be high, he cares for the lowly.
PSALM 138:7

The depiction of biblical scenes in many Renaissance paintings is unintentionally amusing in one small way: the clothing. The painters dressed their ancient subjects almost as they themselves dressed, rendering the flowing robes in exquisite brocades and lustrous silks, trimming them in fur, accessorizing them with gold jewelry set with gems. Thus King David appears in fifteenth-century images in a crown that looks like a European one. The Virgin Mary is smartly attired in the manner of a wealthy young Renaissance woman, reading her ornate Renaissance book in her comfortable Renaissance bedroom. It seemed impossible to depict her as she actually must have been: a simple young Jewish girl, whose modest existence attracted so little attention that it is attested only by Christian sources. Nobody outside that small community noticed her.

The idea that God favors the oppressed is an ancient one. Nobody would seriously question it. But we do not arrange our world to reflect this preference: within churches no less than without, people care a great deal about privilege and power. Many who have never experienced humiliation or oppression assume, without having given the matter much thought, that their power and privilege are directly linked to the divine favor. Sooner or later, life teaches otherwise: if my vision of God's regard for me is tied to my well-being, it is a very weak reed upon which to lean. Thus the people of ancient story—set, as they so often are, in the midst of poverty and disappointment—do not need fancy embroidery to commend them to us. They are fine just as they are.

Your eyes beheld my limbs, yet unfinished in the womb.
PSALM 139:15

Their tiny arms and legs: transparent, yet already traversed by microscopic blood vessels. Their curled-up position as they float in their primitive first sea—a position most adults still assume in sleep, at least part of the time. We see these things now, through miraculous tiny cameras: see the unborn grow, watch them kick their feet, suck their thumbs. We know all about them, it seems: whether they are healthy, whether they are boys or girls. Whether they are alone or in pairs or trios—or more. We perform delicate operations on them. The operations are successful.

This is recent. For the larger piece of human history, their world has been much more mysterious than it is now. Inches away from the mother's heart, the father's hand, just beneath the doctor's listening ear, those yet to be born have held their small secrets close. The technology that gives us such oversight of a process that used to be entirely beyond our control is an awesome thing. Like all human technologies, once introduced, it has immediately been taken for granted.

And yet I sometimes meet expectant parents who choose not to know the sex of their babies. They choose the mystery we accepted without choice. This is interesting: an acknowledgment that there is value in mystery, that allowing life to surprise you is not entirely a bad thing. A reminder that the best of plans do not fully control the mighty and minute process by which the gift of life is given.

They have sharpened their tongues like a serpent.

PSALM 140:3

➤✦

*L*ife of the party, Jim. Tall and handsome, with a quick wit and an opinion on everything. When he was still drinking, he could be so funny he was almost dangerous, given to wild practical jokes and risky stunts. He left that behind in his midforties, though, and in sobriety he calmed down considerably.

Except that Jim had a special way of talking about his wife at parties. Whatever the topic of conversation, there would be an anecdote about her ditsy ways. Something about her ineptness with the Christmas tree at the holiday. A tale about her fender bender if something automotive came up, or about her cooking mistakes if the topic were food. Jim had a way with words: he told these stories well. His wife laughed along with everybody else.

It hurt her, though. Nothing good was ever said—just these casual cruelties under cover of jokes. She was a straight-A student in a competitive graduate degree program. She was a fine mother and kept a beautiful house. She was physically beautiful and had exquisite taste. The main topic of conversation, though, was always her shortcomings. Even in private, he never told her he loved her. I guess he didn't.

Eventually she had had enough Pin the Tail on the Donkey. He was outraged when she left their marriage. Full of self-righteousness about having provided for her all those years, about commitment, about vows made at marriage.

Among the vows we make at marriage, though, is the promise to honor one another. He never struck her. He didn't have to. His words were more than sufficient to convey his regard.

Let my prayer be set forth in your sight as incense.

PSALM 141:2

✦

The children's choir is having an attack of Protestant Throat up in the balcony: coughing and sniffling because of the smoke from the incense wafting up from the sanctuary below. Adults get it, too, those who disapprove of incense: the body enlisted by the mind to protest something perceived as foreign.

The next week, nobody coughs or gasps. Most people stop after the use of incense has been explained. The sweet-smelling smoke layered in the air rises slowly toward the ceiling. It is intended to put us in mind of prayer ascending, leaving the boundaries imposed by the earth. The upward direction of smoke is less about the geographical location of heaven than about freedom from the restrictions earthly reality sets upon us. Whether or not heaven is a place somewhere in the sky is unknowable and, ultimately, unimportant. What heaven *does* matters a lot more than what or where it is.

What heaven does is broaden our experience to include the holy. Without a sense of the holy, I would be left with a life experienced as a series of events, meaningful only while I am around to see them. But the layers of human life are more than that. There is a spiritual community among human beings, more immediate and more lasting than the physical community, which depends so on being able to see and hear one another. Talk to someone who is bereaved—not a recent bereavement, but one a few years along. The relationship between him and the one who has died is far from over, even though it is no longer nourished by daily interchange.

The holy is like that. The communion of saints, in fact, that ongoing relationship we have with the beloved dead, is a piece of it very familiar to us. The prompting of conscience—not to be confused with constant fussy, self-absorbed apology—is another. The discovery of human love is another. There is a kingdom of heaven, a household of God, and here and there in life we have hints of what it is. The incense hangs in the air, sweet and mysterious, untouchable and unknowable, and it rises to heaven.

OCTOBER 3

Bring me out of prison.
PSALM 142:7

✦✦

J. C. finds himself on Rikers Island several times a year. Usually he's picked up for stealing something—an accusation he always denies. He is a crack addict, so his version of the events of his life lacks a certain sense of responsibility for his own actions. Now he has tuberculosis, and the penal system holds him longer than it used to, so that his compliance with the long course of daily medication can be assured. The disease has invaded his bones, rather than his lungs: he has a painful lesion on his spine. This is very dangerous. Although I have not said this to him, I suspect that J. C. does not have long to live. On his next birthday, he will be twenty-nine years old.

He got straight and sober once, at a drug treatment center in Harlem. Six months it lasted, but then his mentor there "went out," and before too long, J. C. followed. Another time he learned to be a plasterer in a Job Corps program. The bits and pieces of his life I have gleaned from my many talks with him are heartbreaking: a father who left the family, a mother so discouraged by her son's lies and abusive behavior that she can no longer allow him to know her address or even her telephone number—they communicate only through me. One Christmas he stole the ornaments right off their tree, to sell for money to buy crack. Once I set up a meeting between them, his mother and stepfather, his sister. J. C. didn't show. His sister cried. I tried again the next week; this time he was there and they didn't come. Bad timing.

I guess he'll be on Rikers again this Christmas. Seems to me he was there last year, too. *Will you help me get an apartment when I get out?* he asks me, and I tell him I will. He can qualify for SSI (supplemental security income) because of his disability. That same disability, of course, will get him kicked out of any apartment we're lucky enough to find. Then he'll be on the street. Before long, he'll be back on Rikers Island. He may get out of jail now and then, but this young man never gets out of prison.

OCTOBER 4

For your servants love her very rubble, and are moved to pity even for her dust.

PSALM 102:14

➤✦

I can't deal with New York anymore, a woman tells me as we sit in a traffic jam in the Bronx. I can certainly understand this. She lives right now in a midwestern city: wide, quiet streets, beautiful lakes right in town, lovely parks and waterfalls, neat houses. All the people who live there are clean and nice. New York is crowded, dirty, dangerous, neurotic, and vulgar. Abandoned cars lie, wheel-less, along our road-ways. Sirens scream at all hours of the day and night. A subway token costs $1.50 now. When I came it was thirty cents, and I know scads of people who remember the nickel fare.

But we love New York. Every crumbling cornice and homicidal cabdriver of it. Here, where you can become homeless in an afternoon, where cars chase you right up on the sidewalks in order to run you over, just going to work and coming home again can give you a real sense of achievement. There is a special feeling of triumph, of having beaten the odds, when you meet somebody you know on the street. We go into the grocery store and emerge with six eggs and two potatoes. Our refrigerators are slightly larger than doll furniture. Two people can barely fit in most of our kitchens. We store our vacuum cleaners in our bedrooms, those of us who have bedrooms. We are content with small things.

Individual life is so circumscribed that we borrow public life and live it vicariously. Our mayors are brash and we like them that way; our tabloids taunt them rudely several times each week, and they dish it right back. Two or three times a week we all hang suspended as somebody's tragedy unfolds: someone's child fights for life after a shooting, someone falls from a roof, someone's building collapses. Ghoulishness fights with human sympathy for possession of our souls.

It is a hard place to be. But I live a few streets over from where W. H. Auden lived, and down the street from where Dylan Thomas drank himself to death. Edgar Allan Poe lived near here. I know a woman who lived near Zora Neale Hurston and knew her. Alexander Hamilton died in a house a couple of blocks from here. The other day I saw Whoopie Goldberg. Interesting neighbors.

Show me the road that I must walk.

PSALM 143:8

>←

I think I'm going to take a semester off, Anna tells me. We're having dinner in our favorite restaurant. *You know, I don't know what I want to do with my life. I mean, there are things I've liked, but nothing I've studied has really captured me. It's dispiriting—I mean, I'm bright enough, and interested in a lot of things, but I'm not on fire.*

She and a lot of folk her age. Why? I'm not sure. I do know that the world greets Generation X with a yawn and an accusing list of reasons why they don't measure up to previous generations in terms of drive. And the idea that a corporation might be interested in making a long-term investment in a young career is laughable today: corporations want cheap temporary workers to whom they owe no benefits and no loyalty. I imagine that *would* be dispiriting.

My heart is in my throat. *Well, take the time off if you think it's best,* I tell her. *Work for a while and see where you are. You'll go back if you really want to.* This is a scary thing for me to say: I know a person who left college needing only one course to graduate and *never went back.* But I am right: she will finish college if she wants to, and it is the fire of wanting that she must somehow discover in herself. Wanting something enough to sacrifice for it. To delay gratification for it.

Did we, whose parenting manuals elevated self-esteem to the status of a religion, injure them by being so delighted with what they were that they are satisfied to remain there? Or did we cow them with our own drivenness? Maybe. Maybe not. We did the best we could, for reasons that made sense at the time. Other generations have had other obstacles; this malaise is theirs. And like the others, they must find their way through it.

Blessed be the Lord my rock! who trains my hands to fight.

PSALM 144:1

➤❖

It's been over a year and I still cry myself to sleep every night, the young woman says. *I miss him so much. It seemed so perfect—it* was *perfect. We were unbelievably compatible.* She sighs heavily. *I just think about him all the time. I worry about whether he's all right.*

There are times when anger is your friend. This might be one of those times, I think as she talks on. She speaks mainly of her concern for the well-being of the man who left her so abruptly. Her solicitude for him prevents her from doing what she needs to do to make herself feel better. Worrying about his well-being is a way of denying that the relationship is really over. *If I still feel responsible for him,* the soul hopes, *then he's not really gone.* The soul can be very wise, but she can also be pretty dumb. He *is* gone. She needs to focus for a while on what that loss has done to her, not on their rosy past, his unknown present, or their fantasy future. Right now, she has received injury at his hands. If she allows herself to feel that as the attack it is, she'll be mad. And her anger will energize her to defend herself, to get her life moving in a way that compassion for the man who spurned her never will.

Please don't misunderstand me: I'm not suggesting that we should all hold fifty-year grudges that never change against those who have hurt us. That's no way to live your life. I'm just saying that it can be a big mistake to rush too quickly to being nice. Even God gets angry, and we can, too. Forgiveness is not an immediate thing; it's a process. It takes some time.

The eyes of all wait upon thee, O Lord, and thou givest them their meat in due season; thou openest thine hand, and fillest all things living with plenteousness.

PSALM 145:16–17

✢

This was the grace that was sung in the refectory before every meal when I was in seminary. It's from an older version of the psalms in our old prayer book. Certain of us who liked to sing took turns leading it; the leader would sing one half of a verse and all the students and faculty would sing back the other half in answer. Every day. A small thing, that grace, but I loved it: a fixed point in lives that were preparing for a big change in a short time.

There was a lot we needed to learn in preparation for that change. Some of it we learned in that place; some we had to learn on the job. Some we have yet to learn. From the beginning, I loved that life. Fifteen years and lots of changes later, I love it even more.

Why have priests? Not every faith does. But, in those that do, what is it that an ordained person can provide for the good of the body? Can't everyone serve God by serving others? Isn't everyone called to be meditative and thoughtful? Shouldn't we all be well-educated in our traditions? Yes, yes, and yes. But spiritual leaders gather the people of God, inviting in them those gifts of service and holiness and wisdom which they received from God and which, each in her own way, they must give back. A happy life is not to be had in selfish pursuits. Now, more than ever, in a world up to its neck in the futility of trying to find happiness in self-absorption, the challenge is to call people to look for joy where true joy can be found.

The Lord opens the eyes of the blind.
PSALM 146:7

✢✢

O ne moment she was laughing, looking up at me with her china-blue eyes. The next she was wailing with pain—*My eye!*—one hand pressed to her left eye. Anna had just turned two. It had not been too long since she had even learned the word.

She had not seen the glass shelf in the store display, and had turned her head. The sharp corner sliced her eye. A clear gelatinous substance splashed down her cheek. A tiny red filament hung from the eye itself. The colored part of her eye was oddly scrambled. She looked like a broken doll. The paramedics came. One of them took a gentle look. *Oh, my God,* he said quietly. We rode in the ambulance.

So little to have such an injury. So many surgeries over the next years. It was not always an easy thing for her. *You know what's weird?* she said after her last operation. She was twenty now. *Sometimes I see out of that eye. Just for a second. Then it goes back to the way it was. Did I ever tell you that when I was little, I thought people who could see with both eyes saw two of everything? You did?* I say, and we both laugh.

Inside I am not really laughing. Why only a second or two of weird vision? Why blindness? Why did that moment twenty years ago have to happen? Why my child? And the answer: no particular reason. Things just are what they are. For my children. For your children. For all of us.

There are miracles, of course. I wouldn't mind one. Neither would you, I imagine. Maybe you've had one. Maybe I've had a few myself. A few seconds of seeing the world in a different, more complete way. Weird.

Praise him, heaven of heavens, and you waters under the heavens.

PSALM 148:4

✣

Do you get the lay of the land here? The ancients believed that there was water under the earth and also water over the sky. This made some sense: if you dig deep enough into the earth, eventually you hit water. And water comes out of the sky when it rains, so there must be some up there, too. Our earth, afloat in its watery bath, with the sky sandwiched in between.

Available water is the primary reason for refugee migration. People cannot stay where there isn't any. This was something the biblical writers understood very well: they lived in a part of the world where water was scarce and therefore precious. Springs of water, water springing from the dry rock, streams of living water—"living water" was what they called water that moved, as the water in rivers does—these water images were often part of their God-talk. Makes sense: human beings think of God primarily in terms of things we ourselves lack. We are thirsty, so God must have access to lots of water. We feel our own weakness, so God is strong. We die, so God lives forever. This is all very well, as far as it goes: God certainly *is* the opposite of human limitation and deprivation. But if we invent God as simply the remedy of all our deficits, we fashion a sort of Super Person, a Paul Bunyan figure— like us, only really big. When we do that, we miss the main thing about God as far as human beings are concerned: God's mystery. We really haven't a clue about the divine reality. Living water? You bet. But also much, much more.

For the Lord takes pleasure in his people.

PSALM 149:4

➤✦

People who don't have children sometimes wonder at the sacrifice involved in having them. When you're a mom or a dad, the majority of your energy is spent on the needs of your children rather than on your own. You learn to regard a slumber with only one interruption as a good night's sleep. Purchases for yourself come only after you've gotten what they need first. Their meals are more important than yours.

This all sounds pretty grim unless you're doing it. The truth is that doing things for your children is fun. Getting them something they want feels as if you've gotten something you wanted. And you have: the happiness of the ones who matter more to you than anything else.

It's such a change, such a reordering of priorities, and it goes on for so long, that when they're grown, many of us have to relearn what it is to consult our own desires first. It feels very odd, at first, to admire something pretty in a store and not have to weigh its purchase against their needs. They see this and are bemused by it. *Go ahead, Mom, get it,* they say, pleased no longer to be the utterly dependent first priorities they were when they were little. They begin to ask questions about your health, questions that sound like the ones a friend might ask you. Or, you think with a start, like your own mother might, if she were still alive.

The community of love and need takes turns. Love sweetens my life with the happiness of the one I love.

Praise him with resounding cymbals.
PSALM 150:5

⇥⇤

*B*uckley loved high school. He was there for a long time—I remember that he was twenty-three when I was a sophomore. I first saw him in the band, a huge round head in the percussion section. His head was like that because he had water on the brain, I was told. That was the first I'd heard of that ailment. It made Buckley walk with a pronounced limp. It made the focus of his eyes uncertain. And it scrambled his thinking.

But he loved the band. Triangle and cymbals were Buckley's instruments: I remember the great round head, dwarfing the little gold triangle he held up in front of his face, watching the conductor intently for his cue. And the crash of his cymbals, sometimes three or four in succession: a great musical moment. And a great moral moment as well: each of us contributing to the common effort as each is able. The way life is supposed to be.

He managed the band as well—Buckley had an uncanny memory for numbers. He knew everybody's homeroom and everybody's schedule within a week or two of the start of school every year. He could organize the music and keep track of the folders. He loved the responsibility of this job he could do well. Today he works in the post office, I hear. The perfect job. I imagine he's memorized every zip code in the United States by now.

To the prom, he took his cousin, a sweet, pretty girl in a pink dress. His mother drove them. My boyfriend danced with her a couple of times at Buckley's request. Pretty darned suave, I thought—not my boyfriend, I mean, but Buckley. Did he know he was brave? I am not sure. But of all the athletes and honor society members I knew, I didn't know anyone who made better use of the gifts he had been given than that injured young man.

OCTOBER 12

*Our iniquities you have set before you, and our secret sins
in the light of your countenance.*
PSALM 90:8

➤✦

I don't know why I'm so jumpy today. Could it be because I had planned to appear at an important church service and have had to cancel? That shouldn't bother me—it's not as if I were the preacher and would be missed; I was just going to *go*, for heaven's sake. I don't have the energy I used to have, and I can't keep up the schedule I used to maintain; everybody knows this, and understands perfectly when I have to say no to something I would have been able to do in days gone by. But I still feel uneasy when I have to cut things out of my schedule.

Or could it be because I can't find my husband's practically-new summer polo shirts anywhere? Attic, no; basement, no. Maybe they're in my office, although what on earth they would be doing there I couldn't tell you. I check; they're not. Matter can be neither created nor destroyed, I remind myself: I will eventually find those shirts. But I feel frantic about it, upset beyond what it's worth.

Or could it be because I forgot to put my watch on this morning and, as a result, Rosie was two minutes late to school? She didn't seem perturbed. The teacher hasn't phoned in a rebuke. There wasn't a message on my machine from the truant officer when I returned from taking her. It really doesn't matter that much. But it upsets me.

An armload of things I didn't do right—or didn't do at all. Ugh. There are days when I can't seem to see the good that is in me, days on which it is outshouted by my shortcomings. Days when I would like to rewind the video of my life and run it again, from the beginning. Or maybe just fast-forward through them and start fresh tomorrow. Days when I'm harder on myself than anyone else would ever be on me.

Here is what I will do: I'll have a little cry—nothing fancy, just a little one to clear the air—and then I will read myself the confession rite from the Book of Common Prayer. I'll put the shirts and Rosie's late arrival at school and the missed church service in there, in the blank where you can list all your sins, and offer the whole mess to God, who is much too loving a presence ever to snicker at how upset I have allowed myself to become over things that don't amount to a hill of beans. And who, after all, knows about some other things I've done that were significantly more serious than misplacing a few shirts.

OCTOBER 13

Do I not hate those, O Lord, who hate you?
PSALM 139:20

✠

Sometimes I discover that two people whom I like very much don't like each other. This is very, very uncomfortable. *I know you're friends with her,* one of them will begin, and then will go on to tell me something about my other friend that I honestly would rather not know.

Do we have to like and dislike what our friends like and dislike? Of course not. And what of the more serious situations, more serious than the matter of taste that determines a great deal of which friendships we will nurture and which we will not—those people the psalmist identifies as hating God? Do we rightly hate people who are bad?

I have a hard time saying yes to that. Do I really know the heart of another well enough to write her off completely? What about the people who have done terrible things—the Jeffrey Dahmers of the world? Many people nodded grimly when he was bludgeoned to death with a broom by another prisoner. Justice was served, they felt. But he was a human being, more than the sum of his actions, however unthinkable those actions were. Clearly society needed his incarceration, and justice demanded his punishment, but what demanded that we hate him? Such a life can only have been the product of some terrible disease. Such a man was far from being his own master.

I am uncomfortable with the idea of justifiable hate. It does several things: it forestalls any hope of healing in either party. It makes reconciliation impossible. And it provides too easy a way to avoid our own shortcomings: conspicuous villains make everyone else feel a little more virtuous, and too much confidence in your own virtue is a dangerous thing.

Take from me the way of lying.
PSALM 119:29

➤✦

Are you finished with the play yet? Q wants to know.

Not exactly, I tell him, when what I mean is *Not at all.* Truth to tell, I haven't even started it yet. This would ordinarily not be such a terrible thing, but we're supposed to present this play in a reading the day after tomorrow.

How many copies of the script will you need? he wants to know.

As many as there are actors, I tell him vaguely, and scuttle away unapprehended. *I'm not lying,* I tell myself guiltily. But I certainly wasn't telling the truth.

This happens much too often. If you can't be utterly candid about what you're doing—or, in my case, what you're *not* doing—then there must be something wrong with it in your own eyes. I don't want to own up to having bitten off about five times what I could chew in saying I would write this play. But come Friday night, when the reading is set to take place, I must either have a play in hand or a reason why I don't have one.

What will the reason be? The dog ate it? We don't have a dog. The house burned? It was stolen? No, no, and no. The solution to this self-created problem is to do what I said I would do and then think twice next time about committing myself beyond my strength. If you don't get yourself into situations you're ashamed of, then you don't have to lie your way out of them.

And if you do? As unimaginable as it sounds before you do it, the most comfortable thing is to tell the truth. People are more understanding than we think they are, and most of them also respect the honest admission of fault a lot more than the frantic—and, usually, painfully obvious—tap dance of prevarication.

The earth has brought forth her increase.
PSALM 67:6

✣

*U**m,* Madeline looks at the ceiling as she tries to remember what she did on yesterday's field trip to the pumpkin farm, *we saw them make apple cider. And they let us drink some. And we picked pumpkins from the pumpkin field. And I got to take one home to keep.*

I remember when her mother used to go to the pumpkin farm with her class. She went back this year, in fact: took the day off from work to chaperone the field trip. *It was fun,* she says, *the kids loved it.* The souvenir pumpkin sits on their living room shelf. Madeline has already moved on to other things: her birthday is coming up, and she's trying to convince her sister to tell her what we've bought her as a gift. I remember her mother's autumn birthdays, how she would wheedle me to tell her about her presents. *Just one early present?* Madeline asks hopefully, trying her luck. Her mother used to say the same thing, with just that facial expression. Twenty years ago she deliberated over frosting colors for her cake, raked leaves into piles for her guests to jump in, wrote out invitations. The autumns were birthdays, school shoes, loose teeth, visits to the pumpkin farm. I remember it all.

I wonder if Madeline's mother knows that she herself is the harvest, the rich reward for my early spring's uninformed, tentative seeding. My little bright pumpkin, all grown up. That when I see her beauty, her intelligence, her motherhood, her humor, I thank God for it. If she doesn't know that, she will—when another little girl, a girl with no name yet, comes into the family to remind her of Madeline, someday when today is long ago. *And I got to take one home to keep.*

He gave their crops to the caterpillar.

PSALM 78:46

✴

Come and look at something, Q says. He's watering things in the garden; I'm sitting at the picnic table reading. His voice sounds a little odd; I look up. His brow furrowed and his mouth straight, he's gazing at the little candlestick pine that grows at the edge of the patio.

I get up and walk over. At first I see nothing. Then he waves his watering can a few inches in front of a branch and it comes to sudden, unusual life: a hundred small green forms rear up as if governed by one brain, writhing away from the spout of the watering can, and then settle back down onto the branches, resuming their hungry sucking of the plant's lifeblood. He does it again; again they writhe up and then subside to their work.

Creepy, I say softly, and he nods. The whole tree is full of them. They weren't here yesterday. In fact, they weren't here just this morning. The caterpillars have descended upon poor Candlestick like Grant through Richmond. Now I see that half of his needles are gone. He will die before the day is out if we don't do something.

Where did they come from so fast? No wonder the ancient people thought caterpillars were a plague: these guys seemed to materialize out of thin air. They are only animals, of course. They are only doing what all living things must do: nourishing themselves in order to survive. What they are doing is not different in kind from what we do when we eat a salad or a hamburger. It seems diabolical because there are so many of them, because they act as one organism, because they arrive unannounced. But they are as much a part of nature as the tree they will destroy.

Q has gone into the house and he returns with a spray bottle in his hand. He unleashes its contents on the tree. Caterpillars fall like Lucifer from heaven. We seep them up and put them in a garbage can. Q then gives Candlestick a nice drink. We feel relieved, as if we have defended the innocent and the good from the insidious powers of the Evil One. But all we have done is choose death for some creatures and life for others, an economy older than our race.

OCTOBER 17

Lord, send us now success!
PSALM 118:25

➵➴

There is a point, during the weeks of rehearsal leading up to the production of a play, when it just doesn't look like things are going to come together. Maybe it doesn't happen to all directors, but it always happens to me: about three weeks before we open, when I'm still missing a minor character and two actors are still walking around with their scripts in their hands, I ride home on the train after rehearsal one night and think, *In three weeks, a hundred people are going to pay twelve dollars to see these guys walk around with scripts in their hands.*

In professional theater, you can fire people and yell at them about things like this, I suppose. In amateur productions, you can't do that; they require more interpersonal skill. You can never forget that the actors are giving you something you can never give back to them: their time. Your job is to help them make this joint effort wonderful, make of themselves the very best they can be, and to blend the skill levels of the thirty-year professionals and the first-time walk-ons so that the audience gets lost in the characters they create.

Some of the shows I've directed have been better than others. But all of them have been the best they could be. Nothing is ever perfect, and the circumstances life throws us are different for everything we undertake. What am I going to do, three weeks from opening night when things look bleak? Quit? No way. We just keep on keepin' on, putting one foot in front of the other, and we get there in the end.

OCTOBER 18

With long life will I satisfy him.
PSALM 91:16

✦

*M*adeline *had a hard night last night,* my daughter says when I call her to see how everybody is. *What happened?* I ask, thinking that she probably had an upset tummy or a fight with her sister. But it was nothing so easily mended: my little granddaughter had abruptly realized that someday her mother would die. Five years old, Madeline. She had been lying on the floor in front of the record player, listening to her Vivaldi record—for some reason, Madeline adores the "Autumn" portion of *The Four Seasons*—and suddenly her mother heard great sobs coming from the living room. The thought of losing her mommy was unbearable. She cried and cried, and would not be comforted. *I don't want to be a person,* she wailed, *if I have to know about it!*

I don't want to be a person because I have to know this. Yes. I know.

I told several friends about this, and they all had the same reaction: *Oh, the poor little thing,* they said, all in the same tone, half surprise and half sad recognition. We all immediately recognized humanity's central pain: *This all has to end. I won't have this forever.* In the midst of life, we are in death. We wish your innocence had not ended so soon, little girl. We, too, wish you didn't have to know this.

I notice that the central figure of this human sorrow for Madeline was her mother: it was the certainty of Mommy's death that made her weep. As harsh an introduction to the facts of life as this realization was, it stopped short of one that is still harsher: Madeline has not yet realized that she, too, will one day die. I wish you decades and decades of such ignorance, little sweet one.

I thought it striking that she was listening to music she loves when this thought came to her. Happy music, too: "Autumn" is bouncy, dancing music, intended to make you imagine jolly peasants celebrating a successful harvest. Madeline already has a lovely, clear treble singing voice, and a good ear, right on pitch—a rarity in her age group. Already I know that music will be an important way into her soul: a way to speak excitement and love. But also a way to speak sorrow, for a keen sensitivity to beauty always knows that beauty is most wonderful because it passes away. Artists know that we cannot hold on to this world forever; they know this, and they know that they must create beauty while there is still time. Already, Madeline has seen the loss that gives meaning to beauty. Yes, it's sad, but now her life begins. Already, she is an artist.

You spoke once in a vision . . .
PSALM 89:19

>+<

I saw Jesus once. I was at Girl Scout camp and dreamed that I got up out of my bunk, grabbed my flashlight, and went outside to the trail. I walked along until I came to a fork in the trail. There he was, in his bathrobe, just like in the pictures. He looked at me and said *Follow me.* Okay, I said, and started back the way I came. That was the end of the dream.

I was seven years old. That was the last direct audience I had, and I'm forty-four now. I do not know if there will be any more. But I don't think this was the last time God spoke to me. In my experience, God is usually not terribly direct. Often, I don't know I'm being addressed at all until sometime after the event. Then I look back, and things slide into place. Sometimes it's a person, like the angel who walked up to me on a street corner in New York a few years ago and announced, *You're beautiful, but you're too damn fat,* and then melted back into the crowd. He had a point. Sometimes it's a book or a magazine article, or even just one sentence: the words I needed right when I needed them. Sometimes it's a life-changing event—God spoke whole paragraphs to me when I was hit by a car a few years back, and I still don't think I've gotten it all.

The things of life speak to us of our destiny. Or, perhaps our several *destinies*—those forks in the road that determine the future so powerfully. My vision of Jesus when I was seven was, you'll remember, at a fork in the road. He said to follow him. Okay, I said. I forgot to ask him where he was going. I still don't know. But I said okay.

Restore our fortunes, O Lord, like the watercourses of the Negev.
PSALM 126:5

⇥⇤

*T*he land would be dry, dry as a whole skeleton's worth of bones, parched from lack of rain. Then the rains would come, and the empty riverbeds would fill. The river bottoms had been baked into hard clay by the hot sun, so the riverbeds would fill to overflowing, and the water would run out into the thirsty land. Thus was the land fertile for another growing season.

The soul's journey is like that. It seems that the dry periods serve no purpose, that they are only to be got through. But it is those times that form the hard floor of your soul, fix its boundaries. So that, when refreshment finally comes to you, you can feel it hit. If we experienced nothing but good we wouldn't really understand what good is: you have to know dryness in order to rejoice in the rain.

But about that hard floor. The pain of making your way through life can create some pretty thick calluses on your soul. There are people who become so tough from living through their hard times that they will not allow themselves to be restored. You know them: so scarred by a bad relationship that no good one is possible. So accustomed to the victim's role that deliverance is wearily refused. Living mainly in their own pasts, responding to new things as if they were the same old enemies. But even in the desert, the rain eventually comes again, and the dry riverbed waits in hope of it.

Make a vow to the Lord your God and keep it.
PSALM 76:11

➳✦

What a lovely wedding. The groom is American: he was in my youth group when he was a boy. The bride is Filipine. The familiar Episcopal ceremony has some touches unfamiliar to me: a large veil symbolizing marital chastity is placed over the couple by two friends. Then a silken cord, with a knot in the middle, is wrapped around them. The knot is God, the bride's mother tells me. A friend hands Devon a small purse with thirteen coins in it. The thirteen coins are Jesus and his twelve disciples. Devon hands it to his new wife: a symbol of sharing all their possessions.

Unfamiliar to me, but very beautiful and meaningful. And not without a few surprises for the bride's folks, too: traditionally, the veil would have been placed only over the bride. The couple balked at that: it's both of us or neither of us, they said. They wanted to be part of these old customs, but in a way that represented them as the people they are. It worked.

You don't have to abandon the faith of your heritage to live honestly in the 1990s. You also don't have to pretend it's *not* the 1990s, that nothing has changed, that every single thing that used to be done must be done now, too, in exactly the same way, or we are unfaithful stewards of the treasures of the past. Nonsense. Of course we've changed. Everything changes.

When I first began performing weddings, many brides chose not to be given in marriage. It seemed to suggest that they were possessions, like sacks of flour, that could be handed from one man to another, and they didn't want to suggest that. That made sense. Now, though, almost every bride who has a father is presented by him, and it's not because they've all suddenly become silly little nitwits who don't know how to support themselves in the world. It's because they want to honor their dads. They do lots of different things these days: sometimes both the mom and the dad walk down the aisle with the bride. Sometimes the groom's folks come, too, and both parties are presented in marriage. Sometimes a couple's children present them. And sometimes they just present themselves.

The important thing about a tradition is not that it never changes. The important thing about it is that it represents something good and true.

OCTOBER 22

While I felt secure, I said, "I shall never be disturbed."
PSALM 30:7

➳

*W*hen things are going well, we usually feel it's because of our strength, our good planning, our competence. Then along comes something that tosses a monkeywrench into the middle of everything: an illness, or loss of a job. We wonder if we have been wrong about ourselves. Where did all my strength go?

When I was hit by a car in broad daylight—while walking on the *sidewalk*, no less—I found myself crushed against the side of a building. I felt many things: physical pain, of course. Fear, of course. Annoyance, even: I didn't have time for this. But the most overwhelming feeling I had may surprise you.

It was shame.

I felt that I was grandstanding in a most self-absorbed manner. I thought I was malingering, making a big fuss over nothing—this, even though it would soon be revealed that I had a broken back. *You get yourself up this minute and go home!* I scolded myself.

Why couldn't I accept this injury as being something other than my own fault? I think it's because of fear. If everything is up to me, if my prosperity is because of my goodness and my setbacks because of my badness, then maybe I can be very, very good and nothing terrible will happen to me. Irrational? Very. But I suspect it goes very deep, in me and a lot of other people. My husband has the flu, and it's taking him longer to recover than he thinks it should. I can tell he feels impatient with himself, as if it were his fault. My friend has had a disappointment in love: her darling has demonstrated that he is incapable of making a commitment. She cannot help but wonder if there is something wrong with her that has made this happen.

But no. I didn't make a car jump up onto the sidewalk and run me down. She didn't make her lover immature; that happened long before they met. Our lives just unfold, and sometimes they bump into the unfolding of other lives, and sometimes somebody ends up getting hurt. Shame doesn't help us much in learning to cope with what happens. We should save our energy for better things.

They did not remember his power.

PSALM 78:42

✦

*Y*ou *have such willpower,* my friend says to me as we sit together at dinner and I do not eat.

Wrong. I have no willpower. Not an ounce. Addicts don't have willpower. I don't even know what willpower is.

All I have is a plan and some friends to help me keep it in the forefront of my mind. And some skills to help me, too, like planning ahead for vulnerable times. That's not willpower. It's the set of things I need precisely because I *have* no willpower.

Probably the bravest thing a human can do is admit to a weakness. This is a world that worships power. We try to amass it; if we don't have it, we try our best to look as if we did. When someone comes along and admits to a vulnerability, the sharks circle. But if he sticks to the truth about himself, they really can't hurt him.

When temptation comes to you, don't think in terms of resisting it all by yourself. Instead, talk to someone—right away—about how you feel. Face the temptation and admit how sorrowful and worthless it makes you feel, and then remind yourself that you are a child of God and not worthless, even though you are not powerful. You have the right to be delivered from the temptation of something that will harm you. Ask to be delivered. And then, move: focus on something you do or something you have that makes you feel happy.

What can they do to me if I tell them I'm weak? Taunt me with it? They won't be telling me anything I don't already know. So don't grip the table's edge with your hands and try to be strong. Let go and let strength come to you.

If I forget you, O Jerusalem, let my right hand forget its skill.
PSALM 137:5

➔←

*T*he hands themselves know things. The way to roll up pie dough and put it in a pan: try to explain to someone just how this is done. The way to peel a potato: people who never do it fill the cutting board with tiny chips of potato skin. It takes them five minutes to peel just one. Experience produces gorgeous long ribbons of transparently thin peel; it takes hands that are used to doing it about one minute to peel five. *Let me just get the feel of it,* my mother used to say when we cooked together; she would take the spoon and stir. She would know from the way the spoon felt in the mixture just how far we were from finished. Ten thousand spoons and ten thousand mixtures later, so do I.

Knowledge imprinted on the body, automatic skill: your hands are not the only part of you that knows what this is. Your soul can tell what's going on by the feel of it, too. It learns a routine and becomes very quick about it: spiritual disciplines that start out difficult become second nature to your soul after a time. This is what enables you to deepen your spiritual life; you don't have to reinvent the wheel every time you try to meditate. The path becomes familiar, and so the soul has time as it walks to notice and respond to the things that are new.

Indeed, I have been wicked from my birth, a sinner from my mother's womb.

PSALM 51:6

➤◄

That seems extreme, doesn't it? Most of us look upon babies as innocent, not as little bundles of sin. When a child suffers, for instance, we are apt to talk about that innocence—*What did a little kid ever do to hurt anyone?* we might say, as if the suffering of morally compromised adults were a lot more understandable.

The admittedly hyperbolic biblical writers, though, aren't always talking about specific infringements of moral codes when they talk about sin. Sometimes they mean a general attitude of self-centeredness, a putting of oneself in the center of creation and expecting everyone else to put us there, too. So, then, this idea of sinful babies begins to make a bit more sense: babies *do* experience themselves and their own needs as the most important things in the world. For a little while, they don't even know there *is* anything else; then, when they grasp that, they assume for a long time that the people and things in their lives exist for them alone. This is the way babies are. And it's the way they have to be; in them, it's not sin.

But it is in people who are not babies. You may have had some contact with someone like that, someone who treated you as if you existed for his convenience alone; if you have, you know how it made you feel. Observe his life, and you see more: not only does this posture toward the world hurt others, it cripples and isolates the one who maintains it even more.

It is easy to see this attitude as sin when someone does it to me. It is less easy to see when I am the one who has put herself at the center of the universe. People who are treating other people as objects don't know that's what they're doing. It doesn't feel wrong to them. It feels like something to which they are entitled.

Bless the person who has the guts to call you on this, should you ever fall into it. Look hard at yourself if there happen to be several of them: it may just be true. Perhaps you are being offered an opportunity to join the human race. Not as a baby, who needs everyone waiting on her, but as the adult you are, a person who can give as well as receive.

OCTOBER 26

I am but skin and bones.
PSALM 102:5

>+<

*W*ell, that's something of an overstatement, I guess: there's still a good deal of me to love. But my cheekbones have emerged from their hiding place, looking none the worse for their years in hibernation, and I can feel my hipbones. So there's progress.

Late in the afternoon, I remember my childhood home at the end of the day. I remember the furniture and the light, the boys reading the paper in the living room, the clatter of pots and pans from the kitchen, the good cooking smells. I remember my father coming home, and my mother. I remember my grandmother's different aprons. That was a time when someone else was responsible for me, when my family made the world safe—a job that has now fallen to me. I put in a long and taxing day. I would like some of that blessed irresponsibility back. I remember it, late in the afternoon of my very different adult days, and I begin to feel a little sad. And what do I do with that vague sadness? Up until recently, what I did was eat. Something hot and savory, usually. A lot of it—a whole meal's worth of calories, sometimes, on an afternoon when I knew I would be eating dinner later on. Did it help? Yes, in a way—for a while. Until the next time I caught sight of myself in a mirror and allowed myself to see what I saw.

It has been only recently that I have understood what late afternoons have always meant to me, why I have been vulnerable to overeating late in the day. My memories of home have not really been conscious ones. Just lingering, faint hopes for the daily homecoming of a family that no longer exists. Almost everyone in it is dead now. Now others need that safety from me.

Just making this unconscious wistfulness explicit has helped me stop the futile attempt to treat sorrow with food. Just facing the fact that I miss them makes me feel better all by itself. Love is precious, even if the only way we can experience it is through the pain of loss.

OCTOBER 27

Who among you loves life, and desires long life to enjoy prosperity?
PSALM 34:12

➤❖

People usually tiptoe around the central fact of an elderly person's life: that it's coming to an end. At a luncheon, I ask a lady if she'd like me to bring her a plate. *Oh, no,* she says, *I'll get my own for as long as I can.* I'm sure that'll be a long time, I say in a polite but silly reflex; what makes me so "sure" that she will live and remain vigorous for a long time? *Oh, I hope not,* she says, and smiles gently. Not a bitter remark: just a mature recognition that the time will come sooner rather than later when she will find life less blessing than burden. In the end, we all lay it down. Old people aren't too stupid to know this. It is young people who have trouble with it.

I have found that many older people welcome a chance to talk about the end of life. That many of them are surprised by how much less fearsome a prospect it is to them, now that it is closer, than it used to be when they were younger. By the time a person is old, many of the great loves of life—parents, spouse—have gone on before. Old people have seen things come and go. They have also seen life linger past its welcome, and the fear that this delay might be theirs is much more vivid than any fear of the end itself.

The reason I bring this up is that I think many relationships could be deepened if the parties to them were more open with one another about these things. We long for the ones we love to know us, yet we skitter away nervously when the talk gets too close to the heart. This is a mistake. We help each other immeasurably when we share our hopes and fears. There is no greater gift one human being can give another.

OCTOBER 28

For they do not plan for peace, but invent deceitful schemes against the quiet in the land.

PSALM 35:20

✦

*M*y father worked for years for what was then called "The War Department." A Pentagon image consultant must have noticed this designation and become alarmed: sometime during my childhood, the War Department became the Department of Defense, a name not nearly so truculent. We would not want to appear to prepare for war with too much zest. Or to seem to prepare for war at all, in fact: it was better to call a war something else, like the Korean "conflict," and to put a gentler spin on what soldiers did, like calling them "advisors," as we did in the early years of the war in Vietnam.

War, a complex human endeavor, takes a tremendous amount of human planning. Everyone pulls together for a war. It brings out some of the best of human virtues: self-sacrifice and courage. People willingly deprive themselves of necessities. They work overtime without a complaint. We seem to be at our best when we are fighting.

And we long for that goodness once again. The sentimentalization of the brief war in the Persian Gulf in the popular mind—the yellow ribbons, the lionization of the generals, of the computer jocks who manned the deadly-accurate electronic missiles: these things were telling. We wanted to be, again, what we had been in the last war everybody felt unambiguous about. We skirted the dubiousness of the cause and went for the good feeling.

Even the best of wars, though, is far from a good thing. Peace has never excited us as war has. Nobody mobilizes for it. Few sacrifice themselves for it. Yet we all say we want it. That will ring more true when we begin to make peace with the enthusiasm with which we now make war.

I hate those who have a divided heart.
PSALM 119:113

❧❧

The psalmists, for the most part, had a simple view of human morality: people were either good or bad, faithful or faithless, and it didn't take a rocket scientist to tell who was who. The idea that good and bad might be combined in an individual personality, while not completely absent from their thought, appears to have been an idea whose time had not yet come.

There's been a real change. St. Paul noticed it, writing in the first century C.E.: *I can will what is right, but I cannot do it. For I do not do the good I want. . . the evil I do not want is what I do.* Many people reading him since then have nodded in understanding. That *is* the way we are: we may know what is right, and want to do it, but we find ourselves doing something south of that a fair amount of the time. We have come to view the person who trumpets his own virtuousness with suspicion.

It's not easy to do the right thing, or even to want it. We are good liars, most of us, coming up with compelling reasons for our behavior that even we believe. The entire edifice of psychotherapy is erected upon our skill at the lie and the damage it does us. *Everyone* has a divided heart. Probably in heaven they know what it is to will one thing, but that's something we hardly ever do down here. That is why it's not a good idea to live in such a way that you don't have to check with anybody else about the things you do; it's easy to get unreal fast when there's nobody around to provide a reality check. It's no accident that individual freedom and utter autonomy feels like a religion to us: we're eager to live in a world without rules. We keep forgetting what life would be like if we really did live in such a world. It would be bloody.

I have become like a leather flask in the smoke.

PSALM 119:83

➤◄

A facial, a makeup consultation, a manicure, and a pedicure arrived via UPS this afternoon: a certificate entitling me to these things at a ritzy New York salon. Sounds wonderful: I could use some hot cloths and clay and cream and whatever on my face. Just thinking about it makes me feel rested. It was a gift from my daughter-in-law, who knows about my diet and rightly guesses my need for a little TLC. She, like other thin people, is more readily able than I have been in the past to see the possibility of any number of personal indulgences that don't involve food. It's not that all I did was eat—far from it. I have always been extremely busy at a number of very interesting things. But a nice time without food in it somewhere would have seemed, until quite recently, like a contradiction in terms.

A leather flask in the smoke becomes hard and brittle. It can no longer expand to hold the liquid for which it was intended. It was actually my impending facial that I thought of first when I read the verse: the older I get, the more leathery my skin. I'm after it all the time with this or that magical cream. But we also get tough and inflexible *inside*, with the passage of time—unless we determine that we will not. For instance, this food thing of mine: my expectation that eating would accompany all fun was rigidly held. I insisted that no day was complete without a luxurious meal, when in fact there are varieties of completeness, all kinds of fun, of which food is but one. My rigidity was injurious to me; it prevented me from seeing the possibilities life has to offer.

My body will enjoy the massage, the creams, the hot towels. And my spirit will enjoy the quiet. And both of us will come away a little softer.

For a thousand years in your sight are like yesterday when it is past.
PSALM 90:4

❧❧

The Halloween parade at Campbell school is at one o'clock. The one at Moss is at one thirty, to allow time for parents to see one and then run to the other, and for the high school band to play for one and then get on the bus and ride to the other. Rose is a cowgirl, wearing her mother's western dancing clothes—the real thing. She looks startlingly grown up. Madeline is a witch, in her mother's black velour minidress, which comes down to her ankles.

I don't know any of the mothers. Some of the teachers I remember are still there, looking older, as I look older. I see another grandmother and wave. It was years ago that I stood and watched my own little pirate girls, fairies, cats, witches parade by, year after year. *Better pick up some candy on the way home,* I think as the parade audience begins to disperse. I remember watching the little figures walking up sidewalks as I stood on the curb, watching them reach up to ring doorbells, watching them stand in ovals of light from open doors.

In the evening I sit in my living room. The doorbell rings from time to time; I open the door, spilling light out into the dark, and hand out tiny chocolate bars. I exclaim over costumes and grisly masks. The children thank me and leave. I see their mothers waiting at the curb and wave, wave not just across my front yard but across years, years made up of strings of days, years it seemed we would always have. I never knew the time would be so short.

For in death no one remembers you; and who will give you
thanks in the grave?

PSALM 6:5

→←

We know from this and many similar lines that the psalmists believed that life ended with the death of the body. There was also, though, a concept in use at the time, or a little later, of a place called Sheol, the place where departed spirits went to hang out after death. Sheol was not like the Christian hell, full of punishment for sins. Nor was it heaven, a place of reward. Sheol seems to have been a pretty quiet place.

God is being addressed here, in very businesslike terms: *If you want us to gratify you by giving thanks for all the good you do us, you'd better start doing us some good, and be quick about it, before we die and it's too late.* How very human: the psalmist assumes that thanks and praise are what God is after. That's a bit more self-centered an image of God than I am accustomed to entertaining: we think a person is a terrible bore if all he wants to talk about is his own good deeds and accomplishments. What makes us think that God is so praise-hungry?

Not as much interested in praise, I think, as in relatedness. What is a partnership between two such unequal partners as God and everybody else likely to be? If our pasts and presents and futures are contained in God's reality, what sorts of things are we to talk about with one another? It's not as if we could tell God something that was news. The fact is, our closest approach to God probably won't have much in the way of words about it. It probably *will be* that awestruck state of mind that people in the past called "adoration." This isn't really about God needing to be adored. It's more about the human being's only possible response to infinity.

My strength fails me because of affliction.
PSALM 31:10

→←

*I*n a movement that used to work just fine, I wedge one toe against the heel of the other foot's boot and pull. Nothing happens. I can't seem to brace on that side anymore, nor can I seem to get out of the habit of trying. Damn.

With my arms full of prayer books, I lean against the sacristy door and push. Nothing happens. I back off and fall against it as hard as I can. It still doesn't move. Somebody comes along and pushes it for me. Thank you. Damn.

The seats on this train—and I've tried them all—are just not designed for those of us with low back pain. I've even tried a sort of half-lying-down position, but I'm too tall to bring it off. Also I look like a drunk. When I step out onto the platform and hobble off into the night, horizontality is all I want. Damn.

I feel as if these things were personal outrages, as if I were being singled out for special persecution. But when archaeologists examine the ancient skeletons of people much younger than I am, they find that most show signs of arthritis advanced enough to have been seriously painful when those people were alive. People worked hard in days gone by. And it took its toll.

Accepting the reality of a physical limitation is no easy task. A strong young body feels like a birthright to its possessor. "Young" and "strong" go together. But now I've begun to notice disabled people more than I did before my own injury—especially disabled young people. Today I passed a young man who was making a phone call from his wheelchair. His legs were small and misshapen; his spine was twisted. Clearly, he had never known what it was to consider bodily strength his birthright. He was young, all right, but he was not strong.

To notice such things is not to buy into that useless old saw about being glad you're not somebody else, as in *You think you've got problems, just be thankful you're not so-and-so.* That's not why I have become more aware of the disabled. All that does is make people feel guilty for feeling badly about something that is indeed sad, about which they have every right to grieve. It's because I feel sad about myself that I see others more clearly. I want to see how others handle their misfortune so I can learn to handle mine. I want help and advice and inspiration. I want to give these things, too, if I have any of them to give.

NOVEMBER 3

Of Zion it shall be said, "Everyone was born in her."
PSALM 87:4

>‹

*I*n just a few weeks it will be Thanksgiving. Families will move heaven and earth to get together, endure crowded train stations, frantic airports, packed turnpikes, and one another. The wonderful smells will begin in the morning and increase as the day continues, smells of foods that bring back mothers and grandmothers dead for decades. The whole country will watch enormous rubber likenesses of cartoon characters glide solemnly down Broadway, as if they meant something to us. The next day's newspapers will feature recipes for turkey croquettes, turkey chili, Turkey Divan, Turkey Tetrazzini.

The Pilgrims will stand modestly in the background, but they will be there. Our forefathers and foremothers in their sober clothing, the men in tall hats, gathered with their new neighbors at the long tables we all remember as if we had been at that dinner ourselves. Never mind that the majority of us have no blood connection to that band of immigrants to these shores: we all feel as if we did. Most of us came later. Some of us came in chains. Some of us came last week in airplanes. It seems not to matter. A feast of thanksgiving with the people we love, a real Norman Rockwell number: it's such a powerful image for all Americans that people who are alone can get pretty depressed at this time of year.

If our national myth is true, though, those pilgrims whom we all pretend were our ancestors were fairly lonely folk, too. Far from their homes, from grandparents, from sisters and brothers—fairly certain never to go home again. Recently bereaved, most of them: more than a third of the Massachusetts Bay Colony had died. So the Thanksgiving we remember as being warm and fuzzy was actually much more like the one many a lonely person will make for himself on this day three hundred fifty years later: find someone with whom to observe it. Those without families make their own.

NOVEMBER 4

Those who sowed with tears will reap with songs of joy.
PSALM 126:6

➤❖

*T*he pain of bereavement is so total it feels eternal. The one who mourns doesn't even *want* to stop: too much pain even to think about its cessation. Moving forward in life is a meaningless concept; all you want to do when a love has died is move *backwards*, back in time, back before this loss happened.

Few things are less helpful in this situation than attempts to focus the attention of the bereaved forward, to the time when this pain will be less intense. He simply doesn't believe you, and it wouldn't matter if he did: the sorrow must be experienced, and it takes the time it takes. It's hard to see someone you care about inconsolably sad. But trying to talk him out of it is the wrong thing to do. The Jews have a very wise practice where this is concerned: they visit the bereaved, who keeps a sort of open house for this purpose for a week, and during the visit they sit in silence. No small talk about the weather. No well-meaning words about God's mysterious plan. Just sitting with the sorrow.

There will be abundant time for your friend to ponder God's plan. The bereaved have nothing *but* time; the decades alone stretch drearily out before them, an endless road with no scenery. As time passes, they do find a way to bring this death into the story of their lives. It turns out that there *is* some scenery, after all. They do find meaning again. They do know joy again—though never about this loss, and the meaning of life is never what it was before. But life fills up again, for each of us in her own time and her own way.

NOVEMBER 5

Save me, O God, for the waters have risen up to my neck.
PSALM 69:1

➤◀

I look at my calendar and realize that I've scheduled myself to appear at two different meetings in two different parts of the city at the same time on the same day. Can't be done. Now I have to decide whom to offend. This happens much too often. It's rather like the situation I sometimes found myself in when I smoked: furiously lighting up a cigarette, only to find I already had one going in the ashtray. Slow down, girl.

I'm taking on water. Better throw a few things overboard.

The only good thing you can say about getting in so deep that you can no longer move is that it does acquaint you with your limits. Temporarily, anyway: I don't seem to retain the lesson very well. I'll get my schedule set up so it's manageable and enjoy it for about two days. Then I'll start stuffing extra commitments into it again until it's even worse than it was before the purge. Then I'll jettison stuff again and start all over. My schedule is bulimic, binging and purging. *I need a personal secretary,* I tell my friend. *No, you don't,* she says, *what you need is a nanny.*

Grownups know when to stop: when to stop eating, when to stop working. Grownups take care of themselves. Children have someone do that for them. I would make a good child, but I'm a little old for that now. My parents are dead, and I don't have a nanny. There is nobody to take care of me but me.

NOVEMBER 6

You have made him but little lower than the angels.

PSALM 8:6

✦

*M*y brother David and I were having a fight about angels. They were all girls, I knew: they all had long hair. *Oh, yeah?* he shot back. *Well look at this, Miss Smarty-Pants.* In our Bible picture book was a dramatic illustration of the expulsion of our first parents from paradise: poor Adam and Eve skulked miserably away in their animal skins, while a muscular and very male angel—whose long hair did absolutely nothing to feminize him—sternly barred the entrance against their return, brandishing an enormous glowing sword. Clearly a boy angel, long hair notwithstanding. David smiled and closed the book in triumph. I went to my grandmother for comfort and enlightenment.

Well, you're only fighting because you each want the angels to be just like you, she said, *isn't that so?* I nodded without speaking; I was still smarting from my defeat. *But nobody knows what they're really like. The person who drew the picture in the book just used his imagination. So you and David just each use yours and stop criticizing each other.*

We hope that the ultimate things will be like us. That the holy will be familiar. That it will even share our prejudices—all those angels in all those picture books were blue-eyed blondes, I seem to recall. But if spiritual things were just like the mundane, what would be spiritual about them? We know a lot about our world. We're learning more all the time. But that knowledge only takes us so far once we inquire beyond its limits.

NOVEMBER 7

Let me not be put to shame.
PSALM 25:19

➤❖

I made him feel this big. The woman measures about three inches between her thumb and forefinger. She wears a triumphant, bitter little smile; her husband has hurt her feelings a lot over the years, and the relationship long ago became one in which his shame over it gave her pleasure—more pleasure, perhaps, than his amendment of life would have. Ongoing anger is like that: it takes on a life of its own. Its host gets used to carrying it around, and before you know it, it's part of the family. Getting rid of it would be an amputation.

Shame feeds it. Shaming your enemy perpetuates your enmity. It may be that putting him to shame will make him stop doing whatever he does that makes you so mad—for now. But he will remember his humiliation, and the memory will be far from neutral. It will make him want to shame you back. An arms race will follow, as the two of you vie with each other to see who can wither whom. In my experience, shaming another never results in permanently changed behavior. It only results in permanent resentment.

So do you just let people walk all over you and never say anything about it? No. You don't have to. You just register your protest in a way intended to heal and not to hurt. You report on how what's going on affects you, not on what you imagine to be the motives or moral values of your antagonist. You don't rejoice when your persecutor feels "this big." You hope instead for a time when he will act his age, and you approach him as if he already were.

NOVEMBER 8

We have had more than enough of contempt.
PSALM 123:4

➔❤

Something strange seems to have happened in the off-year election we just had: negative advertising didn't work. Where we live in New Jersey, our mailbox yielded six or seven lurid flyers every day for weeks before the vote, all of them the same: a picture of a frightened little girl looking up at a menacing stranger and, on the back, a picture that looked like a mug shot of the Democratic candidate. We were to infer from this that the Democrat would be soft on child molesters, this because she had dared to express reservations about a very popular neighborhood-notification law concerning sex offenders that flew hastily through the legislative process in the New Jersey state assembly last year in response to the terrible rape and murder of a child.

For a number of years, people in the know have taken it as an article of faith that you can't win a political office in America unless you are willing to smear your opponent. *Talk as much about him and as little about yourself as you can,* the common wisdom goes, *and you'll be all right. The electorate is so dumb, and so hooked on yellow journalism, that they believe anything you say if it's bad enough. They are bored by accomplishment and ethical behavior, so you needn't bother yourself overmuch about those things.*

Maybe that's not so. Maybe we're not that dumb. Maybe we've had enough ugliness and cynicism in the last twenty years to last us more than a lifetime, and maybe we're ready for a change. People who didn't know his position on a single major political issue sighed for Colin Powell to run for president. A real grownup. An honest-to-God gentleman. Didn't know there were any left.

When the results were in, the candidate in the mug shot won. Handily.

NOVEMBER 9

He led them to safety, and they were not afraid.
PSALM 78:53

>+<

Of course, we are *not* safe.

Terrible things can happen unexpectedly: I know a woman who was brutally raped in her own home. And a man who caught a terrible fever while on vacation and almost died. Any guarantee that you will not, one day, be in one of those wrong places at the wrong time? None whatsoever. You knew that.

Stop and think about all the things that can happen. Why do you suppose we are not more afraid, given how few guarantees of safety there are in life? You may have known someone who *was* afraid, of course: deathly afraid, unable to leave her home, constantly disinfecting the house against the incursions of microbes, terrified when the telephone rang. She lived in mortal fear: *Something bad may happen.* But, while it is certainly true that something bad may indeed happen, we view a person like this as emotionally ill. Most of us don't hide in our houses and disinfect the soap. Some of us get sick and die. But we don't assume that tragedy will be the norm in our lives.

Psychologists write about what makes a person terrified like that. It is complex. But what do you suppose it is that makes the vast majority of us *not* terrified? All of us know of sudden evil, may even have experienced it more than once, but almost all of us go forth into the world every day feeling safe. And life goes on.

Confidence is in our nature. Confidence in the world. Confidence in ourselves. We experience confidence as our normal state, a feeling of trust that makes our lives possible. The same trust that helps us cope when the car does jump the curb, when the microbe does find us. *This is a temporary aberration,* our souls think, *it will pass.* We feel safe. And we *are* safe. Never safe from the outside factors that can explode into our lives, but safe within ourselves.

The Lord is at my side to help me; I will triumph over those who hate me.

PSALM 118:6

>←

I guess it's just my cross to bear, the woman across from me says defeatedly. She has a black eye this morning. Her husband gave it to her. It's not the first. *I'm trying to be forgiving. I'm just trying to turn the other cheek like it says in the Bible.*

Much is made these days, in circles of folk who want to take scripture seriously, of not "picking and choosing" the parts of the Bible upon which to base their lives. They feel that "picking and choosing" is a bad thing, a cowardly attempt to avoid facing uncomfortable truths. *All or nothing,* they say earnestly. The fact is, though, that we all pick and choose among the many viewpoints in scripture, and it is inevitable that we will do so. The Bible is very rich, as is the body of Christian teaching which has made use of it, and the whole of it cannot be stuffed into every discussion.

The idea of forgiveness is one of our teachings which has often been perverted to the ends of the powerful. Victims of domestic abuse have heard all about their duty to forgive many times, and they will hear all about it many times in the future. And yes—it *is* true that an inability to forgive will ultimately retard their own healing. I'm just not sure that they need to hear about it when they are still in the abusive situation. Maybe they need to hear instead about other *equally scriptural* Christian concepts: that God is on the side of the oppressed, for instance. The deliverance of the people of Israel from Pharaoh, not their meekly staying in slavery, was the central sign to the Jewish people of God's presence in history.

Most people think that forgiveness is something we must "come up with" in order to get right with God, when it is actually a gift *from* God, not something *we* come up with at all. Forgiveness does not mean that history has not occurred or that the abuse has some how not happened, or that a psychological "Oh, what the heck, that's okay" state has somehow been achieved. Whatever it means in an individual case, it is certainly something that takes time. Premature emphasis on forgiveness will be difficult for someone accustomed to punishment to hear as anything but counsel to acquiesce in her own abuse. Trying to cover every base, including forgiveness long before an emphasis on it is appropriate, could seriously undercut what *can* happen—the empowering, strengthening, comforting, and challenging of the abused person to focus on God's saving might and how it can show in her life.

NOVEMBER 11

Keep watch over my life.
PSALM 86:2

✦

*T*oday is the first day of my medically supervised fast—the one Oprah did so well on and then blew. And now? She learned from that pain: she's made planning her diet and exercise routine a permanent part of her life. And she just ran her first marathon: looks good and feels good. She's made it her priority to get the support she needs to live the way she wants to live. The lesson: I must never leave this support group or one like it. Never. I must never think myself secure, never think that it's not necessary to plan what I eat very carefully. I never used to plan eating. I just showed up and hoped to be ambushed by food. Now I'm going to plan. And praise myself to the skies. And take it easy.

Don't listen to that very authoritative inner voice a few months hence when it says I don't have to be quite so doctrinaire. I do have to be doctrinaire. Don't listen when it says I'm an adult and I know best. I don't know best. I will lie to myself and others and do anything to gratify myself in the old way. I've done it all my life. I must have a group that helps me tell the truth.

Look at friend Brooke! She has lost eighty pounds. And listen to her: her asthma is gone. As she chanted at the mass last night, her voice was so much stronger, her breath control so much surer. I'm going to e-mail her and tell her so. Best to encourage each other when we can.

I know my high blood pressure is the beginning of my death. I've visited people in hospitals for years. I watched my own parents die of heart disease. I know what I've seen, and this beginning can have only one end. Okay—we have the genes we have. But I can delay it. I already don't smoke. Now I'll reduce weight and blood pressure. You can't drink alcohol on this diet—maybe I won't drink again, either.

Listen, me in a month, returning to this entry on a discouraged day. You were full of trust. You weren't stupid and naive. You were right: with God's help, you will do this and live.

There move the ships.
PSALM 104:27

✙✙

Yesterday was Veterans' Day. As in the past, the old seafarers gathered at Sheepshead Bay in Brooklyn. Now, these grounds are the site of Kingsborough Community College, and thousands of students in jeans and tee shirts fill the classrooms, the cafeteria, and the hallways. During World War II, though, the area was a training center for American seamen. Six weeks at Sheepshead Bay and an Iowa farm boy was a merchant mariner—or at least he was ready to learn what it was really like to be one. Out to sea they went, some of them never to return. More than six thousand merchant seamen perished in that war—a higher percentage of their total number than in any other branch of the armed services. Many died in the terrible cold of the Murmansk Run, supplying the Allied bases in Russia; the Russians never forgot their sacrifice, and struck a medal for American veterans of that run even while America and Russia were still locked in the Cold War. Many died on the way across the Atlantic to England. Many died within sight of the American coastline, the victims of the U-boats that prowled in Eastern seaboard waters in search of them. Some died within sight of the Statue of Liberty, their ships sunk before they even made New Jersey. The only German Raider sunk by an American vessel during the war was sunk by a merchant ship. Cadet Midshipman Edwin O'Hara of the *Stephen Hopkins*, who fired the shots, perished in that encounter. He was eighteen.

We eat lunch in the cafeteria, the dungareed college students regarding us with curiosity sometimes, indifference more often. The men speak of those days, speak almost casually of fearsome things. A widow wears her husband's medals. We pledge allegiance to the flag. We gather at the water's edge and watch as the crew of a Coast Guard cutter drops a wreath into the water of Sheepshead Bay. A white-haired bugler blows taps. I say a prayer, shouting into the wind that comes in from the sea. I ask that we be made worthy of the sacrifice of those who left these shores so many years ago and sailed off into eternity, forever young.

NOVEMBER 13

Sweeter far than honey, than honey in the comb.
PSALM 19:10

➤◄

*L*ast weekend we flew across the country to visit my stepmother. Laura had made many special things for us to eat, foods she knows I love. I knew she would. I was dreading it the whole flight through. I explained my diet to her. She is a retired nurse; she wanted to see the nutritional label on the stuff I'm drinking five times a day. We promised to send her one. Beautiful service dedicating a gospel-book cover in memory of my dad; I preached and people were kind. There was a dangerous reception afterward—St. Dunstan's is full of fabulous cooks—but I carried a cup of coffee around and talked to people. Fabulous-looking cake, but I resisted easily. A loving talking-to, self-administered, before entering these public occasions, helps: *You're not going to eat food, you'll drink coffee. It will be hard, but what you're doing is a lovely gift to your body. You'll be okay. You can do it.*

Here's an idea: if food is love and comfort for me, then getting love and comfort in other ways will help me not to depend on it. We sat and chatted very lovingly through dinner. I did not eat; they did. I'm sure it would have been much harder to go off by myself while they ate. So if I really focus on love, I can feel cared for. And I am loved, by so many more people than I really deserve.

But even if you haven't a living soul in the world who loves you, you carry love in your soul. You were created by it and your life is sustained by it. It breathes with each of your breaths, and nourishes your body with life-giving oxygen. Most importantly for the matter at hand, it plants in you the longing for love of other human beings, and it is on that longing that we all must act. If we've been living the false life destructive behavior brings in its wake for a long time, we may not be very good company. That may well account for our loneliness. But there is nobody who cannot learn to change that.

NOVEMBER 14

"Let us take for ourselves the fields of God as our possession."
PSALM 83:12

➤✦

I was recently at a dinner party at which a well-dressed and obviously intelligent man assured us all that if you want something enough, it will happen. *It's so simple. People don't realize that that's all it takes, but it's true. If you just want something hard enough, it happens.* The Power of Positive Wanting, I guess you'd call that. Several other people nodded serene agreement. I asked if anybody he loved had ever died. He said yes, puzzled, wondering what I was driving at. *Didn't you want her to get well?* I asked. *Oh, well, sure,* he hesitated, *I mean, of course people die.* There was an uncomfortable beat of silence, and then he went on as before. That was rude of me, I thought to myself, to doubt the magical efficacy of his wanting out loud like that. But I guess sometimes it works and sometimes it doesn't.

Our desires feel magical to us sometimes. It seems impossible that they could be denied. We whistle in the dark about their power, steal sidelong glances at people whose hearts' longings are dashed against the rocks, try to think of a strategy that will ensure that we will never be among them, that they have done something incorrectly which we will do correctly and thus avoid their fate. But it is not so. Our wanting something doesn't make it happen or not happen. We are just not that influential. The future is hidden, and will remain so until it comes.

NOVEMBER 15

You lengthen my stride beneath me, and my ankles do not give way.
PSALM 18:37

The first twenty minutes of walking are okay. After that, something odd happens to my right hip—it begins to feel as if it were in a splint, as if the leg attached to it didn't belong to me anymore. A weird feeling. It's been like that for four years. I guess it's going to stay that way. As disabilities go, it sure could be worse.

As well as I know that—and I visit in hospitals a lot, so I see that there is no shortage of human suffering—I'm often surprised by how sad my changed body makes me. How little my cheery it-could-always-be-worse attitude helps in raising my spirits when I am feeling blue about it. What seems to serve me better is a very different approach: looking at myself, for a little while, as if I were my own child. Expressing love and tenderness toward that little me who has hurt herself, rather like the kisses parents bestow upon all manner of invisible injuries their small children bring them. *Here, let Mommy kiss it—there, now, all better!* And the child, satisfied, runs back to play.

When you're all grown up, nobody is going to do that for you. It would be ridiculous. But that doesn't mean that the child you were isn't still alive in you, in need of comfort. We have to mother ourselves, when our mothers are gone. And just that little bit of self-administered tenderness seems to raise my spirits as no amount of resolute cheeriness ever could.

NOVEMBER 16

You shall eat the fruit of your labor.
PSALM 128:2
✦

I don't eat these days, as you know. But I still cook. In fact, I cook better now than I did before I began to fast, with more interest in what I'm preparing. I think about it more. I want the fellowship that always goes with food more than I did when I hid away behind an enormous plate of whatever I could find to put in my mouth. So I lure people into my kitchen with wonderful dishes. Then I watch them eat. I breathe deeply. It smells wonderful.

Thanksgiving is coming. My favorite holiday, naturally, since it involves food. I am the queen of it: I get up early and cook all day. Daughters contribute. Granddaughters set the table. Husband carves the bird. Guests rave over my dressing, my rolls, my pies. My ego needs are satisfied for a month or more.

Will I be able to do this if I'm not eating any of it? Indeed a question. I'll be surrounded throughout the day by that gradual crescendo of wonderful smells. Beholding the table, so beautiful and so full. What will it be like?

I remember the first Thanksgiving after my mother died, how it fell to me to make that dinner without her for the first time. I had learned well in the twenty-nine years I'd watched her doing it, so the meal went off without too many hitches. The food was good. But the meal was sad. She who had made it a celebration of love for all those years was not there. It could have been the best turkey dinner prepared in America that day and I wouldn't have noticed.

As wonderful as food is, it is not love, and love is what makes this holiday the joyous thing it is. There are a lot of places you can get a good meal. But only a few people in your world love you, and you miss them when they're gone.

My table will be full of dear ones. I won't mind not eating at all. I'll have what I really need.

NOVEMBER 17

I will fulfill my vows to the Lord.
PSALM 116:12

➔✦

*T*he old sister opens the convent door for me. She wears one of the old-style coifs, the kind that completely surrounds the face, as well as covering the head; most of the other nuns wear a modified version that just keeps their hair covered and off their faces and hangs down their backs. She is the only surviving member of the original group that founded this order; she has spent more than fifty years in her unusual lifestyle.

Such a weekend we had, she says. *Ninety people in for a wedding reception. Can you imagine—the bride and groom met right here!* I set down my bag and begin to remove my coat. We joke a little about the incongruity of the two lovebirds finding each other in the convent. This is the second time this had happened. *Do you suppose it's something in the water?* I ask, and her eyes crinkle at the corners as she smiles her gentle smile.

Fifty years in fidelity to the same vow. Lots of marriages don't make it that long. I look at her and think of my own past; I feel the quiet consciousness of my own sin that I always feel when I am in the presence of someone who has been more faithful than I have. It's not true, though one often hears people say it, that promises were made to be broken. They are made to be kept. But they often *are* broken, whatever purity of intention they once enjoyed. Many people have difficulty acknowledging their own failures, especially when divorce happens; it is almost always accompanied by significant anger, and it's very easy to blame the other party. Your friends love you, and will help you do that. But it's rarely true that only one party is at fault when marriage dies. It is redemptive to acknowledge the breaking of vows as the failure it is, for both of us, which is not at all the same as wallowing in self-hatred about it.

"If his children forsake my law, and do not walk according to my judgments . . ."
PSALM 89:30

➣⬿

The careful smile on my friend's face when she describes her son's spiritual journey in leaving the religious tradition in which she raised him tells me that she is far from happy about it. She is impaled on the horns of a dilemma: she believes that her son should be free to follow his conscience, but it hurts that he doesn't share her beliefs. She is a very controlled person; she would never admit to being anything but pleased. Her talk about his new faith in an Eastern religion is enthusiastic and affirming. A lot about how good it has been for him. And I'm sure it has. But it has also hurt her.

We've all heard horror stories about parents who disowned their children when the children abandoned their religion. It's hard for me to imagine doing that, and my faith is the most important thing in my life. I think my family is a gift from God. I can't imagine walking away from that gift in God's name.

So how do you handle it if it happens to you? The way my friend does, I think—although I might smile a little less myself. My own kids have had spiritual journeys different from mine in some ways, although they haven't left the Church. Everybody's journey is different, and we are each entitled to our own. These things are too important to be determined for us by someone else, even someone who loves us very much and whom we love. Even by a mom or a dad.

He makes me sure-footed like a deer.
PSALM 18:34

➻➻

Or like a cat. True story: Jenny the cat was on the roof in her accustomed place—she goes there every night and meows until Q comes to get her. I went to a neighboring window, easily twelve feet away, to close it, as it was beginning to rain. For some reason the screen wasn't down. As I struggled with the window, in sailed the cat: a blur of black fur flying effortlessly out into space over a drop of forty feet. What aim. What guts. What stupidity, I guess—I do know of a cat in New York who fell to his death in a similar exercise, so it's not a one-hundred-percent sure thing for them.

But cats are incredibly sure-footed. For hours they will perch on the narrow backs of two opposing living room chairs and glare at each other. From a dead standstill they will leap ninety degrees to a tree branch five feet above their heads. They do these things with what seems to be a powerful sense of purpose, although why it should be suddenly important to leap five feet straight up in the air remains a mystery.

Q came to cat ownership late in life. His cat chose him during a seashore vacation in Q's fifty-eighth year—she came to the door of his rented house to see if he needed anything, and has yet to leave his side. When he and I married, it was clear that Kate did not approve of the match; she may have misunderstood my coming as a reflection on her housekeeping. And I have to say that there hasn't been much movement on her part in six years: I have tried to make friends, but she continues to hold a grudge. When I am away, she sleeps with him. When I return, she goes out marauding all night. I let her in at dawn; she stalks past me with her tail in the air and tosses a hyphenated meow dismissively back over one shoulder as she passes. At meals, she sits by his chair and pats his knee with one possessive paw. He takes her on rides in his car even if she doesn't have to go to the vet; sometimes they pick me up at the train, and there she is in my seat. She scolds and scolds until I feed her; when I do, she sniffs disdainfully at what I have put in her bowl and walks off. She is rude to the cat I brought to the marriage, refusing to give place to Jenny at the feeding bowl, even though Jenny is older. *This is my house,* Kate hisses to her, and Jenny humbly backs away.

So definite, about things that seemingly matter so little. So certain. I don't understand them. So I anthropomorphize them, invent a feline-human love triangle. Do to them what ignorance always does to the stranger: make them over in my own image.

NOVEMBER 20

They have given freely to the poor.
PSALM 112:9

➤✦

I always get a lot of turkeys at this time of year. And I get about fifty cans of cranberry sauce, paper bags left in front of my office door with two or three cans inside each of them. Two years ago, I got six cases of apple cider from the restaurant around the corner, and about twenty pumpkin pies. A Chinese man always brings in a 1000-count carton of fortune cookies.

It's a generous time of year. People appear out of nowhere to volunteer at the Thanksgiving Dinner. A hundred fifty hungry seafarers tuck into the steaming plates of food. One of them, who became a butcher after the war, carves seven or eight turkeys like lightning, and the serving volunteers line up with their platters for more, and more, and more.

It's heaven. People have often pictured heaven as a banquet. More than enough. People sharing, mindful of their blessedness. People are happy when they give, whether they're dropping off a turkey or a check. They're happy when they work, too. Their rueful comments about aching feet and sore backs are mixed with the pride that comes of having extended oneself for something worth doing.

It's a good feeling. Somehow, people remember about this a good feeling at this particular time of year. But the poor get hungry every day. People in hospitals get lonely every day. The homeless need clothing all year long, not just during the holidays. We who do this work know that we'd better be prepared to take full advantage of the annual outpouring of holiday goodwill that begins in mid-November, because we will not see its like again until next year.

But you know those gifts you can buy that come all year? Fruit-of-the-month or whatever, with a different gift arriving each month: apples once, the next month strawberries, then oranges? Or flowers that can be sent that way, or designer beers, or special cigars: I'd love to see people's holiday charity packaged that way sometimes. Send me a turkey in July. With cranberry sauce.

The wicked arrogantly persecute the poor.
PSALM 10:2

＞＜

The transportation centers in any city are the places where people with nowhere else to go wind up. In New York, it's Penn Station and Grand Central Station, the Port Authority Bus Terminal, the World Trade Center, and the Staten Island Ferry. These places see a couple of million travelers pass through each day. They are not homeless shelters, but they participate in the phenomenon of urban homelessness anyway.

A few years ago, they reconfigured some benches in the Port Authority so that people could not stretch out on them. Advocates for homeless people objected: this was discrimination against the homeless. *No, it isn't,* said a spokesperson for the Port Authority. *It's not discrimination. It's just a rule that applies to everyone. We wouldn't let Donald Trump sleep on these benches, either.*

That stuck with me. At the time, Mr. Trump had five or six monumentally tasteless homes in several parts of the country. A dozen or so beds in each one, I'll bet. He's slightly less prosperous now, I understand, and may be twenty or thirty beds down from 1985 levels, but even now he's not likely to need a bench in the Port Authority. The prohibition against sleeping on a bench applies to Mr. Trump all right, but it doesn't hurt him. He has a place to sleep.

I wait for my train out to the New Jersey town where my husband is probably making a nice dinner for us. The only place to sit down in Penn Station now is within a glass-and-metal fence. The only way to get inside the fence is by showing the attendant your train ticket. I reach into my purse to locate mine; the man waves me inside before I find it. Of course he does: I'm clean and middle-class, an obvious commuter.

There was a time when an evening at Penn Station was shared with homeless people who were sleeping, looking through the trash cans, staring into the middle distance. Some of them enjoyed a considerable privacy, conferred on them by their smell—no one wanted to get too close. Some of them were talking to themselves. Some shouted.

Is the train station more pleasant now that they are gone? Oh, absolutely. It is for me, at least: the middle-aged lady whose husband will pick her up from the train and take her to their comfortable home. It's more pleasant to read the *Times* in my comfortable seat within my steel-and-glass fence.

But where have they gone? I don't think they have a ticket. And I know they are not at home.

NOVEMBER 22

How shall we sing the Lord's song upon an alien soil?
PSALM 137:4

➤❦

*I*n an old photograph, my grandparents stand in the sanctuary of their church. I don't know the exact year it was taken—sometime in the 1920s, judging from my grandmother's low-waisted dress. I know they are in America already—Old Glory stands in the corner. The church has evidently just been decorated for Thanksgiving—pumpkins and autumn leaves and cornstalks are everywhere. It looks like a twister just upended a fruit stand and dumped it in the middle of the sanctuary. My grandparents both beam with pride, though: they think it looks wonderful.

I have other pictures—the young couple in front of their home in

England, posing for a formal portrait with their parents and grandparents and brothers and sisters. An elegant Grandfather, young and bespectacled, sitting in his comfortable study, surrounded with books. Dignified and prosperous, they look, and very secure—a different world, indeed, from that of the isolated little frame church on the North Dakota prairie.

Him, I never knew—he had been dead for years by the time I came along. But she lived with us for a time, in her old age. She was a bit tiresome, I recall. But there were hints of another life in her stories that sometimes caught my fancy: what people dressed like when she was a girl, what Sunday was like—it was pretty quiet. What her mother used to cook, what she learned in school—embroidery, for one thing, and she taught me how to do it. The memories of a girlhood somewhat more genteel than the adult life into which she came across the sea. If one of the things we look to religion for is security and familiarity, what must it have been to carry her faith so far from home to follow her husband's ministry?

Among her things were mementos of the coronation of George VI, newspaper clippings, a souvenir booklet, some commemorative china. The photographs, too. An oil painting of her childhood home. Mementos of the land she left, never to return. Bringing me here, long before my birth.

Be seated on your lofty throne, O Most High.
PSALM 7:8

➤✦

One of the things you can see in the Topkapi Palace in Istanbul is the collection of thrones used by the sultans during the height of the Ottoman Empire. One is called the Pearl Throne, and is appropriately inlaid with thousands of magnificent pearls. There is the Jade Throne, carved completely out of one enormous light green stone: a gift from the Emperor of Japan. There is one of solid silver, and another of gold inlaid with diamonds. Thrones from all over the world, gifts from other absolute rulers to the Ottoman Turks: the symbol of the kind of power they all wielded.

I don't know what kinds of gifts the American presidents gave the sultans who lived during their time. I'm sure it wasn't thrones—we wouldn't like linking our president with such a symbol. We do stand when he enters the room, but we would do the same for our own grandmothers.

Turkey no longer has a Sultan. There are still kings and queens and emperors, but there are few absolute rulers in the world. The image of a god enthroned is not as useful for us as it was for the people who sang these psalms. We have little with which to compare it. Authority means something very different for us. In general, it is more communal now than was the authority symbolized by the despot's throne. We think of power as coming from the many, rather than from the one. Just so when modern people try to think of God: that which unites our multiplicity and diversity, that which contains and expresses everything that is. God, who contains all souls, in whom everything is alive that lives. Not solitary and remote, on a throne apart, but here among us.

They tested God in their hearts, demanding food for their craving.
PSALM 78:18

❧

*H*ow am I going to make Christmas cookies if I'm not eating them? I have worried a bit about this. My Thanksgiving experience strengthens me: I cooked for ten hours and didn't eat the meal, and I didn't feel sad and self-pitying—well, maybe a little, but not to an extent that I couldn't handle.

You don't have to make them, you know, Q proposes. *People always give us more than we can eat anyway. You could buy a few at Dean & Deluca's.*

But I *like* to make them. We've always made them: cutout sugar cookies, the Cherry Queens that my mother always used to send to her sister every year as a joke because Harriet couldn't stand them. Swedish Ginger Cookies. Brandy Snaps, rolled while they're still hot around the handle of a wooden spoon to form little tubes. They're fun to make. I don't want to give up fun just because I have to watch what goes into my mouth.

I start out with the Rum Balls, just to see how I do. They're so easy you could make them in your sleep, and they're not my favorite, so I won't be inordinately tempted to taste as I go. I make two batches. I put some in small cellophane bags as gifts for my colleagues, some in a larger bag to go in my stepdaughter's package. Five in a container for Q—they're not his absolute favorite, either. See? It wasn't so hard. I had the fun of doing it. I didn't eat any. I can do this.

Food symbolizes love to us—it is our primordial experience of it. I can still allow that sweet symbolism to permeate my giving, and focus on the satisfaction of love for myself, letting those whose waistlines can afford it do the actual eating.

Crush together (in a food processor or in a plastic bag with a rolling pin):

1 box plain vanilla wafers	*1 cup pecan pieces*
1 cup confectioners' sugar	*3 tablespoons unsweetened cocoa*

Add and mix well:

1/4 cup light corn syrup	*1/4 cup dark rum*

Form into 1-inch balls and roll in confectioners' sugar. Store in airtight container. Best after a day or two; keeps for several weeks. *Makes about three dozen.*

NOVEMBER 25

The Lord is near to the brokenhearted.

PSALM 34:18

›‹

*B*ut a lot of other people are far away.

Many of us crawl into our caves when we are injured. The thought of the world's seeing our pain is overwhelming. And we quickly find that not everyone can handle our misfortune. Your broken heart will scare some of your friends—it will seem too close for comfort to their own fears. One of the saddest things about a broken heart is that it exposes some people whom you thought you could count on as people who are unable to be there for you.

But it also does something else: sometimes comfort and understanding come from an unexpected source, one you hadn't considered or even known about until your sorrow hit. There are friendships born in the crucible of sorrow. They may be enduring ones that last for the rest of your life. Or they may be more limited: the right person at the right place at the right time is there for you, a gift fallen straight from heaven right into your lap. I recollect a couple of each from my own hard times.

Why is this happening to me? almost everybody asks when sorrow comes. Ask this question enough times and the truth dawns: no reason anybody could give would satisfy you. I don't really give a damn why this happened; I just want it not to be. I want history to have been different, not to have produced the situation that is breaking my heart.

When I look at God as the one who has sent sorrow my way, I get nowhere fast. I don't want to be nowhere. I want to have my life as my own. I want to have such joy as I can have in it. So I look and listen for the one who will be sent to me as the agent of my healing. It is often not the one I would have predicted. But there is a way out of every forest of pain, and that way is usually to proceed straight through it. And not to walk alone.

NOVEMBER 26

You only are my portion.
PSALM 119:57

❧

Last night I invented a new cake made with apple cider, raisin, and pecans. I laid it temptingly out on the counter so that it would be the first thing Q saw when he came in the door. He had two pieces. I had none.

Last week we went to see the movie *Persuasion* to celebrate our anniversary. After the show, we went to an Indian restaurant, where he had a lamb dish called *Rogan Josh* and I had water.

On Thanksgiving I began cooking at about six in the morning, like everyone else in America. We had turkey with sausage dressing, boiled rutabagas, green beans with roasted onions, mashed potatoes and giblet gravy, roasted beets with a lemon glaze, sweet potatoes and apples, cranberry sauce, fresh rolls and butter, and a choice of three pies—pecan, green tomato, and pumpkin—for dessert. I was especially proud of the green tomato. Everyone ate a lot. I drank seltzer.

My diet is going well.

I want you to know that I love you and that I'm proud of you, Q tells me after a few days have passed, *but you're cooking me into an early grave. Isn't there some way we can share fellowship that doesn't revolve around food?*

I bridle defensively at first. I am so proud of being able to cook without eating anything myself. But am I covertly making other people do my eating for me? I notice that I am cooking more now than I did before I began this regime. I notice that I want to be around people who are eating. I thought that was a healthy sign, since one of the things I did when I was overeating was to hide myself away with a plate of forbidden food. Now I'm not so sure.

Spiritual progress is like that: just when you think you've got things more or less under control, something happens that makes you take another look. Things may not be what they seem. There may be something within me that I've overlooked. I'll think about this food thing. In the meantime, would you like the recipe for the Apple Cider Cake? Q tells me it's rich, but very good.

VICARIOUS APPLE CIDER CAKE

Sift together:

1 3/4 cups white flour   1 teaspoon cinnamon
1/2 teaspoon ginger   1/4 teaspoon ground cloves
1 1/2 teaspoon baking powder

Set above ingredients aside. Cream together until fluffy:

1/2 cup butter or margarine   *3/4 cup dark brown sugar*

Add:

1 egg

Beat well, then add:

1 cup apple cider   *3/4 cup raisins*
1/4 cup chopped pecans

Add dry ingredients to butter mixture and turn into greased 8-inch-square pan. Bake at 350°F. for 30 minutes. Cut into pieces. Cake is fairly flat and chewy.

NOVEMBER 27

Make me go in the path of your commandments, for that is my desire.
PSALM 119:35

>÷<

The biblical writers knew something we also know: we don't always do what we really want to do. Sometimes we do something else. Our best intentions don't always take us where we know we should go.

Examples abound: repeated resolutions to get the house in order and keep it that way bow their heads in humiliated defeat before growing piles of unanswered mail, sheaves of newspaper clippings, stacks of to-be-filed receipts. Repeated daytime decisions to throw away the cigarettes yield to shame-filled midnight runs to the all-night convenience store for one more pack. I'll never take another drink. I'll never yell at my kid again. I'll never use another credit card. Each goes down—different ones for each of us, but each of us knows what it is to want one thing and do another.

The remedy for this is paradoxical: stop trying. If you find yourself repeatedly unable to do that which you will to do, it is a sign that you are not in control of your own actions. If you were, you'd do it. To continue to try in the same way something which has repeatedly shown itself not to work is crazy. You need new measures if you want new results.

Give up? Not exactly. Just admit defeat. Face inadequacy and name it for what it is. Recovering alcoholics call this painful honesty "hitting bottom." They don't stop drinking until they stop lying to themselves about their ability to manage what has become unmanageable.

Don't keep trying to lift something you can't lift. There is nothing valiant about that. Do yourself a favor and tell the truth: it's too heavy for you to lift by yourself. Then do the sensible thing and go get some help.

NOVEMBER 28

Then shall I have a word for those who taunt me.
PSALM 119:42

➤✦

*I*t never fails: someone says something breathtakingly rude to me and I fire back a brilliant retort—five hours later, when I'm all alone. At the time, I stand there like a wounded moose. Or maybe not like a wounded moose: I believe they attack when injured. I guess I stand there like a *stuffed* wounded moose, then. I'm from Minnesota, and it's just not that easy for us to return fire.

It's probably just as well I can't come up with a cutting response right on the spot. What would that prove? People are never vanquished by the zingers that find their mark—just infuriated. The conflict escalates as you try to outdo each other with your respective rapier-like wits.

The imaginary word wars are satisfying in a grim way. I picture scenarios of my own vindication that would never in a million years actually take place. My dream triumph makes my Walter Mitty–like real-life experience a little easier to endure. What I *should* do, of course, is confront my tormentor like a grownup and ask him or her to treat me with the respect I deserve, please. Once in a while I find the grace and the guts to do this in just the right way, and some justice is done. A friendship has developed from such moments more than once in my life—often enough so that I wish I were always able to be so sensible and poised. Mostly, though, I end up doing the stuffed moose thing and wishing I'd been brilliant later on.

NOVEMBER 29

My soul has longed . . .
PSALM 119:81

✦

Υou may not be troubled by cravings for something you know you shouldn't have. If not, I envy you; the following meditation may seem like a great deal over not very much. But please be patient today, while those of us who do struggle with these things reflect a bit on something I've come up with that helps me immensely. It's a five-step routine for dealing with a food craving (or a nicotine craving, or any longing for something hurtful). Here goes:

1. I acknowledge the craving. I *really want* that Kentucky Fried Chicken.

2. I breathe deeply. If it is the smell of the food that has induced my longing, I breathe even more deeply; if not, I just breathe slowly and deeply. I feel the enjoyment of the wonderful smell. This will not hurt me. Great smells are free. Breathing deeply also calms me down.

3. I assure myself—as if I were speaking to a frightened child—that I have decided not to eat this food and that I will not. *Don't worry,* I say, *we're not going to go down that road.*

4. I acknowledge that this hurts. I want something and it hurts not to have it. But I also acknowledge that I will not die from this hurt. This is more important than a thin person could ever understand—to us, it feels very dangerous not to have what we want. We don't know about the difference between wanting and needing. In this step, I acknowledge both the reality of this and its falseness.

5. I reward myself—with a hot drink, with a magazine article I've been saving, or just with a thought about the loving thing I just did for my body.

This works for me; it helps me do what I want to do for my own good. Hope it works for you.

Happy are they who dwell in your house!

PSALM 84:3

➤✦

I thought maybe we could set aside the Sunday evenings in Advent as special undisturbed times just for us, I tell my husband. Q nods agreeably from behind the stack of exams he's grading. *Sounds good—we can do Christmas cards,* he says.

On the first Sunday of Advent I light one candle in the Advent wreath and get out the cards. He lights a fire. I put on our *Messiah* record. I get through the *B*s in my address book before falling asleep on the couch. He gets very involved writing his first overseas card, and finishes exactly one. We turn off the record player and stumble up the stairs to bed.

On the second Sunday of Advent he's deep in exams. But at least he's here with me, I think. We have a fire again. I put on Bing Crosby. I do some more cards—our family has a lot of *C*s in it. I get out the wrapping paper and wrap some packages, making a big mess in the living room, which I don't clean up because we're not finished yet. This is a mistake.

Third Advent. The living room looks about the same, but now there is an enormous refrigerator box taking up half the kitchen. We need to cut it down to fit around the red wagon we're sending creatively out to Minneapolis, filled with gifts for our grandson and his parents. It is harder to make a box than I remembered. Q estimates his card output at about fifteen. I still haven't gotten out of the *C*s. I have more cookies I want to bake, but I'm not sure I'll get to them. A small package came yesterday. I open it. Cookies.

The fourth Sunday of Advent is Christmas Eve this year. Uh-oh. It's now crystal clear that we won't get everything done. But of course: we never do. Fortunately, I view the season as beginning on December 25th, not ending then, so there's no need to panic. Our Advent Sunday evenings weren't quite as serene as I'd hoped, but they were serene enough. Enough to feel the thrill of preparing. Enough to remember how lucky we are. I put on the medieval carol record. I get out the cards and begin on the *D*s.

DECEMBER 1

There is corruption at her heart; her streets are never free of oppression and deceit.

PSALM 55:12

➢➢

There are two policemen on every street corner down in the fish market. They've been there for weeks now, ever since a building burned down under circumstances that could not even be called suspicious: obviously, the mobsters whose companies were forced out of the market had their people torch it, as a convenient means of destroying the fish market's records and as a reminder to the mayor of just whose part of town this is. The replacement workers who came in to unload the fish on the first morning of the crackdown were surrounded, heckled, and threatened by the angry men they replaced. Obscene graffiti about the mayor bloomed on sidewalk and wall. For the most part, though, the weeks have passed without much trouble— that's if you don't count the fire. Now the papers say that the mayor intends to go after the garbage-hauling business, also a mob industry.

There has never been a time here when corruption didn't live in the streets. Here in New York or in any large city anywhere. The cities of ancient Israel were not unique: people gathered together in large political units just don't treat each all that well. We will watch the mayor as he goes into battle against the garbage bosses, knowing that this will not be the last such engagement.

But the fact that there have always been crooked dealings wherever human beings have lived together shouldn't discourage us from striving to live good lives. My moral agency is mine alone; I am the one who decides how I will behave, and the things I do are no one's responsibility but my own.

DECEMBER 2

That which is worthless is highly prized by everyone.
PSALM 12:8

❖

$\mathcal{A}$n 18-carat-gold bear, studded with two hundred diamonds, two sapphires for the eyes, thirty-six rubies, and twenty emeralds, sits on an 18-carat-gold cushion. He holds a pocket watch that actually tells time. He costs two hundred thousand dollars.

An electric gondola for two, with brass light fixtures, cushioned seats, a built-in ice bucket and tape deck, and a wooden canopy and curtains you can draw back for romantic privacy. Seven thousand four hundred.

An underwater observation bubble mounted on an underwater scooter in different colors: pink for her, yellow for him. You can tool around on these things at depths of up to forty feet, although it doesn't say why you would want to do that instead of swim. Seven thousand five hundred dollars. For another fifteen thousand, you can add on a communication system so the two of you can exchange sweet nothings while you're down there.

A star-shaped evening purse striped with different-colored Austrian crystals is thirty-one hundred dollars. If you're not feeling quite that prosperous just now, you can always just buy the lipstick case; it's only three hundred eighty-five.

I got these out of the Neiman-Marcus Christmas catalog. I watch for it every year—it's famous for including two or three outlandishly expensive gift items, selected for their great expense and utter uselessness. I don't know if anybody ever actually buys this stuff. Most people who have enough money to buy a three-thousand-dollar purse are smart enough not to spend it that way.

Thorstein Veblen, the philosopher of economics, identified this kind of thing as "conspicuous consumption." The way it goes is thus: it's all very well for the things we need and use to be of high quality, but to really demonstrate wealth and power you need to display great expense in things you *don't* need. You need to throw away food, so people will know you've got more than enough, as the Indians of the Pacific Northwest were said to do in the potlatch ceremony. By the same token, I guess you need a two-hundred-thousand-dollar gold bear to tell you the time.

Don't buy the bear. Buy a Timex if you want to know what time it is. Give the other $199,980 to a hunger program.

You have fed them with the bread of tears; you have given them bowls of tears to drink.

PSALM 80:5

⊱⊰

*T*here are times in which sorrow seems inescapable. Wall-to-wall tears. There's just not much of anything anyone can do to make the day on which a loved one dies much better than terrible. Doesn't seem to matter how long you've been expecting it.

What's fascinating to me, though, is that people ordinarily don't seem capable of crying for long, long blocks of time. We get tired of it. After the funeral, back at the house or out in a restaurant with the other mourners, the talk is apt to be quite jolly, even a bit wild and silly. Once in a while someone will remark on it: *I can't believe we're sitting here laughing like this,* someone will say, and everyone will begin to talk more quietly about the deceased. Somehow people feel ready for a laugh, even people whose lives have turned upside down and will assuredly not be right-side up anytime soon.

Grief takes a long time. "Normal" really doesn't exist in grief; what's right for you is right for you, and has nothing at all to do with how long somebody else mourns. But it's a long haul. When a chance to laugh comes, take it. There will be time enough for tears in the months and years to come. Laughter is a respite from sorrow, not a sign that your sorrow is somehow insincere. If a chance to feel some joy comes to those who grieve, it has fallen straight from heaven into sore hearts that need a break.

You will shelter them.

PSALM 5:14

✦

Donna is dead. It has been a while since we saw her at church, but Donna always ebbed and flowed in her church attendance, depending on any one of a number of factors: how her boyfriend was treating her, whether or not he was in jail, where they were living. So, although we knew she was HIV positive, we were taken aback to learn from Joan at the drop-in center that she had died.

Hers was a homeless life. As a child, she was a resident of the notorious Willowbrook psychiatric hospital, closed down in the 1970s amid the furor at revelations of abuses that went on there. And I remember when her mother died: Donna was sad about it, used to go to visit the grave—more involved with the idea of her mother than her mother had ever been with the idea of her. Her father still lives; he works in a restaurant on Staten Island. I remember that once she went to see him at the restaurant—around to the back, where the food is delivered and the trash put out, and waited for him. He came out and told her to go away. *I don't think that's right,* Donna said, and I said I didn't think it was right, either.

Was her relationship with her boyfriend James good or bad? Bad, a lot of the time: he was abusive to her often, and exploited her. Took the money from her SSI check and bought drugs with it. But there were other times: he would buy her a cheap sweatshirt, a plastic bracelet, a garish stuffed animal to add to the menagerie she carried around with her in a plastic garbage bag. He would take her to the hospital for her treatments. She would bow her head and smile when he hugged her; they would sit together at the potluck supper and eat a huge meal, then pack up food to take home, if they had a home at the time. I cannot deny that there were times when Donna was happy with him. He's in jail now, I hear: freaked out after she died, got high, and assaulted a cop.

How did someone with Donna's limitations face death? What did she know? How did she interpret her weakness and her pain? She was used to complying with doctors; she gave them no trouble, I'm sure. She would come quietly into church, her head bowed, her dark eyes watching James for cues about how to behave. I imagine she died like that, not expecting to understand.

We will miss her.

DECEMBER 5

Come quickly to help me, O my God.
PSALM 71:12

➤❖

"*M*e, of all people," said Mr. Seidel to my teacher as he walked through the lunchroom carrying the Star of Bethlehem from its storage place in the boiler room to the gym, where we would be having the Christmas pageant. She laughed; the principal was the only Jewish faculty member in our school. November, and already we were deep in rehearsal: a sixth-grade Mary and Joseph were already being teased about their rosy plastic baby, the three best boy singers were already working hard on their "We Three Kings" solos. I myself was to be a turtledove: this year "The Twelve Days of Christmas" would be interpolated into the Gospel according to St. Luke. Something fresh and exciting, the music teacher said.

This was a public school. But we had a whole-nine-yards Christmas pageant at which religious Christmas carols were sung side by side with "Jingle Bells" and "Frosty the Snowman." We said the Lord's Prayer every morning, and then we pledged allegiance to the flag, the sacred and the secular knit together in the seamless garment of the American civil religion. None of us thought this juxtaposition of sacred and secular the least bit odd. In fact, we didn't know it was a juxtaposition.

Things are different today, of course. The transmission of our religious heritage to our children is our responsibility alone—the public schools will not assume that duty for us. This means, among many other things, that many children will grow up utterly unacquainted with the teachings of any religious faith. Unless we make it our business to be sure they know, it's "Frosty the Snowman" from here on out.

DECEMBER 6

Save us, for the sake of your steadfast love.
PSALM 44:26

➤✦

Life was easier in the 1950s—for some of us, anyway. But ease is not the friend of faith. In a climate of ease, there is no need to prepare. No need to wait. Nothing for which to yearn. Whether we like it or not, faith grows best in a hostile climate. Where in your life history have you felt your soul's presence most keenly? In the sunny meadows of sweet consensus and good times? Has a sense of the holy not come most powerfully into your life when you needed it most: when you stumbled, doubted, sinned grievously and knew it; when you experienced the paucity of your own resources with a force you couldn't deny or explain away?

The facade of the American dream is being chipped away in every part of us: we can no longer paper over our bitter racial divisions, our casual economic cruelties, the lethal cynicism of a public discourse that leaves no institution untouched and no child innocent for long. No amount of compulsive shopping, management lingo, competitive interior decorating, or endorphin-raising workouts can conceal what we fear: that there is ultimately no meaning, no loyalty, no responsibility to anything beyond ourselves. That we are morally alone.

It's not easy to ask for help if you don't think you need any. There are those who wish for that homogenous ease I remember from childhood, that Christian consensus, that people-like-us-ness that looked like faith to us. I remember its gentleness, but I don't want it back. I want to see clearly the dread from which we scurry away, to feel its cold fingers fasten around my heart. Then I know the extent of my need.

DECEMBER 7

How long shall I have perplexity in my mind?
PSALM 13:2

✢

*B*efore falling asleep each night, I think for a little while about the things that are bothering me. Things that happened during the day to make me sad or mad. Things I should have done and didn't. Things that I'm worried about all the time, in a low-level way, like money. I commend these things to God for the night: I don't want them hanging around my bed. Heaven knows they'll all still be around tomorrow when I can do something about them.

I used to wonder, when I was young, if a time would ever come when I had no worries. Now I'm pretty sure there never will be such a time, that one of the principal signs of life in human beings is the presence of problems. The only people who don't have them are the dead. The rest of us live lives filled with loose ends and nagging little guilts and deficits; there are no exceptions.

To just hand them over so you can get a good night's sleep takes some self-coaching: a lot of us feel compelled to turn them over and over in our minds until the wee hours, and then to add to them the worry about the deleterious effects of losing hours of sleep. But we can intervene in our own self-inflicted suffering.

1. Acknowledge your worry. Name it.
2. Admit that worrying over it is doing precisely nothing. It contributes nothing to the problem's solution and drains energy you need to accomplish it. Going peacefully to sleep is not a cowardly avoidance of responsibility: there is nothing responsible about tossing and turning all night.
3. Promise yourself that tomorrow you will take a concrete step toward a solution, and that you will ask for the help you need.
4. At the end of this, I commend my worry to God's love for me, in accordance with my beliefs. I don't know what your beliefs are, so I can't say too much about the exact content of this step for you. But the universe is a big place, and we are small. Rest your care in that vastness.

He gives snow like wool. . . . Who can stand against his cold?
PSALM 147:17–18

✦

*W*e had a few flakes a week or so back. Somebody said it snowed a little yesterday, but I didn't see anything. One of these days, though, the swollen grey skies hanging over the land will open and the soft white snow will fall. The first snowfall is always the best. Even the folks who hate to shovel look at it in wonder as it blankets the earth. So beautiful. So silent.

Q and I will have our annual argument about snow. I'm the one who starts it. *Maybe this year we should think about getting somebody in to clear the drive.* He doesn't say much in response; from experience, I know that this means he will ignore my good advice. I tell him about the dangers of shoveling snow. I speak of massive myocardial infarction, of back strain. Our driveway is long. More silence. *Are you listening to me? Yes,* he says mildly. *Let me just think about it for a little bit.* I have lost again, I know, without a shot having been fired.

I want to set things up so I don't have to worry about him. If I plan things very carefully, I will not lose him to a myocardial infarction in our driveway. But that will be a temporary victory, of course. Sooner or later, I'll lose him to something else. Or he will lose me. Micro-managing his life won't change that.

Billions of tiny flakes of white, each one so light it cannot be felt, but all of them together heavy enough to kill someone. Millions of minutes in life, each one so short, but all of them together the gift of a lifetime of years. Hundreds of loving thoughts, each one so pure and strong, but all of them together insufficient to hold us here past our time.

All your garments are fragrant with myrrh, aloes, and cassia.
PSALM 45:9

✦

I open my dresser drawer and think of my grandmother: the scent of lavender. My favorite. I use it in my bathwater, on my skin. My soap is lavender. I spray it in our bedroom. I sprinkle lavender under the mattress. I bury it in my underwear drawer.

Lavender is one of humankind's oldest perfumes. In the south of France, you drive past fields of it in the hot summer sun: the scent comes through the open window of your car in a warm, spicy wave. Delicious. I smell it and see my grandmother's still room, her lace doilies, her crocheted bags, her collars, her old photographs. Lavender is about age and dignity, quiet wisdom and gentle interest in a world kept at some distance. I am immersed up to my ears in my own noisy world: I like the idea of a still room, a distant world—not enough, apparently, to set about quieting my own life down, but enough to open a bottle of lavender and remember a person who lived that way.

The memories different smells evoke make them more powerful than they are by themselves. I embrace a friend and remember my mother: Chanel No. 5. I get into a taxi and smell a pipe: my father, when I was little. Hints of a past before much of what I have lost had yet flown away.

I lie down in peace; at once I fall asleep; for only you, Lord,
make me dwell in safety.

PSALM 4:8

✦

Rosie was a holy terror at bedtime when she was tiny. If you tried to tiptoe away before she lost consciousness, she would pull herself up by her crib railing, exhausted, and scream bloody murder for a long, long time. She just could not accept the gentle pleasure of drifting into sleep if she was alone. That can only be done from a feeling of safety; I think Rosie was afraid. The descent into a sleep wrenched from fearfulness is terrifying, an irrational yielding to unnamed sinister forces, a state in which "if I should die before I wake" seems like a reasonable expectation. *If I should die. If I should be all alone. Better stay awake just in case.*

A stair creaks outside my closed bedroom door. Adrenaline shoots through me. I know I've locked the front and back doors. I know it's the cat. But I am afraid anyway. I think of an intruder, of certain terrible stories I have heard on the news. I scold myself for being afraid. I am not afraid when my husband is home—a fact that makes me feel like a wimp.

I have been known to call the police on nights like this. They come right over, burly young men who kindly hide the fact that they think I'm silly. That's okay. *I* know I'm silly. They go down in the basement and up in the attic. They check the closets. They glance at the cat, and then at each other. Everything looks okay, they tell me. I apologize twenty or thirty times for being a bother and thank them for coming.

In the morning when I awaken, the house looks bright and safe. Everything is just as I left it the night before. The wooden stairs feel clean and solid beneath my bare feet. I now feel as if being alone at night is no big deal, as if I could do it every night without difficulty. And I could, of course. And will, eventually.

I am grown-up and Rosie was little, but I understand her panicked wailing perfectly. It differed from my calling the police at night only in that it was wordless. At a time like that, presence is what you need. How silly to call the police. How silly to need someone to stay within sight of your crib. Maybe. But it doesn't seem silly at the time.

Sometimes, on a night when my act is somewhat more together, I don't need the police. Sometimes I'm able to reassure myself by thinking about the presence of God. That would be a good thing to do all the time, since that presence is the only utterly dependable presence we have. One of these nights, I *am* going to die before I wake. I pray the Lord my soul to take. And could you also just stay here beside me for a little while, just until I've dropped off?

DECEMBER 11

He led out his people like sheep.
PSALM 78:52

><

Omari is bigger than the other children—much bigger: he is seventeen and they are all between the ages of five and eight. He has about two feet on the tallest of them, and easily a hundred pounds. But Omari is unaware of any significant difference. He feels like one of them.

We are rehearsing the Christmas pageant. Omari is one of the shepherds. *FEAR NOT!* the announcing angel orders, and Omari turns and looks up at the organ loft, where she is perched on the organist's bench. He spreads his arms in amazement. He is utterly convincing. The smaller shepherd turns with him. We go over this surprising event three or four times: each time, Omari turns and spreads his arms in exactly the same way. Perfect. I've worked with professional actors who were nowhere near so consistent.

Here in the church he is accepted and understood. We are glad he can be in the pageant. I wish it were so everywhere. I wish it really didn't matter that he is different. But there will be many times when it will matter—already have been, I'm sure. People can be cruel. A friend whose child is brain-damaged tells of her daughter's tears when she realized that she wouldn't grow out of it someday—she had always hoped she would. That someday she wouldn't "be this way."

Up the aisle comes Omari with the other shepherds. The infant Jesus is waiting on nine-year-old Mary's lap. Like Omari, he sees no significant difference.

DECEMBER 12

I will set no worthless thing before my eyes.
PSALM 101:3

>‹

Just about everything has been bought for the family's Christmas gifts, but still the catalogs come. I am fair game; instead of putting them straight into the recycling, I look at them. Maybe there's a bargain I missed.

As has been the case in recent years, much is made of quality. Eighties glitz is out, and the old-money look is what we're supposed to strive to achieve: so much money, and that money so old, that the need for ostentation passed from life long ago, and all you need for the weekend is a denim work shirt and a pair of jeans. Oh, and a fountain pen that costs $645, but gives you the satisfying old-fashioned ritual of filling it, providing something to do with your hands now that you no longer smoke.

What could a fountain pen have about it that makes it worth that much money? Not much, I'm afraid. But I bet they sell a fair number of them. The aesthetic is a powerful human value. We love beauty. We love it so much, in fact, that we are forever confusing it with morality. The studied nonchalance of this year's catalogs about the expensive things they peddle is both an example of this and a protest against it: you're wearing a nine-hundred-dollar shearling jacket, but you're wearing it to muck out the barn. On your horse farm. Quality.

But if we are good, it's not because we know a fine fountain pen when we see one. Or even a good poem, although the good is like-lier to shine through one of those than through a pen or a purse. Christmas gifts are about love, and only about beauty insofar as it conveys love.

DECEMBER 13

They shall not live out half their days.
PSALM 55:26

✦

This year, the baby Jesus is a girl. This has happened in my Christmas pageants many times before: at that age, who can tell what they are? All she has to do is sit still, more or less, in Mary's lap for twenty minutes. The one rehearsal she has attended went well; I have every confidence in her.

The pediatrician is thrilled at the news, her mother says. *That's so cool,* she said. *We would never do that at my church.* She's happy to see this baby's robust good health. We all are. We remember that Georgeana has an older sister whom she will know only as a sad part of her family's story: Louise was born too soon. She tried and tried, struggled for three long weeks to breathe on her own. Then, in her mother's lap, with her father's arms encircling them both, she died her quiet little death. Now time has passed. Life has begun again, and this time it proceeded safely to its usual conclusion. *Thank God,* we all said.

Well, you'll have another baby Jesus this time next year, Georgie's mother tells me as she bundles her little one into her snowsuit after rehearsal. *We don't know yet if it's a boy or a girl. July, it's due.* Wonderful.

But there will never be a time when little Louise will not have been. She had a life. She has a spirit. She tried her best to live in this world. Sometimes life in this world is far too hard to live. But, however many brothers and sisters Georgie grows up with, there will always be one more.

DECEMBER 14

You made both summer and winter.

PSALM 74:16

❯❮

We awoke this morning to three or four inches of snow. By the time breakfast was over, there were five or six. All my meetings were most deliciously canceled. A whole day stretched unbroken before me. Rosie and Madeline came in to spend it with us: school is canceled but Mommy's work is not. No sooner were they in than they were out, making angels in the snow. Not so long after that, in walked their mother, sent home from a workplace in which she was almost the only person who showed up.

So my world is taking a day off. We could use one: this year Christmas Eve falls on a Sunday, and that always seems somehow to shorten the preparation. Now I can light a fire and look out the window occasionally as the snow continues to fall. Sounds like a great day to me.

The cold has a purpose: it is to slow things down. The earth would exhaust itself if it never took a rest. Many animals sleep through the winter, signaled to do so by the downward turning of temperature. And there is nothing wrong with our taking some time out, too, when we need it.

Now, there will always be somebody who doesn't think you should do that. Somebody who really needs you at that meeting, and can't reschedule it. Somebody who will not look kindly upon your decision to take care of yourself, who will make you feel like a shirker for taking time off. Maybe that tiresome somebody in your life is you. Whoever your nemesis, don't listen—it's probably the devil in a human suit.

The fact of the matter is that there are twenty-four hours in every day. Most of them are spent working. Some of them you use for eating and sleeping and going to the bathroom and paying bills and taking care of other people's needs. And some of them are yours to enjoy.

"Do not let them rejoice at my expense."
PSALM 38:16

>‹

*M*adeline has the giggles. It started when she spilled her milk at dinner. *Good thing her snowpants are waterproof,* Q says. *You mean "milkproof,"* Rosie says, and Madeline begins to laugh. *You mean "noodle-proof,"* Rosie continues, and Madeline laughs harder—deep belly laughs that just go on and on. Rosie keeps on, naming different foods that Madeline might conceivably spill down her front. For some reason, the floodgates are open. Madeline can't stop. She slides weakly off her chair and lies on the floor. Now we are all laughing at her laughter.

I remember this experience so well, being ambushed by laughter. At first it is wonderful—so freeing, so boisterous, so oblivious to propriety. It is when you realize you can't stop that it gets a little scary. *Come on now, Madeline,* I say, *let's get up on your chair and finish your dinner.* "Hamburgerproof," says her sister with a sadistic grin, and Madeline collapses again. Eventually we restore calm. It takes a while. It was fun while it lasted, but now it's time for it to be over.

There are actually any number of times when laughter isn't fun—the slightly scary, out-of-control laughter Madeline couldn't fight is one. Then there is the laughter behind someone else's back, laughter you wouldn't want her to know about: there's something a little dirty about that laughter, a knowledge that it is somehow unworthy of yourself. Then there is the laughter that masks bitter disappointment; it is no fun to experience life as a lengthy and cynical practical joke perpetrated upon oneself.

So laughter in the right place at the right time for the right reason is a gift from God. It is one of the things that make us human: with the exception of some high-functioning chimpanzees, animals don't laugh.

They lurk in ambush in public squares.
PSALM 10:8

✦

The city is getting safer. The current mayor would like to claim credit for it, but the downturn in crime really began at the end of the administration he defeated. He's welcome to claim some credit for its continuation, I suppose. The incidence of violent crime in New York City has decreased by double-digit percentages in each of the last three years, down in every category to levels we have not seen since the early 1970s. This is a statistical fact. It is matched nationwide by another: the incidence of violent crime is also decreasing in the United States as a whole. Not as dramatically as it is here, but then nothing anywhere else is as dramatic as it is here, is it?

But most Americans feel that crime is getting worse, not better. In the lists of things that bother people most, crime is always at the top. Devices intended to foil car thieves and housebreakers sell like hot-cakes. Politicians exploit sensational crimes with knee-jerk legislative schemes named after the victims of terrible crimes, and anyone who questions the efficacy of these quick fixes is painted as supporting heartless killers and child molesters. Neighborhoods hire their own private police. We don't act like a nation whose crime rate is improving; we act like Dodge City.

Fear begets fear. It turns us in upon ourselves and makes us selfish. In a diabolical way, it really makes us less safe: less likely to intervene when we see injustice or cruelty, less able to lift our eyes from the sidewalk of our own lives to see the pain of others, less likely to view a fellow citizen as neighbor and more likely to view him as potential adversary.

I look to my right hand, and find no one who knows me.

PSALM 142:4

✦

It was bitter cold outside. I stood frozen at the window of my neighborhood delicatessen, looking out onto the sidewalk. There a child screamed to her mother that she wanted to hold her hand, and the mother refused, striding angrily along the sidewalk a few paces in front of the little girl, turning back now and then with a savage face, an open hand poised to strike. How could this be happening? What kind of person doesn't hold a child's hand when the child begs for this simple protective act? My mouth went dry. I wanted to do something—could I dash outside and scold the mother? Could I, perhaps, offer her some money and ask her to calm down and tend to her child? Could I call the police? Could I ask her to give me the child, and take her home? All these things and more raced through my mind in a second or two, and then the pair was out of sight.

I did nothing but stand there and shake. The police would not have done anything about a mother who wouldn't take her little girl's hand. I can still see that little girl's curly hair, her red coat. I can still hear her howls. My mouth is dry again at what I see and hear. And I hate myself for doing nothing. I think about her almost every day. I pray for her almost every night. I long for the world to be different, for all the people who want babies to get them. For all the people who shouldn't have them to have the sense not to.

The fear of the Lord is the beginning of wisdom.
PSALM 111:10

❧

I found an interesting message on my answering machine: *You know that line in "Amazing Grace"—" 'Twas grace that taught my heart to fear"? I was wondering what that means. I've been thinking about it and it doesn't really make sense to me, how grace would teach fear. So if you know, call me back, okay?* The caller left her number.

Okay.

Since she was wondering about this, I thought you might be, too.

Grace is that property of God that brings about the good in human beings. What the poet means is this: the knowledge that all is not well with us is often the beginning of the changes that will be necessary to make us well. Talk to any addict who is active in his addiction: he will tell you he's fine. Sure, he may drink a little too much now and then, but he doesn't have a *problem*. He is not conscious of any lack of control on his part. He is a little annoyed that you brought it up. He is definitely not afraid.

He's not going to stop drinking or smoking or binge eating or shooting up or whatever it is he's doing until he *is* afraid. Then something happens that makes it clear that his life is not working, however convincingly he may have been able to make it look like it was. Something happens that lets him know that he can't live without his addiction but can no longer live with it. And then he is paralyzed with fear: he must give up that without which he cannot live. Sort of like *And now you must not breathe*.

He is mistaken about not being able to live clean and sober, of course. There is grace for him, as there is grace for all. But the beginning of that grace was fear.

For the power of the wicked shall be broken.

PSALM 37:18

❖

*F*irst, it became harder to see a bank teller. We were told that it would be easier to call the computer on the telephone if we had questions about our accounts, and to make withdrawals and deposits at ATM machines. Okay. I got so I depended on the machines. Now I hardly ever need to talk to a human being.

So there are fewer tellers now. We use the machines. Soon, we are told, we'll be charged for using the computer on the telephone and the ATM. Something doesn't sound right: tellers lose their jobs so the bank can cut costs, but we also begin paying for the service that made them obsolete? Somebody's doing very well in this equation, and I don't think it's us.

That's why I don't like computers, Mom, Anna says. I look at the keyboard of this machine I adore, that makes so many things possible for me, that sends my words to an editor a thousand miles away, this machine that contains my book, a book that exists nowhere else but in its circuits, and I say nothing. *They're taking over our lives and putting people out of work. A few people are doing well, but some will never do well again.*

I want you to be one of the ones who do, I tell her, *I don't want you to be left behind.* I feel like I'm arguing with her about whether or not to board the Ark, and maybe I am. I feel sand shifting beneath our feet.

So mortals ate the food of angels; he provided for them food enough.
PSALM 78:25

✥

*A*ngels have been really good for business for the last few years: angels on juice glasses, umbrellas, wall hangings, bedsheets, Christmas ornaments, bath towels, wastebaskets, you name it. Slap a chubby cherub on it and it runs out of the store. One pair of Renaissance angels in particular—a couple of bored winged toddlers leaning their chins in their hands—is particularly popular these days, but you also see lovely slim blonde art deco angels and dark, elegant African American angels. You even see some stern, muscular *guy* angels with long hair, who look kind of like the swashbuckling heroes on the covers of romance novels, although the angels who do most of the real selling are women and children.

Why the sudden popularity of our winged friends? I have a theory: the idea of the angel is very consumer-friendly, and not just because you can decoupage one on a wastebasket. The popular understanding of angels is based on the figure of the guardian angel, a sort of heavenly lawyer/personal shopper/agent who will get you out of any trouble in which you may suddenly find yourself and put you on the inside track to making the most of life's opportunities. Right into your lap will fall your heart's desire, brought to you by your very own angel—rather like shopping on television, only you never get a bill.

It makes every bit of sense to me that a generation as materialistic and self-absorbed as ours would be drawn to beings who exist to serve us. Actually, though, there's not a whole lot of evidence in Christian or Jewish scripture or tradition for this understanding of what the angel business is like. Angels in scripture are, to begin with, not deceased human beings who behaved themselves in life and now live in heaven, but beings who were created to serve God in heaven *and*—here is where we come in—to deliver messages to people on earth. So it was an angel with a fiery sword who stood at the gate of paradise after Adam and Eve were cast out and wouldn't let them back in. And it was a trio of angels who came to visit Abraham and Sarah, ate up all the pita in the house, and then assured them that they would have a baby, even though the two of them were older than dirt. Mary learned of *her* unusual pregnancy during another of these angel visits. Nobody seems to place orders with the angels you meet in scripture, and the angels don't seem to have much time to hold people's hands; their visits are brief and to the point: deliver the message and leave.

In scripture, it is *God* who is the guardian and protector—a much more difficult concept, and one so tied up with our feelings about judgment and guilt that it's no wonder we take refuge in friendly little children with wings, or women with wings who look like our mothers did when we were four. Protection and guidance doesn't mean a sure way to win the lotto, or a free ride through the duties of life, however much we might wish it did.

DECEMBER 21

The wicked borrow and do not repay.
PSALM 37:22

✦

Of course, you never lend money you can't afford to lose. I assume the money I lend is gone for good. That way, I feel like I've stumbled on buried treasure if I get it back. I'm intrigued, though, at the number of people who don't seem to feel much of an obligation to repay funds they've borrowed. I don't understand it: do I appear so rich that repaying me would be insulting? If so, I'm communicating an untruth.

Can I borrow a nickel so I can buy dessert? I asked my mother. She was working in the principal's office at my elementary school while the regular secretary was sick, so I had noontime access to her I usually did not enjoy. *Borrow?* she said to the teacher she was chatting with, and they both laughed. I was embarrassed: I knew I was never going to repay the nickel. I had no money except what she gave me. I didn't want to "borrow" it; I wanted her to give it to me. But somehow I couldn't ask for it that way. I needed to hold out the promise of fiscal responsibility, even though it was patently false.

The homeless people who come in to ask me for money sometimes couch their requests in terms of borrowing. *I'll pay you back,* they say, and I nod and say nothing. Some of them do pay me back, at least part of what they have received. I'm always deeply impressed when that happens: their lives are hard. The majority cannot repay, and we both know it from the beginning. They're not wicked. They just can't face the naked assertion of that fact. So they "borrow."

There is something else about their "borrowing": it implies an ongoing relationship. The borrower is not alone. She has someone in the world to whom there is obligation. If I hand you a dollar in passing, I need not even look you in the eye. I just toss it in the paper cup you're shaking and keep right on walking. But if you *borrow* from me, we have a deal. We have a connection. We will meet again, on the day—whenever it is, here or in heaven—that you come to repay what you have received.

Who never do any wrong.

PSALM 119:3

><

The rolls weren't coming out of the pan very well. I kept dropping the hot pan on the counter. I dropped a roll on the floor. Damn it. Corinna was in the kitchen with me. *Here,* I said tensely, *get these out. And I don't want them to look ugly.* I was rattled. I had a dinner to get on the table.

I don't know how to make them beautiful, she said quietly, *and I'm too old to learn.* And she left the kitchen. She must have thought I expected her to put the rolls in the basket wrong. She must have thought that because my words and tone implied it.

My plan had been to seat everybody around the table in the dining room. We wouldn't all fit, I knew, so my plan was to bring the little library table in from the living room and seat four of us there. It looks really nice when we do that. But what with all the services on Christmas Eve and all the present wrapping, and what with hurrying to put together Rosie and Madeline's doll beds on Christmas morning before they came over, I didn't get the tablecloth and napkins ironed. Sitting down in a formal way with unmatching napkins, or none at all? Time for a change of plan. A quick switch to a buffet format: more casual dishes, cutlery rolled up in unmatched napkins. People all over the living room with plates on their laps. Not what I'd pictured, but just as nice in a different way. They had a good meal and they had fun, and that's all you need.

Deliver me, O God, from allowing my perfectionism to hurt the very people I'm trying to delight.

You have cut short the days of his youth.

PSALM 89:45

➺➻

*O*nly five or six people are here at the cathedral for the monthly AIDS memorial service. A woman is here who mourns her niece. She tells the story of her niece's being infected by her husband, closing on a note of grim satisfaction: *At least he died first,* she says, her mouth a straight line. But this thought really doesn't seem to make her feel any better.

The others are here for other reasons. One man has a list of a dozen names; he writes each of them on a card and attaches each card to the Christmas tree that has been set up by the altar. There are already hundreds of cards, each hanging from the tree on a little red ribbon. Another man hangs back a bit, not in the group but listening intently to the service from the periphery. A seminary student sits thoughtfully in his chair. The deacon has a list of names people have given her to remember at the altar; she reads them slowly. We all supply other names of our own.

I am here to celebrate the Eucharist and preach the sermon. Tomorrow will be Christmas Eve. Twenty years ago tomorrow, my baby died. I talk a little about this time of year, how vividly it reminds us of childhood: our own, our children's. How important children are to us at this time of year. How much we want all to be well for all of them, and how cruel it seems to us at this time of year when all is not well. I talk about these lives, cut off in the flower of youth. I talk about my own child's silent, painless death, of how he knew nothing of what he would miss: his was a different death from the fearsome ones the people in the memorial service remember.

Almost everyone we remember died young. Some were children; many were in their twenties and thirties. Life cruelly ended, just as it was beginning. Almost everybody here has wondered if it would have been better for these young people just not to have been at all. Would it have been better that they had never lived, since they had to die so soon, in such sorrow and pain? Almost everybody who has had such a loss has wondered if it would not have been better never to have loved at all than to have loved and lost. But almost everybody who has wondered this has gone beyond these thoughts: no, it would not be better had they never lived. Even the sorrowful early ending of their lives does not cancel out the good of them. Life and love are great gifts. However short or however long, life together is a great treasure. We may mourn its brevity with all our hearts. It may be that the only way to remember it now is through the veil of sorrow at its loss. But we would still rather remember than forget.

DECEMBER 24

I lie down and go to sleep.
PSALM 3:5
➔←

Santa Claus can't come until you go to sleep, I used to tell my girls on the night before Christmas. It worked, too: they weren't about to do anything to impede the elf's arrival. I remember my own frenzy on Christmas Eve when I was little; I think my girls settled down better than I did.

These days things are different. They are grown-up. Corinna has two little girls of her own. Anna plays Santa Claus at our house, stuffing the stockings and setting out certain gifts unwrapped beneath the tree. Over at Corinna's house, the same: Christmas is a movable feast when your grandmother lives in the same town—two visits from the old elf, two sets of stuffed stockings, as I relive the childhood of my children.

This year my granddaughters are angels in the Christmas pageant. When they were tiny they were sheep—you work your way up through the ranks. But all that work will be over by the time of the Christmas Eve sleep. Into bath and into bed they will go, their heads a jumble of images: the extravagance of their imagined gifts, more wonderful than they will really be, more wonderful than any present could actually be. Mary and Joseph and a real baby. The smell of pine. Special words that are starting to sound familiar to them by now: *In those days a decree went out from Caesar Augustus that all the world should be enrolled. . . .*

DECEMBER 25

Bless the Lord, all you servants of the Lord who stand by night in the house of the Lord.

PSALM 134:1

The early hours of Christmas morning, 1975. I walked the halls in my hospital gown and those dumb-looking foam slippers they give you when you come in unexpectedly. The unplanned pregnancy I'd pretty much gotten used to was gone as disconcertingly as it had appeared. The baby I had only recently allowed myself to daydream about had died weakly in the palm of my hand earlier that day. I couldn't go home yet. Now I forget just why—it was a long time ago.

Everybody who could be discharged had been. The floor was dark and quiet. Up ahead in my walk was the nurses' station, a little pool of light spilling out into the dark hallway. There were low voices.

People. I came and stood in the door. They looked up; one of them asked if I needed something. *I just can't seem to sleep,* I said. *I thought I'd walk around a little.* One nurse offered me a plate of Christmas cookies and I took one, a star with red sugar sprinkles on it. We exchanged regrets about having to be where we were on Christmas Eve. I resumed my walk.

My children were asleep at home. Their father had filled their stockings by himself. I was lucky to have them, I thought as I walked and nibbled on the cookie. But I paced the hospital corridor most of the night, as if I were waiting for something. Late the next morning, my family came to take me home. A kind neighbor invited us for Christmas dinner. I still remember how lovely her tree looked.

The hospital had the graciousness not to put me on the floor with other new mothers. I missed church that Christmas Eve, of course. There would be no ecclesiastical welcome of Mary's little child for me; my mind and body were busy absorbing the early return of my own baby to his maker. But he was still in my thoughts, Mary's new baby, that child of uncertainty, of redemption through sorrow.

DECEMBER 26

I am sinking in deep mire.
PSALM 69:2

➤<

I didn't actually intend to start picking up the piles of Q's papers and books that littered a quarter of our bedroom floor, but after I had finished folding the laundry and the room still looked terrible because of them, something just snapped. I picked up a pile and put it on another pile. Rewarded by the sight of our bedroom carpet, I consolidated more piles. It was no time at all until the ten or twelve piles that had obstructed access to the dresser in which I keep my clothes were all one pile. Nothing had been lost or thrown away, of course, and there were still ten or twelve other piles elsewhere in the room, but order was definitely beginning to emerge out of chaos.

Q appeared at the top of the stairs. *You shouldn't be doing that to your back,* he said, seeing me bending over. *Or to your husband,* he added in quite another tone, when he saw what it was I was working on. Something of a little discussion followed. I know he doesn't want me to touch his piles of papers. I don't know what he thinks I'll do to them, but I do know that he is far from neutral on this subject, and I knew it when I started picking up the piles.

His right to privacy. My right not to wade through piles of another person's life. Which right should win out? *You should have asked me before you started,* he said, and I know I should have. *But would anything have changed if I just asked?* I countered. *Did you ask me if you could leave piles of stuff on my bedroom floor?* He feels ruthlessly managed and ordered about. I feel up to my neck in someone else's confusion. I didn't handle this well, but I am afraid to apologize, lest it be understood as assent to further clutter. At this writing, I do not yet know how all this will turn out.

Life together is hard—all kinds of things to take into consideration that you don't have to when you live alone. I seem to remember saying something unkind during our argument about being left with all those piles of paper when he dies. I imagine my bedroom floor then, clean and uncluttered. Our bed now, then mine alone. Our house, silent except for my own footsteps, the pawpats of the cats. I wish now I hadn't said that bit about having the heaps of papers still there when he dies. We're going to have to come to some agreement: I really *would* like the piles to disappear. But not him.

Your paths overflow with plenty.

PSALM 65:12

➤<

I am not eating any solid food yet, just as I was not at Thanksgiving. This has gotten to feel quite normal. We have planned a fabulous dinner and had fun doing it. Brooke will be coming—she's my dieting partner. She is farther along in her program than I am in mine; she's already eating actual food, while I'm still drinking packets of nutrients mixed with water. I have devised a menu that will be completely legal for her and absolutely delicious for everyone: a lean roast tenderloin of beef, roasted mixed vegetables, brussels sprouts with chestnuts. And two desserts: a lemon tart (lots of fat) and a raspberry angel cake (absolutely none). That is my ambition: a wonderful feast in which we all partake. A life in which my weakness doesn't get me into trouble but also doesn't get in other people's way. I don't want to miss out on the pleasures of the table, of which eating is only one.

And I don't. I drink delicious tea and soak up compliments about the food. Brooke enjoys a meal for which nobody need apologize, and so do all the rest at the table. All is well.

THE GREAT ROASTED VEGETABLES
BROOKE HAD AT CHRISTMAS

Preheat oven to 400° F. Spray a baking pan with butter- (or olive oil-) flavored nonstick spray. Arrange in single layer in pan your choice of:

small red potatoes, in their scrubbed skins	*smallish whole onions*
smallish whole scrubbed beets	*whole scrubbed carrots*
smallish whole turnips	*cloves of garlic, unpeeled*
1/2-inch slices of rutabaga	*wedges of radicchio*
	1/2-inch slices of eggplant

Sprinkle with fresh rosemary leaves and grind pepper coarsely over all. Spray with more flavored nonstick spray. Roast for one hour (radicchio for less), turning as needed. *Delicioso*—the roasting concentrates the flavor of vegetables wonderfully, and slightly carmelizes them. And no fat.

DECEMBER 28

I am counted among those who go down to the Pit; I have become like one who has no strength.

PSALM 88:4

>+<

I left a message on her machine, my friend tells me miserably. *I called at a time when I knew she'd be out. I just couldn't face her.* He looks at the ground as he speaks. He is in anguish. The depression he battles every day has the upper hand at the moment, and he's had to bow out of a big commitment he made when he felt better. Now he's convinced that nobody will ever love him again—he's failed his friend and himself. He feels there's no goodness left in him.

Those who haven't felt this way don't really know what a paralyzing thing it is. It's not just being sad. It's not just a mood. I don't know what causes it—chemicals, I understand, and there are some chemicals you can take to make it better, sometimes—but I do know that it tortures some very good people for long stretches of time.

I have some influence over this particular situation. I can intercede for my friend with the person he's letting down, although, if I know her, it won't be necessary. She loves and respects him, and she knows about his affliction. She'll cut him some slack.

It is he who is unforgiving. Others will love him again, but he must learn to love himself if lasting joy is ever to be his. Easy to say, if one is not in depression's grip, but it is also true. One of depression's more diabolical features is that the sufferer's hopelessness prevents him from taking what action he can to help himself. He can't lift the phone. He can't speak. Most pain impels the sufferer toward healing; this pain sabotages it. He abandons the medicine that helps him, sending himself into a horrifying downward spiral of anger, bizarre behavior, and burned bridges. When he begins medication again, it will take a couple of weeks for his blood levels to adjust. A couple of weeks of completely unnecessary pain inflicted on himself and others.

If this is you, go back to your therapist. *Now.* Look at how you're feeling: there is no reason on earth for you to carry on like this with no one to help you. And don't self-medicate with recreational drugs or alcohol—you are deluding yourself and playing with fire. If you don't have a therapist, seek out a professional you can trust and get a referral; a clergy person with his or her head on straight can help you find one.

If this is someone you care about, keep advising treatment until he goes for it. Keep pointing out how bad this is when he gives you the seven reasons why he can't see a therapist, and keep telling him that you care.

God does not create us so that we will be miserable. God intends our joy. Trust in God in the midst of depression always involves trust in another human being, one put there in your path for your poor soul's own good. Grab hold and allow yourself to be lifted up.

He struck down the firstborn of their land, the firstfruits of all their strength.
PSALM 105:36

>✦<

We have neighbors in for New Year's dinner every year. Every year I make an invitation in the form of a funny cartoon to send out with the Christmas cards. Years ago, it featured our cats making smart remarks about the party. Now, it's our grandchildren: one year in a bubblebath, another in front of the television—always with their backs to us, since I'm not a good enough cartoonist to draw their faces. The cartoons are pretty funny, if I do say so myself.

This year, though, I just didn't get around to the cartoon. Or to the cards, for that matter. The old grey mare, she ain't what she used to be. It's Thursday. New Year's Day is Monday. Oh, well. I start calling people on the phone. *Are you sure you want to do this?* Mary asks when I call her. *I really do,* I tell her. *I look forward to it. I just got a little behind, I guess. You know me: time management is not exactly my long suit.* It turns out that everyone I called has been wondering about the party, and most of them have the time available. No harm done.

Today is the Feast of the Holy Innocents, commemorating the senseless slaughter of male children under age two by mad Herod the King in a vain attempt to kill the Christ Child. A time when all such tragedies are remembered, from the one that decimates a nation to the one that blasts a ragged hole in the heart of one family. You didn't get all your cards out, either? You didn't get everything done perfectly? There are worse things in life than late party invitations. Among the many bits of spiritual nourishment a sober feast like this one gives us is this: lighten up on the details. Save your anguish for something worth it.

Remember, Lord, how short life is, how frail you have made all flesh.
PSALM 89:47

>✦<

Morris Stores has closed. They've been saying they'd close in November since about April, and they finally did. They were in business in Metuchen for forty-seven years, all under the ownership of the same family.

I didn't want to believe it would happen. I got my little girls' dresses there until they weren't little girls anymore. Or sometimes, when I was feeling down in the mouth, I'd pop in and buy them a little something pretty. I got Girl Scout things there. I got the Carter's underwear and blanket sleepers there. When Rosie and Madeline came along, I got their outfits there, too. When my mother-in-law was in a nursing home, I bought there the elastic-waist trousers, snap-front nightgowns, and knee-high stockings the nurses told us to get—things my mother-in-law never would have selected to wear when she was well. I would find myself in Morris Stores at some point every Christmas Eve, sandwiching some last-minute shopping in between my three hundred church services.

But the things they had weren't exactly . . . I mean . . . My friend didn't finish her sentence, and she didn't have to. I knew what she meant: tastes had definitely changed by the end of the forty-seven years, and Morris Stores hadn't quite kept up. But that wasn't the point; she is new in town. It wasn't that they had the best things, or the lowest prices—although they had some fabulous sales. It was the fact that they were *ours* that mattered. They were our store. They anchored Main Street. They sponsored a beauty contest each year: Miss Merry Christmas—in a town with a large Jewish population, from a store owned by a Jewish family, for heaven's sake—with such cheerful disregard of any potential irony contained in that tradition that, to my knowledge, nobody was ever offended. They knew who we were, and we knew them.

Main Street can't compete with the malls. Shopping where you live is slipping into the past all across the country, joining running boards and wringer washers in the quaintness of time gone by. The malls gleam, huge and unnatural, their marble floors and complicated lighting fixtures, their temperature controls and canned music inhuman intrusions into a sense of community already too fragile in our culture. Me, I'm against it. I'll go to any length not to go to one.

When the doors were closed for the last time, the store owner put placards in the darkened windows, along with the framed newspaper clippings of all the Miss Merry Christmas contests throughout the years. They're still there, until something else is done with the building. The placards all read:

TO OUR FAITHFUL CUSTOMERS
SERVING YOU THESE PAST 47 YEARS
GAVE US THE GREATEST OF PLEASURES.
THE ZUTZ FAMILY OF MORRIS STORES

I know it was just a store. But tears sting my eyes every time I walk by.

I was brought very low, and he helped me.

PSALM 116:5

✦

Phil almost died a couple of years ago. He had a car crash and suffered a severe concussion. He was nineteen years old then, the first person among Anna's friends whose life had ever been in danger. The young people were subdued: the end of life was a new and unfamiliar thought.

After a long time in intensive care, Phil made a complete recovery. Today he says he is very different than he was before the accident: *I was a complete pessimist then, but now I'm optimistic.* Why is that? *Because it's a waste of time to be pessimistic. You feel terrible, and you never get back the minute you've spent feeling terrible. You waste it.*

In my work, I am often in conversation with people who have come very near to death. Or who are facing it in the very near future. I have heard it before, this urgency about the value of time. The threat of death puts a person in mind of how sweet life is, and how short. How uncertain. The day you spend mourning about something that hasn't happened yet is a day you will not be given again. Use it well and find a way to be joyful in it, for tomorrow it will be gone and so may you. You will have chosen to be grim instead of choosing joy.

And it *is* a choice. Nobody knows what tomorrow holds—it's no smarter to assume the worst than the best. This is not to recommend ignoring the reasonable warning signs of trouble and the opportunities life presents to deal with them: if you're ill or in trouble, no amount of positive thinking is going to make it just go away. You do have steps to take in turning things around. But are you likely to take those steps if your habitual attitude is "Oh, what's the use"? I think not.

Getting better from a major setback is hard work. You need all your faculties. A pessimistic outlook on life gets in your way and slows you down. People who are fighting their way back need to believe they can do it.

About the Author

BARBARA CRAFTON is an Episcopal priest and author whose books include *Finding Time for Serenity: Every Woman's Book of Days* and *The Sewing Room: Uncommon Reflections on Life, Love, and Work*. She has served congregations in New Jersey and New York, from a stint as a port chaplain on the New York waterfront for the Seamen's Church Institute to one at Trinity Church, Wall Street. She is currently rector of St. Clement's Episcopal Church in Manhattan's theater district. An accomplished actress and theatrical director, she founded two theater companies resident in Episcopal churches, and directs and performs often in New York City. She is a frequent retreat leader and keynoter throughout the country on subjects ranging from the relationship between faith and the arts to discovering everyday spirituality. She has been profiled extensively in national television, and radio and print media, and is seen frequently on the Faith and Values television network. Her articles and revues have appeared in *The New York Times, Reader's Digest, New Woman, Family Circle, Glamour, Trinity News, Episcopal Life,* and many other publications. She is a wife, a mother, and a grandmother, who divides her time between New York City and New Jersey.